THE TALE OF THE GREAT MUTINY

First published 1903
This edition published by Lector House in 2023

ISBN: 978-93-5800-777-0

Lector House LLP
Registered Office: H. No. 96, Block C, Tomar Colony,
Burari, Delhi – 110084, India
info@lectorhouse.com
www.lectorhouse.com

THE TALE OF THE GREAT MUTINY

WILLIAM HENRY FITCHETT

2023

LECTOR HOUSE LLP

FIELD-MARSHAL EARL ROBERTS, V.C., G.C.B.

From an engraving of the portrait by W. W. Ouless, R.A., *by permission of* Henry Graves & Co., *Ltd.*

THE TALE OF THE GREAT MUTINY

BY

W. H. FITCHETT, B.A., LL.D.

AUTHOR OF "DEEDS THAT WON THE EMPIRE," "FIGHTS FOR THE FLAG,"
"HOW ENGLAND SAVED EUROPE," "WELLINGTON'S MEN," ETC.

WITH PORTRAITS AND MAPS

THIRD IMPRESSION

CONTENTS

LIST OF ILLUSTRATIONS

LIST OF MAPS

THE TALE OF THE GREAT MUTINY

CHAPTER I

MUNGUL PANDY

The scene is Barrackpore, the date March 29, 1857. It is Sunday afternoon; but on the dusty floor of the parade-ground a drama is being enacted which is suggestive of anything but Sabbath peace. The quarter-guard of the 34th Native Infantry—tall men, erect and soldierly, and nearly all high-caste Brahmins—is drawn up in regular order. Behind it chatters and sways and eddies a confused mass of Sepoys, in all stages of dress and undress; some armed, some unarmed; but all fermenting with excitement. Some thirty yards in front of the line of the 34th swaggers to and fro a Sepoy named Mungul Pandy. He is half-drunk with bhang, and wholly drunk with religious fanaticism. Chin in air, loaded musket in hand, he struts backwards and forwards, at a sort of half-dance, shouting in shrill and nasal monotone, "Come out, you blackguards! Turn out, all of you! The English are upon us. Through biting these cartridges we shall all be made infidels!"

The man, in fact, is in that condition of mingled bhang and "nerves" which makes a Malay run amok; and every shout from his lips runs like a wave of sudden flame through the brains and along the nerves of the listening crowd of fellow-Sepoys. And as the Sepoys off duty come running up from every side, the crowd grows ever bigger, the excitement more intense, the tumult of chattering voices more passionate. A human powder magazine, in a word, is about to explode.

Suddenly there appears upon the scene the English adjutant, Lieutenant Baugh. A runner has brought the news to him as he lies in the sultry quiet of the Sunday afternoon in his quarters. The English officer is a man of decision. A saddled horse stands ready in the stable; he thrusts loaded pistols into the holsters, buckles on his sword, and gallops to the scene of trouble. The sound of galloping hoofs turns all Sepoy eyes up the road; and as that red-coated figure, the symbol of military authority, draws near, excitement through the Sepoy crowd goes up uncounted degrees. They are about to witness a duel between revolt and discipline, between a mutineer and an adjutant!

Mungul Pandy has at least one quality of a good soldier. He can face peril coolly. He steadies himself, and grows suddenly silent. He stands in the track of the galloping horse, musket at shoulder, the man himself moveless as a bronze image. And steadily the Englishman rides down upon him! The Sepoy's musket suddenly flashes; the galloping horse swerves and stumbles; horse and man roll in the white dust of the road. But the horse only has been hit, and the adjutant struggles, dusty and bruised, from under the fallen beast, plucks a loaded pistol from the holster, and runs straight at the mutineer. Within ten paces of him he lifts his pistol and fires. There is a flash of red pistol-flame, a puff of white smoke, a gleam of whirling sword-blade. But a man who has just scrambled up, half-stunned, from a fallen horse, can scarcely be expected to shine as a marksman. Baugh has missed his man, and in another moment is himself cut down by Mungul Pandy's tulwar. At this sight a Mohammedan Sepoy—Mungul Pandy was a Brahmin—runs out and catches the uplifted wrist of the victorious Mungul. Here is one Sepoy, at least, who cannot look on and see his English officer slain—least of all by a cow-worshipping Hindu!

Again the sound of running feet is heard on the road. It is the English sergeant-major, who has followed his officer, and he, too—red of face, scant of breath, but plucky of spirit—charges straight at the mutinous Pandy. But a sergeant-major, stout and middle-aged, who has run in uniform three-quarters of a mile on an Indian road and under an Indian sun, is scarcely in good condition for engaging in a single combat with a bhang-maddened Sepoy, and he, in turn, goes down under the mutineer's tulwar.

How the white teeth gleam, and the black eyes flash, through the crowd of excited Sepoys! The clamour of voices takes a new shrillness. Two sahibs are down before their eyes, under the victorious arm of one of their comrades! The men who form the quarter-guard of the 34th, at the orders of their native officer, run forward a few paces at the double, but they do not attempt to seize the mutineer. Their sympathies are with him. They halt; they sway to and fro. The nearest smite with the butt-end of their muskets at the two wounded Englishmen.

A cluster of British officers by this time is on the scene; the colonel of the 34th himself has come up, and naturally takes command. He orders the men of the quarter-guard to seize the mutineers, and is told by the native officer in charge that the men "will not go on." The colonel is, unhappily, not of the stuff of which heroes are made. He looks through his spectacles at Mungul Pandy. A six-foot Sepoy in open revolt, loaded musket in hand—himself loaded more dangerously by fanaticism strongly flavoured with bhang—while a thousand excited Sepoys look on trembling with angry sympathy, does not make a cheerful spectacle. "I felt it useless," says the bewildered colonel, in his official report after the incident, "going on any further in the matter.... It would have been a useless sacrifice of life to order a European officer of the guard to seize him.... I left the guard and reported the matter to the brigadier." Unhappy colonel! He may have had his red-tape virtues, but he was clearly not the man to suppress a mutiny. The mutiny, in a word, suppressed him! And let it be imagined how the spectacle of that hesitating colonel added a new element of wondering delight to the huge crowd of swaying Sepoys.

At this moment General Hearsey, the brigadier in charge, rides on to the parade-ground: a red-faced, wrathful, hard-fighting, iron-nerved veteran, with two sons, of blood as warlike as their father's, riding behind him as aides. Hearsey, with quick military glance, takes in the whole scene—the mob of excited Sepoys, the sullen quarter-guard, the two red-coats lying in the road, and the victorious Mungul Pandy, musket in hand. As he rode up somebody called out, "Have a care; his musket is loaded." To which the General replied, with military brevity, "Damn his musket!" "An oath," says Trevelyan, "concerning which every true Englishman will make the customary invocation to the recording angel."

Mungul Pandy covered the General with his musket. Hearsey found time to say to his son, "If I fall, John, rush in and put him to death somehow." Then, pulling up his horse on the flank of the quarter-guard, he plucked a pistol from his holster, levelled it straight at the head of the native officer, and curtly ordered the men to advance and seize the mutineer. The level pistol, no doubt, had its own logic; but more effective than even the steady and tiny tube was the face that looked from behind it, with command and iron courage in every line. That masterful British will instantly asserted itself. The loose line of the quarter-guard stiffened with instinctive obedience; the men stepped forward; and Mungul Pandy, with one unsteady glance at Hearsey's stern visage, turned with a quick movement the muzzle of his gun to his own breast, thrust his naked toe into the trigger, and fell, self-shot. He survived to be hanged, with due official ceremonies, seven days afterwards.

It was a true instinct which, after this, taught the British soldier to call every mutinous Sepoy a "Pandy." That incident at Barrackpore is really the history of the Indian Mutiny in little. All its elements are there: the bhang-stimulated fanaticism of the Sepoy, with its quick contagion, running through all Sepoy ranks; the hasty rush of the solitary officer, gallant, but ill-fated, a single man trying to suppress a regiment. Here, too, is the colonel of the 34th, who, with a cluster of regiments on the point of mutiny, decides that it is "useless" to face a dangerously excited Sepoy armed with a musket, and retires to "report" the business to his brigadier. He is the type of that failure of official nerve—fortunately very rare—which gave the Mutiny its early successes. General Hearsey, again, with his grim "D—— his musket!" supplies the example of that courage, swift, fierce, and iron-nerved, that in the end crushed the Mutiny and restored the British Empire in India.

The Great Mutiny, as yet, has found neither its final historian, nor its sufficient poet. What other nation can show in its record such a cycle of heroism as that which lies in the history of the British in India between May 10, 1857—the date of the Meerut outbreak, and the true beginning of the Mutiny—and November 1, 1858, when the Queen's proclamation officially marked its close? But the heroes in that great episode—the men of Lucknow, and Delhi, and Arrah, the men who marched and fought under Havelock, who held the Ridge at Delhi under Wilson, who stormed the Alumbagh under Clyde—though they could make history, could not write it. There are a hundred "Memoirs," and "Journals," and "Histories" of the great revolt, but the Mutiny still waits for its Thucydides and its Napier. Trevelyan's "Cawnpore," it is true, will hold its readers breathless with its fire, and movement, and graphic force; but it deals with only one picturesque and dreadful episode of the Great Mutiny. The "History of the Mutiny," by Kaye and Malleson, is laborious, honest, accurate; but no one can pretend that it is very readable. It has Kinglake's diffuseness without Kinglake's literary charm. The work, too, is a sort of literary duet of a very controversial sort. Colonel Malleson, from the notes, continually contradicts Sir John Kaye in the text, and he does it with a bluntness, and a diligence, which have quite a humorous effect.

Not only is the Mutiny without an historian, but it remains without any finally convincing analysis of its causes. Justin McCarthy's summary of the causes of the Mutiny, as given in his "History of Our Own Times," is a typical example of wrong-headed judgment. Mr. McCarthy contemplates the Mutiny through the lens of his own politics, and almost regards it with complacency as a mere struggle for Home Rule! It was not a Mutiny, he says, like that at the Nore; it was a revolution, like that in France at the end of the eighteenth century. It was "a national and religious war," a rising of the many races of India against the too oppressive Saxon. The native princes were in it as well as the native soldiers.

The plain facts of the case are fatal to that theory. The struggle was confined to one Presidency out of three. Only two dynastic princes—Nana Sahib and the Ranee of Jhansi—joined in the outbreak. The people in the country districts were passive; the British revenue, except over the actual field of strife, was regularly paid. If their own trained native soldiery turned against the British, other natives thronged in thousands to their flag. A hundred examples might be given where native loyalty and valour saved the situation for the English.

There were Sepoys on both sides of the entrenchment at Lucknow. Counting camp followers, native servants, &c., there were two black faces to every white face under the British flag which fluttered so proudly over the historic Ridge at Delhi. The "protected" Sikh chiefs, by their fidelity, kept British authority from temporary collapse betwixt the Jumna and the Sutlej. They formed what Sir Richard Temple calls "a political breakwater," on which the fury of rebellious Hindustan broke in vain. The Chief of Pattalia employed 5000 troops in guarding the trunk road betwixt the Punjaub and Delhi, along which reinforcements and warlike supplies were flowing to the British force on the Ridge. This enabled the whole strength of the British to be concentrated on the siege. The Chief of Jhind was the first native ruler who appeared in the field with an armed force on the British side, and his troops took part in the final assault on Delhi. Golab Singh sent from his principality, stretching along the foot of the Himalayas, strong reinforcements to the British troops besieging Delhi. "The sight of these troops moving against the mutineers in the darkest hour of British fortunes produced," says Sir Richard Temple, "a profound moral effect on the Punjaub."

If John Lawrence had to disband or suppress 36,000 mutinous Sepoys in the Punjaub, he was able to enlist from Ghoorkas and Sikhs and the wild tribes on the Afghan borders more than another 36,000 to take their places. He fed the scanty and gallant force which kept the British flag flying before Delhi with an ever-flowing stream of native soldiers of sufficient fidelity. At the time of the Mutiny there were 38,000 British soldiers in a population of 180,000,000. If the Mutiny had been indeed a "national" uprising, what chances of survival would the handful of British have had?

It is quite true that the Mutiny, in its later stages, drew to itself political forces, and took a political aspect. The Hindu Sepoy, says Herbert Edwardes, "having mutinied about a cartridge, had nothing to propose for an Empire, and fell in, of necessity, with the only policy which was feasible at the moment, a Mohammedan king of Delhi. And so, with a revived Mogul dynasty at its head, the Mutiny took the form of a struggle between the Moslem and the Christian for empire, and this agitated every village in which there was a mosque or a mollah." But the emergence of the Mogul dynasty in the struggle was an afterthought, not to say, an accident. The old king at Delhi, discrowned and almost forgotten, was caught up by the mutineers as a weapon or a flag.

The outbreak was thus, at the beginning, a purely military mutiny; but its complexion and character later on were affected by local circumstances. In Oude, for example, the Mutiny was welcomed, as it seemed to offer those dispossessed by the recent annexation, a chance of revenge. At Delhi it found a centre in the old king's palace, an inspiration in Mohammedan fanaticism, and a nominal leader in the representative of the old Mogul dynasty. So the Mutiny grew into a new struggle for empire on the part of some of the Mohammedan princes.

Many of the contributing causes of the Mutiny are clear enough. Discipline had grown perilously lax throughout Bengal; and the Bengal troops were, of all who marched under the Company's flag, the most dangerous when once they got out of hand. They consisted mainly of high-caste Brahmins and Rajpoots. They burned with caste pride. They were of incredible arrogance. The regiments, too, were made up largely of members of the same clan, and each regiment had its own complete staff of native officers. Conspiracy was easy in such a body. Secrets were safe. Interests and passions were common. When the British officers had all been slaughtered out, the regiment, as a fighting machine, was yet perfect. Each regiment was practically a unit, knit together by ties of common blood, and speech, and faith, ruled by common superstitions, and swayed by common passions.

The men had the petulance and the ignorance of children. They believed that the entire population of England consisted of 100,000 souls. When the first regiment of Highlanders landed, the whisper ran across the whole Presidency, that there were no more men in England, and that, in default of men, the women had been sent out! Later on, says Trevelyan, the native mind evolved another theory to explain the Highlanders' kilts. They wore petticoats, it was whispered, as a public and visible symbol that their mission was to take vengeance for the murder of English ladies.

Many causes combined to enervate military discipline. There had been petty mutinies again and again, unavenged, or only half avenged. Mutineers had been petted, instead of being shot or hanged. Lord Dalhousie had weakened the despotic authority of the commanding officers, and had taught the Sepoy to appeal to the Government against his officers.

Now the Sepoy has one Celtic quality: his loyalty must have a personal object. He will endure, or even love, a despot, but it must be a despot he can see and hear. He can be ruled; but it must be by a person, not by a "system." When the commander of a regiment of Sepoys ceased to be a despot, the symbol and centre of all authority, and became only a knot in a line of official red tape, he lost the respect of his Sepoys, and the power to control them. Said Rajah Maun Singh, in a remarkable letter to the Talookdars of his province: "There used to be twenty to twenty-five British officers to every 1000 men, and these officers were subordinate to one single man. But nowadays there are 1000 officers and 1000 kings among 1000 men: the men are officers and kings themselves, and when such is the case there are no soldiers to fight."

Upon this mass of armed men, who had lost the first of soldierly habits, obedience, and who were fermenting with pride, fanaticism, and ignorance, there blew what the Hindus themselves called a "Devil's wind," charged with a thousand deadly influences. The wildest rumours ran from barracks to barracks. One of those mysterious and authorless predictions which run before, and sometimes cause, great events was current. Plassey was fought in 1757; the English raj, the prediction ran, would last exactly a century; so 1857 must see its fall. Whether the prophecy was Hindu or Mohammedan cannot be decided; but it had been current for a quarter of a century, and both Hindu and Mohammedan quoted it and believed it. As a matter of fact, the great Company did actually expire in 1857!

Good authorities hold that the greased cartridges were something more than the occasion of the Mutiny; they were its supreme producing cause. The history of the greased cartridges may be told almost in a sentence. "Brown Bess" had grown obsolete; the new rifle, with its grooved barrel, needed a lubricated cartridge, and it was whispered that the cartridge was greased with a compound of cow's fat and swine's fat, charged with villainous theological properties. It would destroy at once the caste of the Hindu, and the ceremonial purity of the Mohammedan! Sir John Lawrence declares that "the proximate cause of the Mutiny was the cartridge affair, and nothing else." Mr. Lecky says that "recent researches have fully proved that the real, as well as the ostensible, cause of the Mutiny was the greased cartridges." He adds, this is "a shameful and terrible fact." The Sepoys, he apparently holds, were right in their belief that in the grease that smeared the cartridges was hidden a conspiracy against their religion! "If mutiny," Mr. Lecky adds, "was ever justifiable, no stronger justification could be given than that of the Sepoy troops."

But is this accusation valid? That the military authorities really designed to inflict a religious wrong on the Sepoys in the matter of the cartridges no one, of course, believes. But there was, undoubtedly, much of heavy-handed clumsiness in the official management of the business. As a matter of fact, however, no greased cartridges were actually issued to any Sepoys. Some had been sent out from England, for the purpose of testing them under the Indian climate; large numbers had been actually manufactured in India; but the Sepoys took the alarm early, and none of the guilty cartridges were actually issued to the men. "From first to last," says Kaye, "no such cartridges were ever issued to the Sepoys, save, perhaps, to a Ghoorka regiment, at their own request."

When once, however, the suspicions of the Sepoys were, rightly or wrongly, aroused, it was impossible to soothe them. The men were told that they might grease the cartridges themselves; but the paper in which the new cartridges were wrapped had now, to alarmed Sepoy eyes, a suspiciously greasy look, and the men refused to handle it.

The Sepoy conscience was, in truth, of very eccentric sensitiveness. Native hands made up the accused cartridges without concern; the Sepoys themselves used them freely—when they could get them—against the British after the Mutiny broke out. But a fanatical belief on the part of the Sepoys, that these particular cartridges concealed in their greasy folds a dark design against their religion, was undoubtedly the immediate occasion of the Great Mutiny. Yet it would be absurd to regard this as its single producing cause. In order to assert this, we must forget all the other evil forces at work to produce the cataclysm: the annexation of Oude; the denial of the sacred right of "adoption" to the native princes; the decay of discipline in the Sepoy ranks; the loss of reverence for their officers by the men, &c.

The Sepoys, it is clear, were, on many grounds, discontented with the conditions of their service. The keen, brooding, and somewhat melancholy genius of Henry Lawrence foresaw the coming trouble, and fastened on this as one of its causes. In an article written in March 1856, he says that the conditions of the Indian Army denied a career to any native soldier of genius, and this must put the best brains of the Sepoys in quarrel with the British rule. Ninety out of every hundred Sepoys, he said in substance, are satisfied; but the remaining ten are discontented, some of them to a dangerous degree; and the discontented ten were the best soldiers of the hundred! But, as it happened, the Mutiny threw up no native soldier of genius, except, perhaps, Tantia Topee, who was *not* a Sepoy!

"The salt water" was undoubtedly amongst the minor causes which provoked the Mutiny. The Sepoys dreaded the sea; they believed they could not cross it without a fatal loss of caste, and the new form of military oath, which made the Sepoy liable for over-sea service, was believed, by the veterans, to extend to them, even though they had not taken it: and so the Sepoy imagination was disquieted.

Lord Dalhousie's over-Anglicised policy, it may be added, was at once too liberal, and too impatient, for the Eastern mind, with its obstinacy of habit, its hatred of change, its easily-roused suspiciousness. As Kaye puts it, Lord Dalhousie poured his new wine into old bottles, with too rash a hand. "The wine was good wine, strong wine, wine to gladden the heart of man;" but poured into such ancient and shrunken bottles too rashly, it was fatal. It was because we were "too English," adds Kaye, that the great crisis arose; and "it was only because we were English that, when it arose, it did not overwhelm us." We trod, in a word, with heavy-footed British clumsiness on the historic superstitions, the ancient habitudes of the Sepoys, and so provoked them to revolt. But the dour British character, which is at the root of British clumsiness, in the end, overbore the revolt.

The very virtues of the British rule, thus proved its peril. Its cool justice, its steadfast enforcement of order, its tireless warfare against crime, made it hated of all the lawless and predatory classes. Every native who lived by vice, chafed under a justice which might be slow and passionless, but which could not be bribed, and in the long-run could not be escaped.

Some, at least, of the dispossessed princes, diligently fanned these wild dreams and wilder suspicions which haunted the Sepoy mind, till it kindled into a flame.

The Sepoys were told they had conquered India for the English; why should they not now conquer it for themselves? The chupatties—mysterious signals, coming whence no man knew, and meaning, no man could tell exactly what—passed from village to village. Usually with the chupatti ran a message—"Sub lal hojaega" ("everything will become red")—a Sibylline announcement, which might be accepted as a warning against the too rapid spread of the English raj, or a grim prediction of universal bloodshed. Whence the chupatties came, or what they exactly meant, is even yet a matter of speculation. The one thing certain is, they were a storm signal, not very intelligible, perhaps, but highly effective.

That there was a conspiracy throughout Bengal for the simultaneous revolt of all Sepoys on May 31, cannot be doubted, and, on the whole, it was well for the English raj that the impatient troopers broke out at Meerut before the date agreed upon.

Sir Richard Temple, whose task it was to examine the ex-king of Delhi's papers after the capture of the city, found amongst them an immense number of letters and reports from leading Mohammedans—priests and others. These letters glowed with fanatical fire. Temple declared they convinced him that "Mohammedan fanaticism is a volcanic agency, which will probably burst forth in eruptions from time to time." But were Christian missions any source of political peril to British rule in India? On this point John Lawrence's opinion ought to be final. He drafted a special despatch on the subject, and Sir Richard Temple, who was then his secretary, declares he "conned over and over again every paragraph as it was drafted." It represented his final judgment on the subject. He held that "Christian things done in a Christian way could never be politically dangerous in India." While scrupulously abstaining from interference in the religions of the people, the Government, he held, "should be more explicit than before"—not less explicit—"in avowing its Christian character."

The explanation offered by the aged king of Delhi, is terse, and has probably as much of truth as more lengthy and philosophical theories. Colonel Vibart relates how, after the capture of Delhi, he went to see the king, and found him sitting cross-legged on a native bedstead, rocking himself to and fro. He was "a small and attenuated old man, apparently between eighty and ninety years of age, with a long white beard, and almost totally blind." Some one asked the old king what was the real cause of the outbreak at Delhi. "I don't know," was the reply; "I suppose my people gave themselves up to the devil!"

The distribution of the British forces in Bengal, in 1857, it may be noted, made mutiny easy and safe. We have learned the lesson of the Mutiny to-day, and there are now 74,000 British troops, with 88 batteries of British artillery, in India, while the Sepoy regiments number only 150,000, with 13 batteries of artillery. But in 1857, the British garrison had sunk to 38,000, while the Sepoys numbered 200,000. Most of the artillery was in native hands. In Bengal itself, it might almost be said, there were no British troops, the bulk of them being garrisoned on the Afghan or Pegu frontiers. A map showing the distribution of troops on May 1, 1857—Sepoys in black dots, and British in red—is a thing to meditate over. Such a map is pustuled with black dots, an inky way stretching from Cabul to Calcutta; while the red points gleam faintly, and at far-stretched intervals.

All the principal cities were without European troops. There were none at Delhi, none at Benares, none at Allahabad. In the whole province of Oude there was only one British battery of artillery. The treasuries, the arsenals, the roads of the North-West Provinces, might almost be said to be wholly in the hands of Sepoys. Betwixt Meerut and Dinapore, a stretch of 1200 miles, there were to be found only two weak British regiments. Never was a prize so rich held with a hand so slack and careless! It was the evil fate of England, too, that when the storm broke, some of the most important posts were in the hands of men paralysed by mere routine, or in whom soldierly fire had been quenched by the chills of old age.

Of the deeper sources of the Mutiny, John Lawrence held, that the great numerical preponderance of the Sepoys in the military forces holding India, was the chief. "Was it to be expected," he asked, "that the native soldiery, who had charge of our fortresses, arsenals, magazines, and treasuries, without adequate European control, should fail to gather extravagant ideas of their own importance?" It was the sense of power that induced them to rebel. The balance of numbers, and of visible strength, seemed to be overwhelmingly with them.

Taken geographically, the story of the Mutiny has three centres, and may be covered by the tragedy of Cawnpore, the assault on Delhi, and the heroic defence and relief of Lucknow. Taken in order of time, it has three stages. The first stretches from the outbreak at Meerut in May to the end of September. This is the heroic stage of the Mutiny. No reinforcements had arrived from England during these months. It was the period of the massacres, and of the tragedy of Cawnpore. Yet during those months Delhi was stormed, Cawnpore avenged, and Havelock made his amazing march, punctuated with daily battles, for the relief of Lucknow. The second stage extends from October 1857, to March 1858, when British troops were poured upon the scene of action, and Colin Campbell recaptured Lucknow, and broke the strength of the revolt. The third stage extends to the close of 1858, and marks the final suppression of the Mutiny.

The story, with its swift changes, its tragical sufferings, its alternation of disaster and triumph, is a warlike epic, and might rather be sung in dithyrambic strains, than told in cold and halting prose. If some genius could do for the Indian Mutiny what Napier has done for the Peninsular War, it would be the most kindling bit of literature in the English language. What a demonstration the whole story is, of the Imperial genius of the British race! "A nation," to quote Hodson—himself one of the most brilliant actors in the great drama—"which could conquer a country like the Punjaub, with a Hindoostanee army, then turn the energies of the conquered Sikhs to subdue the very army by which they were tamed; which could fight out a position like Peshawur for years, in the very teeth of the Afghan tribes; and then, when suddenly deprived of the regiments which effected this, could unhesitatingly employ those very tribes to disarm and quell those regiments when in mutiny—a nation which could do this, is destined indeed to rule the world!"

These sketches do not pretend to be a reasoned and adequate "history" of the Mutiny. They are, as their title puts it, the "Tale" of the Mutiny—a simple chain of picturesque incidents, and, for the sake of dramatic completeness, the sketches are grouped round the three heroic names of the Mutiny—Cawnpore, Lucknow, and Delhi. Only the chief episodes in the great drama can be dealt with in a space so brief, and they will be told in simple fashion as tales, which illustrate the soldierly daring of the men, and the heroic fortitude of the women, of our race.

On the evening of May 10, 1857, the church bells were sounding their call to prayer across the parade-ground, and over the roofs of the cantonment at Meerut. It had been a day of fierce heat; the air had scorched like a white flame; all day long fiery winds had blown, hot as from the throat of a seven times heated furnace. The tiny English colony at Meerut—languid women, white-faced children, and officers in loosest undress—panted that long Sunday in their houses, behind the close blinds, and under the lazily swinging punkahs. But the cool night had come, the church bells were ringing, and in the dusk of evening, officers and their wives were strolling or driving towards the church. They little dreamed that the call of the church bells, as it rose and sank over the roofs of the native barracks, was, for many of them, the signal of doom. It summoned the native troops of Meerut to revolt; it marked the beginning of the Great Mutiny.

Yet the very last place, at which an explosion might have been expected, was Meerut. It was the one post in the north-west where the British forces were strongest. The Rifles were there, 1000 strong; the 6th Dragoons (Carabineers), 600 strong; together with a fine troop of horse artillery, and details of various other regiments. Not less, in a word, than 2200 British troops, in fair, if not in first-class, fighting condition, were at the station, while the native regiments at Meerut, horse and foot, did not reach 3000. It did not need a Lawrence or a Havelock at Meerut to make revolt impossible, or to stamp it instantly and fiercely out if it were attempted. A stroke of very ordinary soldiership might have accomplished this; and in that event, the Great Mutiny itself might have been averted.

The general in command at Meerut, however, had neither energy nor resolution. He had drowsed and nodded through some fifty years of routine service, rising by mere seniority. He was now old, obese, indolent, and notoriously incapable. He had agreeable manners, and a soothing habit of ignoring disagreeable facts. Lord Melbourne's favourite question, "Why can't you leave it alone?" represented General Hewitt's intellect. These are qualities dear to the official mind, and explain General Hewitt's rise to high rank, but they are not quite the gifts needed to suppress a mutiny. In General Hewitt's case, the familiar fable of an army of lions commanded by an ass, was translated into history once more.

On the evening of May 5 cartridges were being served out for the next morning's parade, and eighty-five men of the 3rd Native Cavalry refused to receive or handle them, though they were the old familiar greased cartridges, not the new, in whose curve, as we have seen, a conspiracy to rob the Hindu of his caste, and the Mohammedan of his ceremonial purity, was vehemently suspected to exist. The men were tried by a court-martial of fifteen native officers—six of them being Mohammedans and nine Hindus—and sentenced to various terms of imprisonment.

At daybreak on the 9th, the whole military force of the station was assembled to witness the military degradation of the men. The British, with muskets and cannon loaded, formed three sides of a hollow square; on the fourth were drawn up the native regiments, sullen, agitated, yet overawed by the sabres of the Dragoons, the grim lines of the steady Rifles, and the threatening muzzles of the loaded cannon. The eighty-five mutineers stood in the centre of the square.

One by one the men were stripped of their uniform—adorned in many instances with badges and medals, the symbols of proved courage and of ancient fidelity. One by one, with steady clang of hammer, the fetters were riveted on the limbs of the mutineers, while white faces and dark faces alike looked on. For a space of time, to be reckoned almost by hours, the monotonous beat of the hammer rang over the lines, steady as though frozen into stone, of the stern British, and over the sea of dark Sepoy faces that formed the fourth side of the square. In the eyes of these men, at least, the eighty-five manacled felons were martyrs.

The parade ended; the dishonoured eighty-five marched off with clank of chained feet to the local gaol. But that night, in the huts and round the camp fires of all the Sepoy regiments, the whispered talk was of mutiny and revenge. The very prostitutes in the native bazaars with angry scorn urged them to revolt. The men took fire. To wait for the 31st, the day fixed for simultaneous mutiny throughout Bengal, was too sore a trial for their patience. The next day was Sunday; the Sahibs would all be present at evening service in the church; they would be unarmed. So the church bells that called the British officers to prayer, should call their Sepoys to mutiny.

In the dusk of that historic Sabbath evening, as the church bells awoke, and sent their pulses of clangorous sound over the cantonment, the men of the 3rd Native Cavalry broke from their quarters, and in wild tumult, with brandished sabres and cries of "Deen! Deen!" galloped to the gaol, burst open the doors, and brought back in triumph the eighty-five "martyrs." The Sepoy infantry regiments, the 11th and 20th, ran to their lines, and fell into rank under their native officers. A British sergeant, running with breathless speed, brought the news to Colonel Finnis of the 11th. "For God's sake, sir," he said, "fly! The men have mutinied."

Finnis, a cool and gallant veteran, was the last of men to "fly." He instantly rode down to the lines. The other British officers gathered round him, and for a brief space, with orders, gesticulations, and appeals, they held the swaying regiments steady, hoping every moment to hear the sound of the British dragoons and artillery sweeping to the scene of action. On the other side of the road stood the 20th Sepoys. The British officers there also, with entreaties and remonstrances and gestures, were trying to keep the men in line. For an hour, while the evening deepened, that strange scene, of twenty or thirty Englishmen keeping 2000 mutineers steady, lasted: and still there was no sound of rumbling guns, or beat of trampling hoofs, to tell of British artillery and sabres appearing on the scene. The general was asleep, or indifferent, or frightened, or helpless through sheer want of purpose or of brains!

Finnis, who saw that the 20th were on the point of breaking loose, left his own regiment, and rode over to help its officers. The dusk by this time had deepened almost into darkness. A square, soldierly figure, only dimly seen, Finnis drew bridle in front of the sullen line of the 20th, and leaned over his horse's neck to address the men. At that moment a fiercer wave of excitement ran across the regiment. The men began to call out in the rear ranks. Suddenly the muskets of the front line fell to the present, a dancing splutter of flame swept irregularly along the front, and Finnis fell, riddled with bullets. The Great Mutiny had begun!

The 11th took fire at the sound of the crackling muskets of the 20th. They refused, indeed, to shoot their own officers, but hustled them roughly off the ground. The 20th, however, by this time were shooting at every white face in sight. The 3rd Cavalry galloped on errands of arson and murder to the officers' houses. Flames broke out on every side. A score of bungalows were burning. The rabble in the bazaar added themselves to the mutineers, and shouts from the mob, the long-drawn-out splutter of venomous musketry, the shrieks of flying victims, broke the quiet of the Sabbath evening.

Such of the Europeans in Meerut that night as could make their escape to the British lines were safe; but for the rest, every person of European blood who fell into the hands of the mutineers or of the bazaar rabble was slain, irrespective of age or sex. Brave men were hunted like rats through the burning streets, or died, fighting for their wives and little ones. English women were outraged and mutilated. Little children were impaled on Sepoy bayonets, or hewn to bits with tulwars. And all this within rifle-shot of lines where might have been gathered, with a single bugle-blast, some 2200 British troops!

General Hewitt did, indeed, very late in the evening march his troops on to the general parade-ground, and deployed them into line. But the Sepoys had vanished; some on errands of murder and rapine, the great body clattering off in disconnected groups along the thirty odd miles of dusty road, barred by two rivers, which led to Delhi.

One trivial miscalculation robbed the outbreak of what might well have been its most disastrous feature. The Sepoys calculated on finding the Rifles, armed only with their side-arms, in the church. But on that very evening, by some happy chance, the church parade was fixed for half-an-hour later than the previous Sunday. So the Native Cavalry galloped down to the lines of the Rifles half-an-hour too soon, and found their intended victims actually under arms! They wheeled off promptly towards the gaol; but the narrow margin of that half-hour saved the Rifles from surprise and slaughter.

Hewitt had, as we have seen, in addition to the Rifles, a strong troop of horse artillery and 600 British sabres in hand. He could have pursued the mutineers and cut them down ruthlessly in detail. The gallant officers of the Carabineers pleaded for an order to pursue, but in vain. Hewitt did not even send news to Delhi of the revolt! With a regiment of British rifles, 1000 strong, standing in line, he did not so much as shoot down, with one fierce and wholesome volley, the budmashes, who were busy in murder and outrage among the bungalows. When day broke Meerut showed streets of ruins blackened with fire, and splashed red with the blood of murdered Englishmen and Englishwomen. According to the official report, "groups of savages were actually seen gloating over the mangled and mutilated remains of their victims." Yet Hewitt thought he satisfied all the obligations of a British soldier by peacefully and methodically collecting the bodies of slaughtered Englishmen and Englishwomen. He did not shoot or hang a single murderer!

It is idle, indeed, to ask what the English at Meerut did on the night of the 10th; it is simpler to say what they did not do. Hewitt did nothing that night; did nothing with equal diligence the next day—while the Sepoys that had fled from Meerut were slaying at will in the streets of Delhi. He allowed his brigade, in a helpless fashion, to bivouac on the parade-ground; then, in default of any ideas of his own, took somebody else's equally helpless advice, and led his troops back to their cantonments to protect them!

General Hewitt explained afterwards that while he was responsible for the district, his brigadier, Archdale Wilson, was in command of the station. Wilson replied that "by the regulations, Section XVII.," he was under the directions of General Hewitt, and, if he did nothing, it was because that inert warrior ordered nothing to be done. Wilson, it seems, advised Hewitt not to attempt any pursuit, as it was uncertain which way the mutineers had gone. That any attempt might be made to dispel that uncertainty did not occur, apparently, to either of the two surprising officers in command at Meerut! A battery of galloper guns outside the gates of Delhi might have saved that city. It might, indeed, have arrested the Great Mutiny.

But all India waited, listening in vain for the sound of Hewitt's cannon. The divisional commander was reposing in his arm-chair at Meerut; his brigadier was contemplating "the regulations, Section XVII.," and finding there reasons for doing nothing, while mutiny went unwhipped at Meerut, and was allowed at Delhi to find a home, a fortress, and a crowned head! It was rumoured, indeed, and believed for a moment, over half India, that the British in Meerut had perished to a man. How else could it be explained that, at a crisis so terrible, they had vanished so completely from human sight and hearing? Not till May 24—a fortnight after the outbreak—did a party of Dragoons move out from Meerut to suppress some local plunderers in the neighbourhood.

One flash of wrathful valour, it is true, lights up the ignominy of this story. A native butcher was boasting in the bazaar at Meerut how he had killed the wife of the adjutant of the 11th. One of the officers of that regiment heard the story. He suddenly made his appearance in the bazaar, seized the murderer, and brought him away a captive, holding a loaded pistol to his head. A drum-head court-martial was improvised, and the murderer was promptly hanged. But this represents well-nigh the only attempt made at Meerut during the first hours after the outbreak to punish the mutiny and vindicate law.

Colonel Mackenzie, indeed, relates one other incident of a kind to supply a grim satisfaction to the humane imagination even at this distance of time. Mackenzie was a subaltern in one of the revolting regiments—the 3rd Bengal Light Cavalry. When the mutiny broke out he rode straight to the lines, did his best to hold the men steady, and finally had to ride for his life with two brother officers, Lieutenant Craigie and Lieutenant Clarke. Here is Colonel Mackenzie's story. The group, it must be remembered, were riding at a gallop.

> The telegraph lines were cut, and a slack wire, which I did not see, as it swung across the road, caught me full on the chest, and bowled me over into the dust. Over my prostrate body poured the whole column of our followers, and I well remember my feelings as I looked up at the shining hoofs. Fortunately I was not hurt, and regaining my horse, I remounted, and soon nearly overtook Craigie and Clarke, when I was horror-struck to see a palanquin-gharry—a sort of box-shaped venetian-sided carriage—being dragged slowly onwards by its driverless horse, while beside it rode a trooper of the 3rd Cavalry, plunging his sword repeatedly through the open window into the body of its already dead occupant—an unfortunate European woman. But Nemesis was upon the murderer. In a moment Craigie had dealt him a swinging cut across the back of the neck, and Clarke had run him through the body. The wretch fell dead, the first Sepoy victim at Meerut to the sword of the avenger of blood.

For the next few weeks Hewitt was, probably, the best execrated man in all India. We have only to imagine what would have happened if a Lawrence, instead of a Hewitt, had commanded at Meerut that night, to realise for how much one fool counts in human history. That Hewitt did not stamp out mutiny or avenge murder in Meerut was bad; his most fatal blunder was, that he neither pursued the mutineers in their flight to Delhi, nor marched hard on their tracks to the help of the little British colony there.

Lord Roberts, indeed, holds that pursuit would have been "futile," and that no action by the British commanders at Meerut could have saved Delhi; and this is the judgment, recorded in cold blood nearly forty years afterwards, by one of the greatest of British soldiers. Had the Lord Roberts of Candahar, however, been in command himself at Meerut, it may be shrewdly suspected the mutineers would not have gone unpursued, nor Delhi unwarned! Amateur judgments are not, of course, to be trusted in military affairs; but to the impatient civilian judgment, it seems as if the massacres in Delhi, the long and bitter siege, the whole tragical tale of the Mutiny, might have been avoided if Hewitt had possessed one thrill of the fierce energy of Nicholson, or one breath of the proud courage of Havelock.

CHAPTER II

DELHI

Delhi lies thirty-eight miles to the south-west of Meerut, a city seven miles in circumference, ancient, stately, beautiful. The sacred Jumna runs by it. Its grey, wide-curving girdle of crenellated walls, is pierced with seven gates. It is a city of mosques and palaces and gardens, and crowded native bazaars. Delhi in 1857 was of great political importance, if only because the last representative of the Grand Mogul, still bearing the title of the King of Delhi, resided there in semi-royal state. The Imperial Palace, with its crowd of nearly 12,000 inmates, formed a sort of tiny royal city within Delhi itself, and here, if anywhere, mutiny might find a centre and a head.

Moreover, the huge magazines, stored with munitions of war, made the city of the utmost military value to the British. Yet, by special treaty, no British troops were lodged in Delhi itself; there were none encamped even on the historic Ridge outside it.

The 3rd Cavalry, heading the long flight of mutineers, reached Delhi in the early morning of the 11th of May. They spurred across the bridge, slew the few casual Englishmen they met as they swept through the streets, galloped to the king's palace, and with loud shouts announced that they had "slain all the English at Meerut, and had come to fight for the faith."

The king, old and nervous, hesitated. He had no reason for revolt. Ambition was dead in him. His estates had thriven under British administration. His revenues had risen from a little over £40,000 to £140,000. He enjoyed all that he asked of the universe, a lazy, sensual, opium-soaked life. Why should he exchange a musky and golden sloth, to the Indian imagination so desirable, for the dreadful perils of revolt and war? But the palace at Delhi was a moral plague-spot, a nest of poisonous insects, a vast household in which fermented every bestial passion to which human nature can sink. And discontent gave edge and fire to every other evil force. A spark falling into such a magazine might well produce an explosion. And the shouts of the revolted troopers from Meerut at its gates supplied the necessary spark.

While the old king doubted, and hesitated, and scolded, the palace guards opened the gates to the men of the 3rd Cavalry, who instantly swept in and slaughtered the English officials and English ladies found in it. Elsewhere mutiny found many victims. The Delhi Bank was attacked and plundered, and the clerks and the manager with his family were slain. The office of the *Delhi Gazette* shared the same fate, the unfortunate compositors being killed in the very act of setting up the "copy" which told of the tragedy at Meerut. All Europeans found that day in the streets of Delhi, down to the very babies, were killed without pity.

There were, as we have said, no white troops in Delhi. The city was held by a Sepoy garrison, the 38th, 54th, and 74th Sepoy regiments, with a battery of Sepoy artillery. The British officers of these regiments, when news of the Meerut outbreak reached them, made no doubt but that Hewitt's artillery and cavalry from Meerut would follow fierce and fast on the heels of the mutineers. The Sepoys were exhorted briefly to be true to their salt, and the men stepped cheerfully off to close and hold the city gates against the mutineers.

The chief scene of interest for the next few hours was the main-guard of the Cashmere Gate. This was a small fortified enclosure in the rear of the great gate itself, always held by a guard of fifty Sepoys under a European officer. A low verandah ran around the inner wall of the main-guard, inside which, were the quarters of the Sepoys; a ramp or sloping stone causeway led to the summit of the gate itself, on which stood a small two-roomed house, serving as quarters for the British officer on duty. From the main-guard, two gates opened into the city itself.

The guard on that day consisted of a detachment of the 38th Native Infantry. They had broken into mutiny, and assisted with cheers and laughter at the spectacle of Colonel Ripley, of the 54th N.I., with other officers of that regiment, being hunted and sabred by some of the mutinous light cavalry who had arrived from Meerut. Two companies of the 54th were sent hurriedly to the gate, and met the body of their colonel being carried out literally hacked to pieces.

Colonel Vibart, one of the officers of the 54th, has given in his work, "The Sepoy Mutiny," a vivid account of the scene in the main-guard, as he entered it. In one corner lay the dead bodies of five British officers who had just been shot. The main-guard itself was crowded with Sepoys in a mood of sullen disloyalty. Through the gate which opened on the city could be seen the revolted cavalry troopers, in their French-grey uniforms, their swords wet with the blood of the British officers they had just slain. A cluster of terrified English ladies—some of them widows already, though they knew it not—had sought refuge here, and their white faces added a note of terror to the picture.

Major Abbott, with 150 men of the 74th N.I., presently marched into the main-guard; but the hold of the officers on the men was of the slightest, and when mutiny, in the mass of Sepoys crowded into the main-guard, would break out into murder, nobody could guess.

Major Abbott collected the dead bodies of the fallen officers, put them in an open bullock-cart, covered them with the skirts of some ladies' dresses, and despatched the cart, with its tragic freight, to the cantonments on the Ridge. The cart found its way to the Flagstaff Tower on the Ridge, and was abandoned there; and when, a month afterwards, the force under Sir Henry Barnard marched on to the crest the cart still stood there, with the dead bodies of the unfortunate officers—by this time turned to skeletons—in it.

Matters quickly came to a crisis at the Cashmere Gate. About four o'clock in the afternoon there came in quick succession the sound of guns from the magazine. This was followed by a deep, sullen, and prolonged blast that shook the very walls of the main-guard itself, while up into the blue sky slowly climbed a mighty cloud of smoke. Willoughby had blown up the great powder-magazine; and the sound shook both the nerves and the loyalty of the Sepoys who crowded the main-guard. There was kindled amongst them the maddest agitation, not lessened by the sudden appearance of Willoughby and Forrest, scorched and blackened by the explosion from which they had in some marvellous fashion escaped.

Brigadier Graves, from the Ridge, now summoned Abbott and the men of the 74th back to that post. After some delay they commenced their march, two guns being sent in advance. But the first sound of their marching feet acted as a match to the human powder-magazine. The leading files of Abbott's men had passed through the Cashmere Gate when the Sepoys of the 38th suddenly rushed at it and closed it, and commenced to fire on their officers. In a moment the main-guard was a scene of terror and massacre. It was filled with eddying smoke, with shouts, with the sound of crackling muskets, of swearing men and shrieking women. Here is Colonel Vibart's description of the scene:—

> The horrible truth now flashed on me—we were being massacred right and left, without any means of escape! Scarcely knowing what I was doing, I made for the ramp which leads from the courtyard to the bastion above. Every one appeared to be doing the same. Twice I was knocked over as we all frantically rushed up the slope, the bullets whistling past us like hail, and flattening themselves against the parapet with a frightful hiss. To this day it is a perfect marvel to me how any one of us escaped being hit. Poor Smith and Reveley, both of the 74th, were killed close beside me. The latter was carrying a loaded gun, and, raising himself with a dying effort, he discharged both barrels into a knot of Sepoys, and the next moment expired.

The struggling crowd of British officers and ladies reached the bastion and crowded into its embrasures, while the Sepoys from the main-guard below took deliberate pot-shots at them. Presently a light gun was brought to bear on the unhappy fugitives crouching on the summit of the bastion. The ditch was twenty-five feet below, but there was no choice. One by one the officers jumped down. Some buckled their sword-belts together and lowered the ladies. One very stout old lady, Colonel Vibart records, "would neither jump down nor be lowered down; would do nothing but scream. Just then another shot from the gun crashed into the parapet; somebody gave the poor woman a push, and she tumbled headlong into the ditch beneath." Officers and ladies scrambled up the almost perpendicular bank which forms the farther wall of the ditch, and escaped into the jungle beyond, and began their peril-haunted flight to Meerut.

Abbott, of the 74th, had a less sensational escape. His men told him they had protected him as long as they could; he must now fly for his life. Abbott resisted long, but at last said, "Very well. I'm off to Meerut; but," he added, with a soldier's instinct, "give me the colours." And, carrying the colours of his regiment, he set off with one other officer on his melancholy walk to Meerut.

**LIEUTENANT GEORGE WILLOUGHBY,
BENGAL ARTILLERY**

Reproduced, by kind permission of his niece, Miss Wallace, *from a photograph of an unfinished water-colour drawing, taken about 1857*

The most heroic incident in Delhi that day was the defence and explosion of the great magazine. This was a huge building, standing some 600 yards from the Cashmere Gate, packed with munitions of war—cannon, ammunition, and rifles—sufficient to have armed half a nation, and only a handful of Englishmen to defend it. It was in charge of Lieutenant Willoughby, who had under him two other officers (Forrest and Raynor), four conductors (Buckley, Shaw, Scully, and Crowe), and two sergeants (Edwards and Stewart); a little garrison of nine brave men, whose names deserve to be immortalised.

Willoughby was a soldier of the quiet and coolly courageous order; his men were British soldiers of the ordinary stuff of which the rank and file of the British Army is made. Yet no ancient story or classic fable tells of any deed of daring and self-sacrifice nobler than that which this cluster of commonplace Englishmen was about to perform. The Three Hundred who kept the pass at Thermopylae against the Persian swarms, the Three, who, according to the familiar legend, held the bridge across the Tiber against Lars Porsena, were not of nobler fibre than the Nine who blew up the great magazine at Delhi rather than surrender it to the mutineers.

Willoughby closed and barricaded the gates, and put opposite each two six-pounders, doubly loaded with grape; he placed a 24-pound howitzer so as to command both gates, and covered other vulnerable points with the fire of other guns. In all he had ten pieces of artillery in position—with only nine men to work them. He had, indeed, a score of native officials, and he thrust arms into their reluctant hands, but knew that at the first hostile shot they would run.

But the Nine could not hope to hold the magazine finally against a city in revolt. A fuse was accordingly run into the magazine itself, some barrels of powder were broken open, and their contents heaped on the end of the fuse. The fuse was carried into the open, and one of the party (Scully) stationed beside it, lighted portfire in hand. Willoughby's plan was to hold the magazine as long as he could work the guns. But when, as was inevitable, the wave of mutinous Sepoys swept over the walls, Willoughby was to give the signal by a wave of his hat, Scully would instantly light the fuse, and the magazine—with its stores of warlike material, its handful of brave defenders, and its swarm of eager assailants—would vanish in one huge thunderclap!

Presently there came a formal summons in the name of the King of Delhi to surrender the magazine. The summons met with a grim and curt refusal. Now the Sepoys came in solid columns down the narrow streets, swung round the magazine, and girdled it with shouts and a tempest of bullets. The native defenders, at the first shot, clambered down the walls and vanished, and the forlorn but gallant Nine were left alone. Hammers were beating fiercely on the gates. A score of improvised scaling-ladders were placed against the walls, and in a moment the Sepoys were swarming up. A gate was burst open, but, as the assailants tried to rush in, a blast of grape swept through them. Willoughby's nine guns, each worked by a single gunner, poured their thunder of sound, and storm of shot, swiftly and steadily, on the swaying mass of Sepoys that blocked the gate.

Lieutenant Forrest, who survived the perils of that fierce hour, has told, in cool and soldierly language, its story:—

> Buckley, assisted only by myself, loaded and fired in rapid

> succession the several guns above detailed, firing at least four rounds from each gun, and with the same steadiness as if standing on parade, although the enemy were then some hundreds in number, and kept up a hot fire of musketry on us within forty or fifty yards. After firing the last round, Buckley received a musket ball in his arm above the elbow; I, at the same time, was struck in the left hand by two musket balls.

When, before or since, has there been a contest so heroic or so hopeless? But what can Nine do against twice as many hundreds? From the summit of the walls a deadly fire is concentrated on the handful of gallant British. One after another drops. In another moment will come the rush of the bayonets. Willoughby looks round and sees Scully stooping with lighted port-fire over the fuse, and watching for the agreed signal. He lifts his hand. Coolly and swiftly Scully touches the fuse with his port-fire. The red spark runs along its centre; there is an earth-shaking crash, as of thunder, a sky-piercing leap of flame. The walls of the magazine are torn asunder; bodies of men and fragments of splintered arms fly aloft. The whole city seems to shake with the concussion, and a great pillar of smoke, mushroom-topped and huge, rises slowly in the sky. It is the signal to heaven and earth of how the Nine British, who kept the great magazine, had fulfilled their trust.

Of those gallant Nine, Scully, who fired the train, and four others vanished, along with hundreds of the mutineers, in one red rain. But, somehow, they themselves scarcely knew how, Willoughby, with his two officers, and Conductor Buckley found themselves, smoke-blackened and dazed, outside the magazine, and they escaped death, for the moment at least.

The fugitives who escaped from the Cashmere Gate had some very tragical experiences. Sinking from fatigue and hunger, scorched by the flame-like heat of the sun, wading rivers, toiling through jungles, hunted by villagers, they struggled on, seeking some place of refuge. Some reached Meerut, others Umballa, but many died. Of that much-enduring company of fugitives, it is recorded that the women often showed the highest degree of fortitude and patience. Yet more than one mother had to lay her child, killed by mere exposure or heat, in a nameless jungle grave; more than one wife had to see her husband die, of bullet or sword-stroke, at her feet.

But the fate of these wanderers was happier than that of the Europeans left in the city. Some twenty-seven—eleven of them being children and eight women—took refuge in a house near the great mosque. They held the house for three days, but, having no water, suffered all the agonies of thirst. The Sepoys set vessels of water in front of the house, and bade the poor besieged give up their arms and they should drink. They yielded, gave up the two miserable guns with which they had defended themselves, and were led out. No water was given them. Death alone was to cool those fever-blackened lips. They were set in a row, the eleven children and sixteen men and women, and shot. Let tender-hearted mothers picture that scene, transacted under the white glare of the Indian sun!

Some fifty Europeans and Eurasians barricaded themselves in a strong house in the English quarter of the city. The house was stormed, the unhappy captives were dragged to the King of Delhi's palace, and thrust into an underground cellar, with no windows and only one door. For five days they sweltered and sickened in that black hole. Then they were brought out, with one huge rope girdling them—men, women, and children, a pale-faced, haggard, half-naked crowd, crouching under one of the great trees in the palace garden. About them gathered a brutal mob of Sepoys and Budmashes, amongst whom was Abool Bukr, the heir-apparent to the King of Delhi. The whole of the victims were murdered, with every accompaniment of cruelty, and it is said that the heir-apparent himself devised horrible refinements of suffering.

Less than six months afterwards Hodson, of Hodson's Horse, shot that princely murderer, with a cluster of his kinsfolk, under the walls of Delhi, and in the presence of some 6000 shuddering natives, first explaining, that they were the murderers of women and children. Their bodies were brought in a cart through the most public street of the city, laid side by side, under the tree and on the very spot where they had tortured and murdered our women.

Mutiny grows swiftly. On Sunday night was fired, from the ranks of the 20th Sepoys, the volley that slew Colonel Finnis, and was, so to speak, the opening note in the long miserere of the Mutiny. At four o'clock on Monday afternoon the thunder of the great magazine, as it exploded, shook the walls of Delhi. Before the grey light of Tuesday morning broke over the royal city every member of the British race in it was either slain or a captive.

When a powder-magazine is fired, the interval of time between the flash of the first ignited grain and the full-throated blast of the explosion is scarcely measurable. And if the cluster of keen and plotting brains behind the Great Mutiny had carried out their plans as they intended, the Mutiny would have had exactly this bewildering suddenness of arrival. There is what seems ample evidence to prove that Sunday, May 31, was fixed for the simultaneous rising of all the Sepoy regiments in Bengal. A small committee of conspirators was at work in each regiment, elaborating the details of the Mutiny. Parties were to be told off in each cantonment, to murder the British officers and their families while in church, to seize the treasury, release the prisoners, and capture the guns. The Sepoy regiments in Delhi were to take possession of that great city, with its arsenal.

The outbreak at Meerut not merely altered the date, it changed the character of the revolt. The powder-magazine exploded, so to speak, in separate patches, and at intervals spread over weeks. It was this circumstance—added to the fact that the Sepoys had rejected the greased cartridges, and with them the Enfield rifle, against which Brown Bess was at a fatal disadvantage—that, speaking humanly, robbed the Mutiny of half its terror, and helped to save the British Empire in India.

But, even allowing for all this, a powder-magazine—although it explodes only by instalments—is a highly uncomfortable residence while the explosion is going on; and seldom before or since, in the long stretch of human history, have human courage and fortitude been put to such a test, as in the case of the handful of British soldiers and civilians who held the North-West Provinces for England during the last days of May 1857.

Sir George Campbell, who was in Simla at the time, has told the story of how he stood one day, early in June, beside the telegraph operator in Umballa, and listened while the wire, to use his own words, "seemed to repeat the experience of Job." "First we heard that the whole Jullunder brigade had mutinied, and were in full march in our direction, on the way to Delhi. While that message was still being spoken, came another message, to tell us that the troops in Rajpootana had mutinied, and that Rohilcund was lost; following which, I heard that the Moradabad regiment had gone, and that my brother and his young wife had been obliged to fly."

Let it be remembered that the revolted districts equal in area France, Austria, and Prussia put together; in population they exceeded them. And over this great area, and through this huge population, the process described by the telegrams, to whose rueful syllables Sir George Campbell listened, was being swiftly and incessantly repeated. The British troops did not number 22,000 men, and they were scattered over a hundred military stations, and submerged in a population of 94,000,000. Let the reader imagine fifteen or sixteen British regiments sprinkled in microscopic fragments over an area so vast, and amongst populations so huge!

The Sepoy army in Bengal numbered 150,000 men, and within six weeks of the shot which killed Colonel Finnis at Meerut, of its 120 regiments of horse and foot, only twenty-five remained under the British flag, and not five of these could be depended upon! A whole army, in a word, magnificently drilled, perfectly officered, strong in cavalry, and yet more formidable in guns, was in open and murderous revolt. Some idea of the scale and completeness of the Mutiny can be gathered from the single fact that every regiment of regular cavalry, ten regiments of irregular cavalry out of eighteen, and sixty-three out of seventy-four regiments of infantry, then on the strength of the Bengal army, disappeared finally and completely from its roster!

In each cantonment during the days preceding the revolt, the British officers on the spot were—to return to our figure—like men shut up in a powder-magazine with the train fired. There might be a dozen or twenty British officers with their families at a station held by a battery of native artillery, a couple of squadrons of native horse, and a regiment of native infantry—all plotting revolt and murder! Honour forbade the British to fly. To show a sign of mistrust or take a single visible precaution would be to precipitate the outbreak. Many of the old Bengal officers relied on their Sepoys, with a fond credulity that nothing could alarm, and that made them blind and deaf to the facts about them. "It was not," says Trevelyan, "till he saw his own house in flames, and not till he looked down the barrels of Sepoy muskets, and heard Sepoy bullets whizzing round his ears, that an old Bengal officer could begin to believe that his men were not as staunch as they ought to be."

But all officers were not so blind as this. They knew their peril. They saw the tragedy coming. They walked day after day in front of the line of their men's muskets on parade, not knowing when these iron tubes would break into red flame and flying bullets. They lay down night after night, knowing that the Sepoys in every hut were discussing the exact manner and time of their murder. Yet each man kept an untroubled brow, and went patiently the round of his duty, thanking God when he had no wife and child at the station to fall under the tender mercies of the mutineers. Farquhar, of the 7th Light Cavalry, writing to his mother at the time, said, "I slept every night dressed, with my revolver under my pillow, a drawn sword on my bed, and a loaded double-barrelled gun just under my bed. We remained in this jolly state," he explained, "a fortnight."

When the outbreak came, and the bungalows were in flames, and the men were shouting and firing on the parade-ground, it was a point of honour among the officers to hurry to the scene and make one last appeal to them, dying too often under the bullets of their own soldiers. The survivors then had to fly, with their women and children, and hide in the hot jungle or wander over the scorching plains, on which the white heat burns like a flame, suffering all the torments of thirst and weariness, of undressed wounds, and of wearing fever. If some great writer, with full knowledge and a pen of fire, could write the story of what was dared and suffered by Englishmen and Englishwomen at a hundred scattered posts throughout the North-West Provinces, in the early stages of the Mutiny, it would be one of the most moving and heroic tales in human records.

Sir Joseph Fayrer tells how, early in 1857, he was a member of a tiger-shooting expedition into the Terai. It was a merry party, and included some famous shots and great civil officials. They had killed their eleventh tiger when the first news of the rising reached the party. "All my companions," says Fayrer, "except Gubbins, were victims of the Mutiny during the year. Thomason was murdered at Shah Jehanpore; Gonne in the Mullahpore district; Colonel Fischer was killed by the men of his own regiment; Thornhill was murdered at Seetapore; Lester was shot through the neck during the siege of Lucknow; Graydon was killed after the first relief of Lucknow." Swift-following deaths of this sort have to be multiplied over the whole area of the Mutiny, before we can realise what it cost in life.

Fayrer, as a single example of the sort of tragedies which took place on every side, tells how his brother, who was an officer in a regiment of irregular cavalry, was killed. He was second in command of a detachment supposed to be of loyalty beyond suspicion. It had been sent by Lawrence from Lucknow to maintain order in the unsettled districts. There was no sign that the men intended to rise. The morning bugle had gone, the troop was ready to start, and young Fayrer, who had gone out, walked to a well with his charger's bridle over his arm, and was drinking water from a cup. Suddenly one of his own troopers came up behind him and cut him down through the back of the neck with his tulwar. "The poor lad—only twenty-three—fell dead on the spot, gasping out the word 'mother' as he fell." The troopers instantly rode at the three other British officers of the detachment. One of these slew three Sepoys before he was killed himself; the second, ill mounted, was overtaken and slain; the third, a splendid rider, made a reckless leap over a nullah, where his pursuers dared not follow, and so escaped.

Before describing the great drama at Cawnpore, or Lucknow, or Delhi, it is worth while to give, if only as hasty vignettes, some pictures of what happened at many of the stations scattered through Oude and the Punjaub. They are the opening episodes of a stupendous tragedy.

According to Sir Herbert Edwardes, it was the act of an English boy that saved the Punjaub. A very youthful operator—a mere lad—named Brendish, was by some accident alone in the Delhi Telegraph Office. When the Mutiny broke out he had to flee like the rest; but, before leaving, he wired a somewhat incoherent message to Umballa. "We must leave office," it ran; "all the bungalows are on fire, burning down by the Sepoys of Meerut. They came in this morning.... Nine Europeans are killed." That message reached Umballa, was sent on to Lahore, and was read there as a danger-signal so expressive, that the authorities at once decided to disarm the native troops at that station. The cryptic message was then flashed on to Peshawur, and was there read in the same sense, and acted upon with the same promptitude. Brendish was one of the few who afterwards escaped from Delhi.

At some of the stations, where cool heads and steadfast courage prevailed, the Sepoys were disarmed with swiftness and decision. This was especially the case in the Punjaub, where the cause of England was upheld by the kingly brain of John Lawrence, the swift decision of Herbert Edwardes, and the iron courage of Neville Chamberlain and of John Nicholson.

Lord Roberts has told how, on May 12, he was present as scribe at a council of war held in Peshawur. Round the table sat a cluster of gallant soldiers, such as might well take charge of the fortunes of a nation in the hour of its deadliest peril. Herbert Edwardes was there, and Neville Chamberlain, and Nicholson. They had to consider how to hold the Punjaub quiet while all Bengal was in a flame of mutiny. The Punjaub was a newly conquered province; its warlike population might well be expected to seize the first opportunity of rising against its conquerors. It was held by an army of over 80,000 troops, and of these only 15,000 were British—the rest, some 65,000, were almost sure to join the Mutiny. For every British soldier in the Punjaub, that is, there were four probable mutineers, while behind these was a warlike population, just subdued by the sword, and ready to rise again.

But the cool heads that met in that council were equal to their task. It was resolved to disarm all doubtful regiments, and raise new forces in their stead in the Punjaub itself, and from its wild frontier clans. A movable column, light-footed, hard-hitting, was to be formed under Neville Chamberlain's command, with which to smite at revolt whenever it lifted its head. So the famous Movable Column came into being, commanded in turn by Chamberlain and by Nicholson. That column itself had to be purged heroically again and again to cleanse it from mutinous elements, till it practically came to consist of one field-battery, one troop of horse-artillery, and one infantry regiment, all British. Then it played a great part in the wild scenes of the Mutiny.

Before new levies could be raised in the Punjaub, however, the English had to give some striking proof of decision and strength. No Indian race will fight for masters who do not show some faculty for command. The crisis came at Peshawur itself, towards the end of May. The Sepoys had fixed May 22 for rising against their officers. On the 21st the 64th Native Infantry was to march into Peshawur, and on the following morning the revolt was to take place. Herbert Edwardes and Nicholson, however, were the last men in the world to be caught off their guard. At 7 A.M. on the morning of the 21st, parade was held, and, as the result of some clever manœuvres, the five native regiments found themselves confronted by a line of British muskets, and ordered to "pile arms." The intending mutineers were reduced, almost with a gesture, to the condition of an unarmed mob, and that lightning-stroke of decision saved the Punjaub. Levies poured in; new regiments rose like magic; a loyal army became possible.

Little more than a fortnight afterwards, Neville Chamberlain discovered a plot in the 35th Native Infantry, and promptly blew two ringleaders from the guns, the first instance of that dramatic form of punishment in the Mutiny. Later, when Nicholson took command of the Movable Column, he was compelled to disarm two native regiments, the 35th and the 33rd. The 33rd was on its march to join the column, and Nicholson conducted the business with so nice an adjustment of time and method that the 35th had been disarmed, and their muskets and belts packed in carts and sent off to the fort, just as the 33rd marched up. As it halted it found itself, not side by side with a regiment of accomplices, but in front of a long and menacing line of British infantry and guns, and Roberts himself rode forward with the order to its colonel to pile arms. "What! disarm my regiment?" said that astonished officer, who was serenely unconscious that there was a mutinous brain under every shako in his regiment. When the order was repeated, the old colonel broke into actual tears. But there were sterner wills and stronger brains than his in command, and the 33rd was, in turn, reduced to harmlessness.

At Lahore, again, the Sepoys had an elaborate plot to kill their officers, overpower the European troops, and seize the treasury and the guns. Lahore was a city of 90,000 inhabitants, with a garrison of 2500 Sepoys in the city itself. The city troops were to rise first, and their success was to be signalled to Meanmeer, the military cantonment, six miles distant. Mutiny at Lahore was to be followed by revolt through all the military stations of the district, from the Rabee to the Sutlej. The plot, however, was discovered. General Corbett, a cool and gallant soldier, resolved to disarm the whole native garrison.

On the night of May 12, three days before the date fixed for the Mutiny, a military ball was to be held. This arrangement was not changed, lest the suspicions of the Sepoys should be aroused, and dancing was kept up till two o'clock in the morning. Then the officers at grey dawn hurried to the parade-ground, where, by instructions issued the day before, the whole brigade was assembled, nominally to hear some general orders read. These were read in the usual fashion at the head of each regiment. Then some brigade manœuvres followed, and these were so adroitly arranged that, at their close, the native regiments found themselves in quarter-distance column, with five companies of a British regiment, the 81st, opposite them in line, the guns being still in the rear of the 81st.

In a single sentence, brief and stern, the order was given for the native regiments to "pile arms." The Grenadiers of the 16th, to whom the order was first addressed, hesitated; the men began to handle their arms; for one breathless moment it was doubtful whether they would obey or fight. But simultaneously with the words "pile arms," the 81st had fallen back, coolly and swiftly, between the guns, and the Sepoys, almost at a breath, found themselves covered by a battery of twelve pieces loaded with grape, the artillerymen standing in position with burning port-fires, whilst along the line of the 81st behind ran the stern order, "Load," and already the click of the ramrods in the muskets was heard.

The nerve of the Sepoys failed! Sullenly they piled arms, and 600 English, by adroitness and daring, disarmed 2500 Sepoys without a shot! What five minutes before had been a menace to the British power was made harmless.

Montgomery, the chief civil officer at Lahore, divides with Corbett the honour of the brilliant stroke of soldiership which saved the city. Never was there a less heroic figure in outward appearance than that of Montgomery. He was short, stout, soft-spoken, rubicund-faced, and bore, indeed, a ludicrous resemblance to Mr. Pickwick as depicted by the humorous pencil of "Phiz." He was familiarly known, as a matter of fact, to all Englishmen in his province by the sobriquet of "Pickwick." But nature sometimes conceals an heroic spirit within a very unheroic-looking body. If in outward look there was something sheep-like in Montgomery's appearance, there was a lion-like strain in his courage. He had only a hint of the coming storm. A couple of scanty telegrams brought in the news of the mutiny at Meerut and the seizure of Delhi. With quick vision Montgomery read the temper of the native troops at Meanmeer, and, with swifter decision than even that of Corbett, he advised that they should be instantly disarmed. That decision averted a great disaster.

The whole story shows what is possible to clear judgment and resolute courage; but where these failed, or where some old Bengal officer retained his blind and fond credulity as to the "staunchness" of his men, then great tragedies became possible.

Thus at Futteghur, some seventy miles from Cawnpore, the 10th Native Infantry, with some irregular troops, held the cantonments. General Goldie was divisional commander; Colonel Smith held command of the 10th, and cherished a piously confident belief in the loyalty of his Sepoys. The civilians, with a shrewder insight into the state of affairs, believed mutiny certain, and murder highly probable, and determined to leave the station. On June 4 a little fleet of boats, laden with almost the entire English colony in the place—merchants, shopkeepers, missionaries, with their wives and children—started down the river, to the huge disgust of Colonel Smith, who thought their departure a libel on his beloved Sepoys. Part of the company found refuge with a friendly Zemindar, while three boats, containing nearly seventy persons—of whom forty-nine were women and children—pushed on to Cawnpore. In Cawnpore, however, though they were in ignorance of the fact, Wheeler and his gallant few were already fighting for life against overwhelming odds.

News soon reached the Sepoy lines at Cawnpore that three boat-loads of Sahibs were on the river, and a rush was made for them. The poor victims had pulled in to the bank and were enjoying "afternoon tea" when the horde of mutineers burst upon them. Some tried to hide in the long grass, which was set on fire above them. The rest, scorched, wounded, half-naked, with bleeding feet—mothers trying to shelter or carry their children—were dragged to the presence of Nana Sahib. The ladies and children were ordered to sit on the ground; their husbands, with their hands tied, were arranged in careful order behind them. Being thus picturesquely arranged for easy murder, some files of the 2nd Cavalry were marched up to kill the whole. The process was lengthy, wives clinging to their husbands, mothers trying to shelter their little ones with their own bodies from the keen cavalry swords. Nana Sahib watched the whole process with the leisurely and discriminating interest of a connoisseur.

On June 18 Colonel Smith's trusted Sepoys broke into open revolt at the station, whence these poor fugitives had fled. The little British garrison, consisting of thirty fighting men, with sixty ladies and children, took refuge in a low mud fort, and held it for nearly three weeks. Then they fought their way to their boats and fled. They were fiercely pursued. One boat grounded, and its miserable passengers were summarily murdered. Death by bullets, by sunstroke, by drowning, pursued the rest. One boat-load escaped, but escaped only to reach Cawnpore, and to perish amid the horrors of the slaughter-house there.

One survivor has left a record of that dreadful voyage. He was in the boat that first grounded and was boarded by the Sepoys. He describes how the passengers were shot, and how "Major Robertson, seeing no hope, begged the ladies to come into the water rather than fall into their hands. While the ladies were throwing themselves into the water I jumped into the boat, took up a loaded musket, and, going astern, shot a Sepoy.... Mr. and Mrs. Fisher were about twenty yards from the boat; he had his child in his arms, apparently lifeless. Mrs. Fisher could not stand against the current; her dress, which acted like a sail, knocked her down, when she was helped up by Mr. Fisher.... Early the next morning a voice hailed us from the shore, which we recognised as Mr. Fisher's. He came on board, and informed us that his poor wife and child had been drowned in his arms."

For skill, daring, and promptitude, nothing exceeded the fashion in which the incipient mutiny at Multan was trampled out. At no other post were the conditions more perilous. The garrison consisted of a troop of native horse-artillery, two regiments of native infantry, and the 1st Irregular Cavalry; the only English troops were 50 artillerymen in charge of the magazine. Here, then, were 50 British artillerymen, without guns, opposed to over 3000 Sepoys—horse, foot, and artillery!

The decisive factor in the problem was the character of the British commander, Major Chamberlain. His strong will and genius for command held the 1st Irregular Cavalry steady. They were Hindus from the neighbourhood of Delhi, with a full measure of the superstition and pride of caste which swept away other regiments. But they believed in their commander. He swayed their imaginations as with a touch of magic. The spell of his looks and voice, his imperious will, overbore the impulse to revolt. His men declared they would follow him to the death! Chamberlain resolved to disarm the other native regiments, and he performed the perilous feat, not only with miraculous audacity, but with a miraculous nicety of arrangement.

The 2nd Punjaub Infantry and the 1st Punjaub Cavalry were to arrive at the station on a given day. They were native troops, but could—for the moment at least—be trusted. The new troops came in at nightfall. At 4 A.M. the next morning the two Sepoy regiments and a troop of native artillery were marched out as if for an ordinary parade. They were suddenly halted; the Punjaub troops quietly marched betwixt them and their lines; the fifty English gunners took their places beside the guns of the native artillery, and a little band of Sikh cavalry that could be trusted rode up to the flank of the guns.

Then Chamberlain gave the order to the suspected regiments to "pile arms." One Sepoy shouted, "Don't give up your arms! Fight for them;" but his English adjutant instantly grasped him by the throat, shook him as a terrier would shake a rat, and flung him on the ground. The mutinous Sepoys hesitated; their courage sank; they meekly piled arms, were marched back weaponless to their barracks, and the station was saved. But it was a great feat to disarm a whole garrison with only fifty English gunners. The regiment of irregular cavalry was permanently saved by the spell of Chamberlain's authority, and, as a reward, is still the 1st Regiment of Bengal Cavalry.

Some of the revolting regiments, it is satisfactory to know, had very distressful experiences. They found that mutiny was a bad investment. Let the tale of the 55th, for example, be told. The regiment broke into open mutiny at Mardan on May 22, fired on their officers, and marched off to the hills with the regimental colours and treasure. Its colonel, Spottiswoode, blew out his brains in mingled grief and despair when he saw his "faithful" Sepoys in open revolt.

Meanwhile, the most menacing figure in all the great drama of the Mutiny—that of Nicholson—made its appearance on the track of the mutineers. Nicholson overtook them on the 24th, after a ride of seventy miles, slew 150, captured another 150 with the stolen colours, and promptly executed forty of his prisoners by blowing them from his guns. The rest of the broken regiment crossed the border, were hunted down by the hill-tribes, fell into the hands of Mohammedan fanatics, were "converted" by the argument of whip and sword, or were sold as slaves. "One fat old subahdar," says Mr. Cave-Browne, "was sold for four annas (sixpence)"! Mutiny, it is clear, proved a very bitter experience for the unhappy 55th! The legend that has grown round the wanderings of this broken regiment is told by Mr. Rudyard Kipling in his vivid story, "The Lost Legion."

CHAPTER III

STAMPING OUT MUTINY

Perhaps the most characteristic story of Sepoy outbreak is that at Allahabad. The city stands at the junction of the Ganges and the Jumna, 500 miles from Calcutta, and, with its strong fortress and great arsenal, was a strategic point scarcely second in importance to Delhi. It had a population of 75,000, highly fanatical in temper. Its arsenal was one of the largest in India, having arms for 40,000 men and great stores of artillery. Yet, with the exception of the magazine staff, there was not a British soldier in the city! It was garrisoned by the 6th Native Infantry, a wing of a Sikh regiment, the 9th, a battery of native artillery, and some native cavalry.

Colonel Simpson of the 6th, who was in command, cherished the most enthusiastic faith in his men. He looked on his cherished Sepoys as a regiment of mere dusky-skinned Sir Galahads; each one of them was as faithful as Milton's Abdiel! Some sixty superannuated British artillerymen, the youngest of them over fifty years of age, had been thrown hurriedly into the fort itself as a garrison; and Colonel Simpson strongly urged that his regiment should be taken into the fort in their place as "a proof of confidence." This would have been like putting a committee of wolves inside the fold!

At evening parade on June 6, Colonel Simpson read to his Sepoys the formal thanks of the Governor-General for their virtuous offer to go out and fight the wicked mutineers at Delhi. He added a glowing eulogium of their loyalty on his own account. The Sepoys cheered, Colonel Simpson and his fellow-officers adjourned to the mess-room, and no doubt discoursed with great comfort on the much-enduring fidelity of their men. Within four hours of being thanked by Lord Canning and praised by Colonel Simpson, the "faithful" Sepoys of the 6th Infantry had murdered seventeen officers and all the women and children of English blood they could capture, and were in full march to Delhi.

The tale is typical. At nine o'clock a bugle call sounded from the lines—it was the signal for revolt. The men rushed to arms. The Sepoy artillerymen holding the bridge swung their guns round, and opened fire on their officers. Harward and Alexander, in command of the Native Irregular Horse, and both officers of great promise, leaped into their saddles, and galloped fiercely to the bridge to recapture the guns. When they gave the order to charge, their treacherous followers suddenly pulled up; and, followed by only three troopers, the officers rode at the guns. Alexander, rising in his stirrups for one gallant sword-stroke, was shot through the heart; and Harward had to gallop for his life.

Simpson and his officers in the meanwhile ran to the parade-ground to "expostulate" with their men. Five officers were instantly shot down. Colonel Simpson was beginning to address a new series of compliments to his faithful Sepoys, but they turned their muskets upon him, and interrupted his eloquence with a volley. By some miracle he escaped and galloped off to the fort. He had to ride past the mess-house, and the mess guard turned out and took pot shots at him as he rode. The unhappy colonel reached the gate of the fort with a dying horse, a wounded arm, and an entirely new theory of Sepoy loyalty.

But was the fort itself safe? Its garrison consisted of the sixty odd superannuated artillerymen, a few civilian volunteers, the wing of a Sikh regiment, and a company of the 9th Native Infantry. These men held the gate, and were, of course, only waiting to open it to their revolted comrades. If the Sikhs joined hands with them, there remained nothing but hopeless massacre for the British. And only five days before, at Benares, it must be remembered, a Sikh regiment had opened fire on its officers! As a matter of fact, the Sikhs in the fort were effervescing with excitement. Mutiny was in the air. Upon whom the Sikh muskets might be turned, their owners themselves scarcely knew. It was a crisis of the sort which overwhelms weak men, but gives a man of heroic will a supreme opportunity. And, fortunately, a man with all the decision and courage the moment needed was on the spot.

Lieutenant Brasyer had fought as a private in the ranks through the Sutlej campaigns, and won a commission by his coolness and daring. He possessed exactly the genius needed for commanding irregular soldiery. He was an athlete, a fine swordsman, a man of the swiftest decision and most gallant courage. He is not unworthy, indeed, to be ranked for leadership and personal daring with Hodson of "Hodson's Horse." Brasyer had first to master his Sikhs, trembling on the verge of revolt themselves. Archibald Forbes has described his method: "Standing over the magazine with a red-hot iron in his hand, he swore by Nanac, Ram Das, Govind, and all other Gooroos of the Sikhs, that if his men did not promptly fall in and obey his orders he would blow the regiment to the Sikh equivalent of Hades."

Brasyer's glance and voice, his imperious will and daring, mastered the Sikhs, and they fell obediently into rank. He instantly marched them down, with loaded muskets, to the gate, and, with the help of the artillerymen with their port-fires, drove out the company of Sepoys that held it, and the fort was saved! But to master Sepoys in open revolt, by Sikhs on the edge of revolt, was a great feat, and shows for how much, at such a crisis, one clear heroic will counts.

That night Allahabad was given up to outrage and murder. Only above the fort itself flew the flag of England, and in the fort the handful of British officers, determined that the great arsenal should not fall into the hands of mutineers, were preparing to copy Willoughby's desperate example at Delhi. Russell, of the artillery, who was in charge of the magazine, ran trains of powder into it, and stood ready to blow it up in the event of capture.

In the city itself every European or Eurasian was hunted like a rat through the streets, and slain with every accompaniment of cruelty. Outrage, in the ordinary sense, was not, on the whole, a marked feature of the Great Mutiny. The

Sepoys, that is, were on fire with cruelty rather than with lust. But their cruelty spared neither age nor sex. The wife of a captain, according to one story current at the time—and perhaps not true—was literally boiled alive in ghee, or melted butter. Children were tossed on bayonets, men roasted in the flames of their own bungalows; women were mutilated and dismembered. The Sepoys plundered the Treasury, carrying off some £300,000 in booty.

One detail of the Allahabad massacre peculiarly shocked the imagination of British soldiers wherever the tale was told. At the mess-table of the 9th, that fatal night, there sat eight fresh-faced and boyish cadets just out from England. They had not yet joined their regiments, and military life, with all its fun and excitement, lay in the glamour of the unknown before them. When the bugle rang out on the parade-ground these eight unposted boy ensigns ran out with the other officers. They fell into the hands of the mutineers, and seven had their throats cut like sheep. The eighth, a boy of sixteen, was left for dead, but survived in spite of horrible wounds for four days, hiding himself in a ravine. On the fifth day he was discovered, dragged to the native lines, and thrust into a hut as a prisoner.

He found there a Christian catechist, who had formerly been a Mohammedan, and who was being tortured by the Sepoys to make him renounce his faith. The catechist's courage had given way, but the gallant English lad—himself only sixteen years of age—urged the unhappy catechist, "Don't deny Christ! Never deny Christ!" Neill reached Allahabad in time to rescue both catechist and ensign. But the ensign, Arthur Cheek, died of his wounds four days after Neill's arrival. He had joined his regiment just eighteen days when murdered in this tragical fashion by his own men. It may be imagined how the massacre of the "poor little griffins" moved the British soldier to wrath everywhere.

For a few days mutiny and riot reigned supreme at Allahabad. Then, hot from Benares, there appeared on the scene Neill with a handful of his "Lambs," as the Madras Fusileers, with admiring irony, were called. "Thank God, sir," said the sentry at the gate of the fort, as Neill rode in; "you'll save us yet!"

Neill is one of the cluster of great soldiers thrust into sudden fame by the crisis of the Mutiny, and is hardly to be judged by the standard of smaller men and of a tamer period. He was of Scottish blood, an Ayrshire man, with a vehement fighting quality, and a strain of iron resolve, which had come to him, perhaps, from a line of Covenanting ancestry. He was a veteran soldier, accustomed to govern wild clans and irregular troops, and had held high command in the Turkish contingent in the Crimea. On the domestic side, he was, as many stern and rough-natured men are, of singular tenderness. He was strongly religious, too, though he borrowed his religion rather from the Old Testament than the New.

When the Mutiny broke out Neill found himself in command of the Madras Fusileers, a regiment which included many wild spirits in its ranks, but which, in fighting quality, was a warlike instrument of singular efficiency. Neill and his "Lambs" were summoned from Madras by the crisis in Bengal, and Neill's best qualities, as well as his worst—his fighting impulse, his Scottish pride of race, the natural vehemence of his temper, his soldierly hate of mutiny, the wrath of a strong man at outrages on women and children, and his fierce contempt for the feebleness shown by some of the "arm-chair colonels" of the Bengal Army—all threw their owner into a mood in which he was prepared to dare anything to crush the Mutiny and to punish the mutineers.

The Fusileers landed on the railway wharf at Calcutta, as night fell, on May 23. The great city of Benares was on the verge of revolt, and Neill's "Lambs" were to be hurried up by express to its rescue. The station-master told Neill that unless he could get his men ashore in three minutes the train would start without them. But Neill was not the man to allow a railway time-table to stand betwixt him and the suppression of a mutiny. With an abrupt gesture, he put the station-master in charge of a sergeant and a file of Fusileers. The unhappy official shouted for help, but in another second stokers, firemen, and guard were in a row against the station wall, with a couple of "blue-caps" in charge of each. At the double the Fusileers came up the wharf, filed into the carriages, and the train, carrying the left wing of the regiment, moved off to Raneegange; thence the detachment was carried by bullock-carts to Benares. Leaving the bulk of his men to follow, Neill pushed on with the leading detachment to Benares.

Nowhere, perhaps, did English courage shine out with a clearer flame than at Benares. Benares is the holy city of Hinduism; it had a population of 300,000, fanatical and turbulent in the highest degree. The cantonment was held by three Sepoy regiments—all pledged to revolt—150 men of a British regiment, the 10th, and some thirty British gunners, with half a battery of artillery, under the command of Olpherts. But the cluster of soldiers and civilians responsible for the city—Tucker the commissioner, Frederick Gubbins the judge, Lind the magistrate, Ponsonby the brigadier, and Olpherts in command of the guns—held on to their post; by mere cool audacity kept the turbulent city in awe, and the mutinous Sepoys from breaking out; and sent on to other posts in greater peril than their own such scanty reinforcements of British troops as reached them. In the Commissioner, Tucker, at least, this heroic courage had a religious root. "The twenty-second chapter of 2 Samuel," he wrote to Lord Canning, "was their stand-by." "The Lord is my rock, and my fortress, and my deliverer," is the opening verse of David's song in that chapter; "the God of my rock; in Him will I trust. He is my shield, and the horn of my salvation, my high tower, and my refuge."

Neill reached the city on June 3, and found himself on the very edge of a tragedy. The Sepoys had arranged for an outbreak on the night of June 4. The native troops numbered over 2000; the British troops, as we have seen, consisted of 150 men of the 10th, and thirty artillerymen with three guns. To these Neill added sixty of his "Lambs" whom he had brought with him. Neill put the impress of his vehement will on the brigadier, Ponsonby, in charge of the station, and at half-an-hour's notice it was resolved to disarm the Sepoys.

The business was ill-managed. The Sepoys commenced to shoot, the Sikhs turned on their officers. Ponsonby, an old man, found "the sun" and the strain of the scene too much for him, and visibly broke down. He dismounted, and Neill, who had been grimly watching the scene, said abruptly, "General, I assume command." Ponsonby assented in silence, and Neill instantly opened on the mutineers with grape and musketry fire, and, after a few minutes' furious shooting, Sikh and Sepoy fled. The 250, that is, destroyed, in a military sense, the 2000!

Having stamped out the Mutiny—or, rather, scattered the mutineers—Neill devoted the next two or three days to punishing it. The Governor-General telegraphed orders to push on to Allahabad, but Neill believed in making thorough work, and he wired back, "Can't move; wanted here." And for the next three days he kept the gallows busy, and hanged without pause or pity. The Sepoys had shot down their officers, and murdered women and children, and Neill was bent on showing that this was a performance which brought in its track swift and terrible punishment. "Colonel Neill's hangings" were, no doubt, of heroic scale, and, looked at through the cold perspective of forty years, wear a very black aspect. But Neill, rightly or wrongly, held that to strike, and to strike hard, and to strike swiftly, was the one policy in such a crisis.

Benares being secure, Neill pushed on across the seventy miles of dusty, heat-scorched road to Allahabad. He started with only forty-four of his "Lambs," and covered the seventy miles in two night marches. When they reached the Ganges, almost every fourth man was down with sunstroke, Neill himself being amongst the number, and his men only kept him up by dashing buckets of water over his head and chest. The boat pushed from the bank; it was found to leak at a dozen points, and began to sink. The "blue-caps" relanded, and their officer, Spurgin, called for volunteers to beat the banks of the river in search of another boat.

Almost every man able to walk volunteered, and, in the heavy sand of the river-bank, with the furnace-like heat of an Indian sun setting on fire the very air they breathed, the Fusileers began their search for a boat to carry them across to Allahabad. More than one brave fellow fell and died from heat and exhaustion. But a boat was found, the gallant forty crossed, and marched—as many of them as could still keep their feet—a tiny but dauntless band, through the gates of the fort.

Other detachments followed quickly, and Neill flung himself with all the fire of his Scottish blood into the task of restoring the British raj in the great city. At daybreak he opened with his guns, from the fort, on the suburb held by the revolted Sepoys, and then sallied out with his scanty force, and burnt it over their rebel heads. "I myself," he wrote to his wife, "was almost dying from complete exhaustion;" but his fierce spirit overbore the fainting body that carried it. He armed a river steamer with a howitzer and a party of volunteer riflemen, and employed it as a river patrol. He launched the fierce Sikhs—by this time heartily loyal—on the villages.

They were wild soldiers, gaunt, sinewy, and eager—the "Singh log" ("the lion people"), as they called themselves. Maude has left a graphic picture of the Sikhs who, at Allahabad, followed Brasyer as, with his flowing white beard, he led them in pursuit of the broken Sepoys, or hung with soldierly obedience on Neill's stern orders. "When no fighting was on hand," he says, "squads of the tall, upright, Hebraic-visaged Sikhs used to march into their commanding officer's tent, where they stood at attention, in silence, with one hand raised at the orthodox salute. 'What do you want, my men?' was the question in Hindustani. 'May it please the protector of the poor, we want two days' leave.' 'What for?' 'To get drunk, Sahib!' And their request, being considered reasonable, was usually granted!"

Neill, by the way, had to use these by no means ascetic Sikhs to keep his own "blue-caps" sober. The stocks of all the merchants in the city were practically without owners, and the finest champagnes and brandies were selling at 6d. per bottle. For a day or two it seemed probable that Neill's little force would be swept out of existence in a mere ignoble torrent of drunkenness. Neill threatened the whip and the bullet in vain; and finally marched up the Sikhs and took peremptory possession of all intoxicating drinks.

On June 18 the fighting was over, the British were masters both of fort and city, where, fourteen days before, they had been little better than prisoners or fugitives. Then was repeated, in yet sterner fashion, the retribution which had struck terror through Benares. The gallows in Allahabad groaned under its heavy and quick-following burdens. In his diary Neill wrote: "God grant that I may have acted with justice. I know I have with severity, but, under all the circumstances, I trust for forgiveness. I have done all for the good of my country, to re-establish its prestige and power, and to put down this most barbarous and inhuman insurrection." Then he recites cases of outrage and mutilation on English ladies and on little children, with details that still chill the natural blood with horror to read.

The Sepoys, it is to be noted, when the fighting was over, took their penalty with a sort of composed fatalism, to the Western imagination very amazing. Sir George Campbell tells the story of the execution of an old native officer, a subhadar, which he witnessed. "He was very cool and quiet, and submitted to be executed without remonstrance. But the rope broke, and he came down to the ground. He picked himself up, and it was rather a painful scene for the spectators. But he seemed to feel for their embarrassment, and thought it well to break the awkwardness of the situation by conversation, remarking that it was a very bad rope, and talking of little matters of that kind till another rope was procured, which made an end of him!"

It would be easy to write, or sing, a new and more wonderful Odyssey made up of the valiant combats, the wild adventures, and the distressful wanderings of little groups of Englishmen and Englishwomen, upon whom the tempest of the Mutiny broke.

Forbes-Mitchell, for example, tells the story of Robert Tucker, the judge at Futtehpore. Tucker was a great hunter, and also, like many Indian officials, an earnestly religious man, with an antique sense of duty. When the Mutiny broke out he despatched every European to Allahabad, but refused to move himself. This solitary Englishman, in a word, was determined to defend Futtehpore against all comers! Believing the native officer in charge of the police to be loyal, he sent a message to him asking him to come and make arrangements for the protection of the Treasury. This "loyal" official sent back word that the judge Sahib need not trouble himself about the Treasury; that, in the cool of the evening, he, with his "loyal" police, would come down and dismiss the dog of a judge himself to Hades!

Tucker had a hunter's armoury—rifles, smooth-bores, and hog spears. He loaded every barrel, barricaded every door and window, and waited quietly, reading his Bible, till, when the cool breath of evening began to stir, he saw the police and the local budmashes, with the green banner of Islam fluttering over their heads, marching down to attack him. Tucker was offered his life on condition that he abandoned his Christianity. Then the fight broke out. For hours the musketry crackled, and was answered by the sharp note of Tucker's rifle. Before midnight the brave judge lay, riddled with bullets and pierced with many spear-thrusts, dead on his own floor. But all round his house were strewn the bodies of those who had fallen before his cool and deadly aim.

Later on, at Kotah, a similar tragedy took place, the story of which is told by George Lawrence. Major Burton, the Resident at Kotah, with his two sons—one aged twenty-one, the other a lad of sixteen—and a single native servant, held the Residency for four hours against native troops with artillery, and a huge crowd of rioters. The Residency was at last set on fire, and Major Burton proposed to surrender on condition that the lives of his sons were spared. The gallant lads indignantly refused to accept the terms. They would all die together, they declared. They were holding the roof of the Residency against their assailants, and, as Lawrence tells the story, "they knelt down and prayed for the last time, and then calmly and heroically met their fate." The mob by this time had obtained scaling-ladders. They swept over the roof, and slew the gallant three. Major Burton's head was cut off, paraded round the town, and then fired from a gun.

One of the most surprising of these personal adventures was that which overtook the Deputy Commissioner of Delhi, Sir T. Metcalfe. Wilberforce, in his "Unrecorded Chapter of the Indian Mutiny," tells the tale, and says he heard it twice over from Sir T. Metcalfe's own lips—though Wilberforce's stories sometimes are vehemently suspected to belong to the realm of fiction rather than of sober history. His account of Metcalfe's adventure, however, is at least *ben trovato*.

Metcalfe escaped from Delhi on horseback, hotly pursued by some native cavalry. His horse broke down, and in despair Metcalfe appealed to a friendly-looking native to conceal him from his pursuers. The man led him to a cave, told him he would save him if possible, and, striking his horse on the flank, sent it galloping down the road, while Metcalfe crept through the black throat of the cave into concealment. Presently Metcalfe heard his pursuers ride up, fiercely question his protector, and finally propose to search the cave.

> On this my friend burst out laughing, and, raising his voice so that I must hear, he said, "Oh yes, search the cave. Do search it. But I'll tell you what you will find. You will find a great red devil in there; he lives up at the end of the cave. You won't be able to see him, because the cave turns at the end, and the devil always stands just round the turn, and he has got a great long knife in his hand, and the moment your head appears round the corner he will slice it off, and then he will pull the body in to him and eat it. Go in; do go in—the poor devil is hungry. It is three weeks since he had anything to eat, and then it was only a goat. He loves men, does this red devil; and if you all go in he will have such a meal!"

Metcalfe guessed that he was intended to hear this speech and act upon it. The cave, a short distance from the entrance, turned at right angles. He stood with his sword uplifted just round the corner, while a line of dismounted cavalry, in single file, one daring fellow leading, came slowly up the cave. As soon as the leader put his head in the darkness round the corner, Metcalfe smote with all his strength. The fellow's head rolled from his body, and his companions, with a yell of terror, and tumbling one over another in the darkness, fled. "Did you see him?" demanded Metcalfe's friend outside. "Do go back; he wants more than one." But the rebel cavalry had had enough. The men who had gone up the cave declared that they had actually seen the red fiend, and been scorched by the gleam of his eyes; and, mounting their horses, they fled.

"Why did you save my life?" Metcalfe asked his protector. "Because you are a just man," was the reply. "How do you know that?" asked Metcalfe. "You decided a case against me in your court," was the unexpected reply. "I and all my family had won the case in the inferior courts by lying, but you found us out, and gave judgment against us. If you had given the case for me I would not have saved your life!"

Wilberforce tells another tale which graphically illustrates the wild adventures of those wild days. Early one morning he was on picket duty outside Delhi, and in the grey dawn saw two men and a boy hurrying along the road from the city. They were evidently fugitives, and, telling his men not to fire on them, Wilberforce went forward to meet them. When the group came up the boy ran forward, threw his arms round Wilberforce's neck, and, with an exclamation in English, kissed him. The "boy" was a woman named Mrs. Leeson, the sole survivor of the Delhi massacre. She had been concealed for more than three months by a friendly native, and had at last escaped disguised as an Afghan boy.

When the Mutiny broke out she, with some other ladies and a few Englishmen, took refuge in a cellar, and for nearly three days maintained a desperate defence against the crowds attacking them. The hero of the defence was a Baptist missionary, a former shipmate of Wilberforce's, "a very tall and powerful man, with a bloodless face, grey eyes, a broad jaw, and a determined mouth." One by one the men holding the cellar fell. Food failed, the ammunition was exhausted, and at last, behind the bodies of the fallen, piled up as a breastwork, stood only the brave missionary, with nothing but his sword to protect the crouching women and children. "Stripped to the waist, behind the ghastly rampart of the dead, the hero stood; and for hours this Horatius held his own. At last he fell, shot through the heart, and the bloodthirsty devils poured in." Mrs. Leeson was covered by some of the dead bodies, and so escaped the doom of the other ladies, and at night crept out of that pit of the dead. She wandered through the dark streets, the only living Englishwoman in the great city, and saw, hanging up on the trees in the dusk, the headless trunks of white children and the mutilated bodies of Englishwomen. By happy chance she met a pitying native, who concealed her until she escaped in the fashion described, with more or less of imagination, by Wilberforce.

CHAPTER IV

CAWNPORE: THE SIEGE

> The annals of warfare contain no episode so painful as the story of this siege. It moves to tears as surely as the pages in which the greatest of all historians tells, as only he can tell, the last agony of the Athenian host in Sicily. The sun never before looked on such a sight as a crowd of women and children cooped within a small space, and exposed, during twenty days and nights, to the concentrated fire of thousands of muskets and a score of heavy cannon.

In these words Sir George Trevelyan sums up the famous struggle round the low mud-walls of Wheeler's entrenchments at Cawnpore more than forty years ago; a struggle in which Saxon courage and Hindu cruelty were exhibited in their highest measure, and which must always form one of the most heartbreaking and yet kindling traditions of the British race. Volumes have been written about Cawnpore, but Trevelyan's book remains its one adequate literary record. The writer has a faculty for resonant, not to say rhythmic prose, which recalls the style of his more famous uncle, Macaulay, and in his "Cawnpore" his picturesque sentences are flushed with a sympathy which gives them a more than literary grace.

Cawnpore at the time of the Mutiny was a great city, famous for its workers in leather, standing on the banks of the sacred Ganges, 270 miles S.E. from Delhi, and about 700 miles from Calcutta. It was a military station of great importance. Its vast magazine was stored with warlike material of every sort. It was the seat of civil administration for a rich district. But the characteristic British policy, which allows the Empire to expand indefinitely, without any corresponding expansion of the army which acts as its police and defence, left this great military station practically in the hands of the Sepoys alone. The British force at Cawnpore, in May 1857, consisted of sixty men of the 84th, sixty-five Madras Fusileers, fewer than sixty artillerymen, and a group of invalids belonging to the 32nd. The Sepoy force consisted of three strong infantry regiments and the 2nd Native Cavalry—a regiment of very evil fame.

Here, then, were all the elements of a great tragedy—a rich treasury and a huge arsenal, lying practically undefended; a strong force of Sepoys, bitter with mutiny; a turbulent city and crowded cantonments festering with crime; and only a handful of British soldiers to maintain the British flag! Had the British consisted merely of fighting men, though they counted only 300 bayonets against four regiments of splendidly trained Sepoys, and a hostile population of 60,000, their case would not have been desperate. But the little British garrison had under its guard a great company of women and children and sick folk—civilian households, the wives and families of the 32nd, and many more. For every fighting man who levelled his musket over Wheeler's entrenchments during the siege, there were at least two non-combatants—women, or little children, or invalids. A company so helpless and so great could not march; it could not attack; it could only stand within its poor screen of mud-walls and, with the stubborn and quenchless courage natural to its blood, fight till it perished.

General Sir Hugh Wheeler, who was in command at Cawnpore, was a gallant soldier, who had marched and fought for fifty years. But he had the fatal defect of being over seventy-five years of age. A little man, slender of build, with quick eye and erect figure, he carried his seventy-five years with respectable energy. But a man, no matter how brave, in whose veins ran the chill and thin blood of old age, was tragically handicapped in a crisis so fierce. Wheeler, moreover, who had married a Hindu wife, was too weakly credulous about the loyalty of his Sepoys. On May 18, scarcely a fortnight before the Mutiny, he telegraphed to Calcutta: "The plague is stayed. All well at Cawnpore!" He had been warned that Nana Sahib was treacherous, yet he called in his help, and put the Treasury in his charge for safety! This was committing the chickens, for security, to the benevolence and "good faith" of the fox! Not four days before the outbreak Wheeler actually sent back to Lucknow fifty men of the 84th who had been sent to him as a reinforcement. There was chivalry in that act, but there was besotted credulity too.

But Wheeler's most fatal mistake was in the choice he made of the place where the British garrison was to make its last stand. The Cawnpore magazine itself was a vast walled enclosure, covering three acres, with strong buildings and exhaustless store of guns and ammunition, with the river guarding one front, and a nullah acting as a ditch on another. Here would have been shelter for the women and the sick, a magnificent fighting position for the men, abundant water, and a great store of cannon.

Wheeler, for reasons which nobody has ever yet guessed, neglected this strong post. He allowed its stores of cannon to be turned against himself. He chose, instead of this formidable and sheltered post, a patch of open plain six miles distant, with practically no water supply. He threw up a slender wall of earth, which a musket-ball could pierce, and over which an active cow could jump, and he crowded into this the whole British colony at Cawnpore.

"What do you call that place you are making out on the plain?" asked the Nana's Prime Minister, Azimoolah, of a British officer. "You ought to call it the 'Fort of Despair.'" "No, no," answered the Englishman, with the pluck of his race, "we'll call it the 'Fort of Victory!'" Nevertheless, when Wheeler made that evil choice of a place of defence, he was constructing a veritable Fort of Despair.

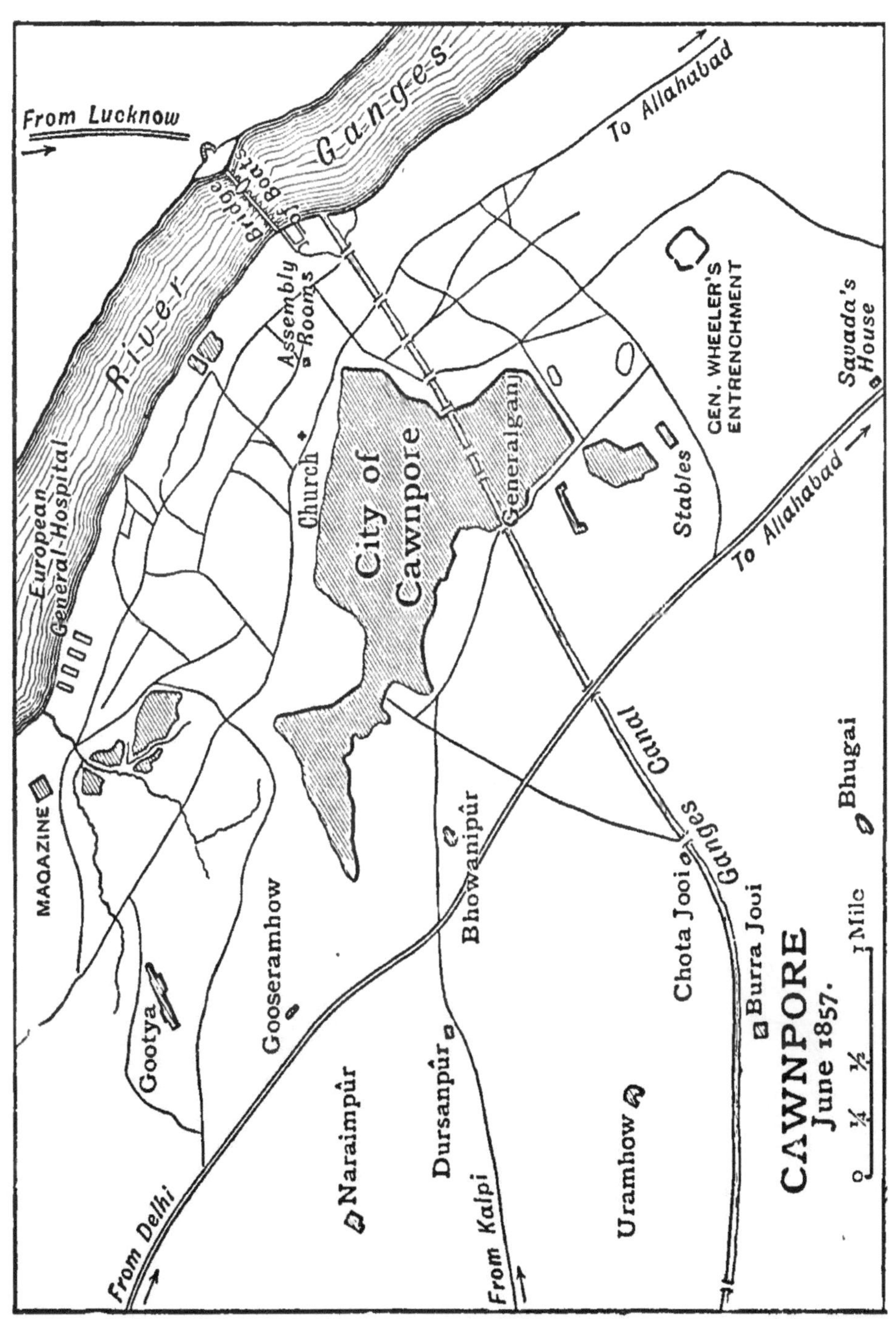

CAWNPORE, JUNE 1857.

Walker & Cockerell sc.

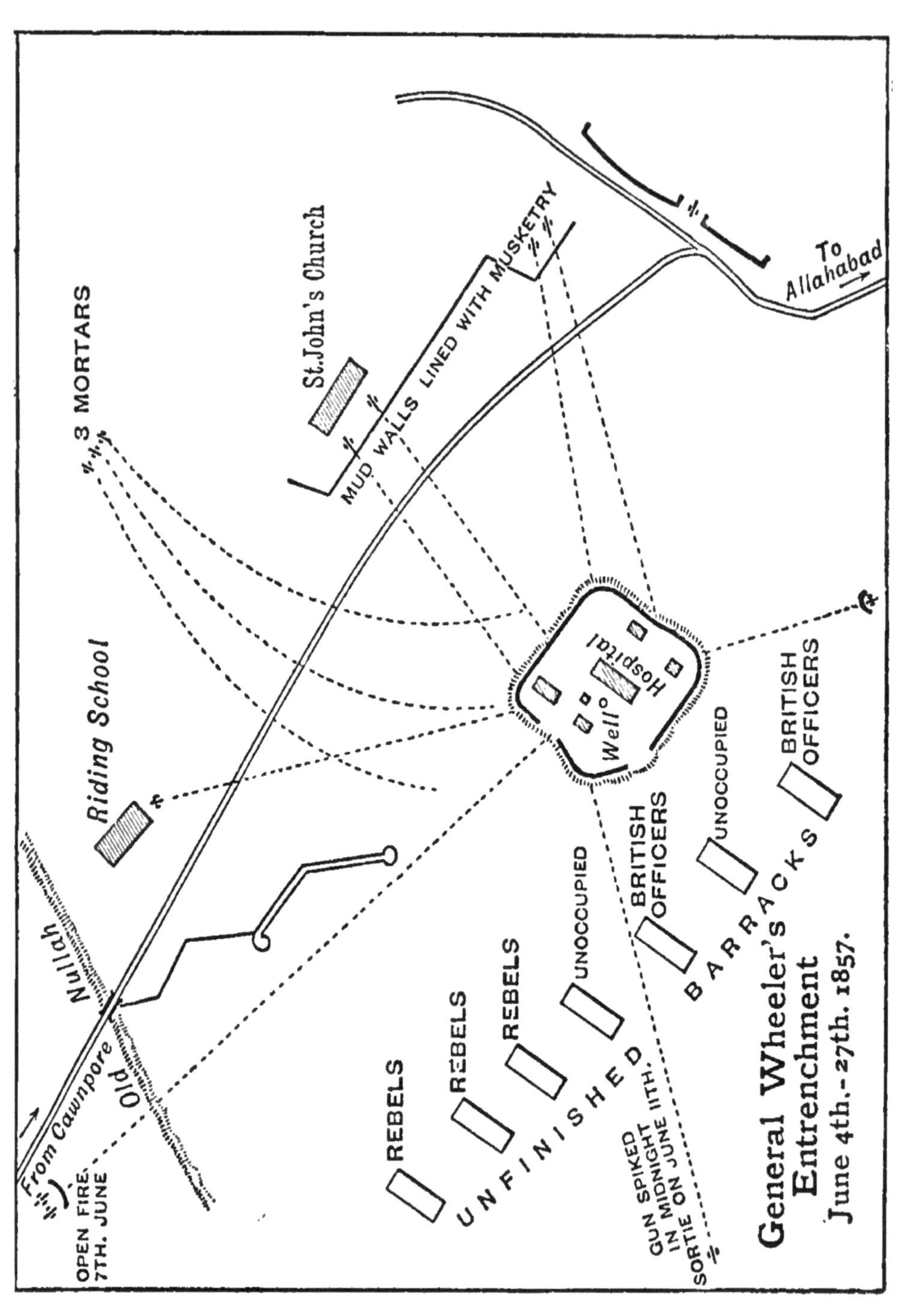

GENERAL WHEELER'S ENTRENCHMENT, JUNE 4TH.-27TH. 1857.

Walker & Cockerell sc.

Wheeler, it seems, did not occupy the magazine, as it was held by a Sepoy guard, and it would have "shown mistrust," and might have precipitated a conflict, if he had attempted to move into it. But what more expressive and public sign of "mistrust" could be imagined than the construction of the entrenchment in the open plain? And what could more fatally damage British prestige than the spectacle of the entire British community, military and civilian, crowding into these worthless defences!

If Wheeler did not occupy the magazine, he might have blown it up, and with that act have turned to smoke all the resources of the rebels. This was left to be done by Sepoy hands six weeks later. Meanwhile, Wheeler left almost unlimited resources of guns and munitions of war in the hands of the mutineers—to be employed against himself!

In the grim pause, while waiting for the outbreak, the British garrison showed a cool and gallant patience. The women, children, and civilians took up their quarters every night within the earthworks, where some ten light guns were mounted. But to "show their confidence" in their men, and, if possible, still to hold them back from mutiny, the British officers slept with their regiments. To lead a forlorn hope up the broken slope of a breach, or to stand in an infantry square while, with thunder of galloping hoofs, a dozen squadrons of cavalry charge fiercely down, needs courage. But it was a finer strain of courage still which made a British officer leave his wife and children to sleep behind the guns, standing loaded with grape, to protect them from a rush of mutineers, while he himself walked calmly down to sleep—or, at least, to feign sleep—within the very lines of the mutineers themselves!

On the night of June 4 came the outbreak. The men of the 2nd Cavalry rushed to their stables, mounted, and, with mad shouts and wild firing of pistols, galloped off to seize the magazine and to "loot" the Treasury; and as they went they burnt and plundered and slew. The 1st Sepoys followed them at once; the other two Sepoy regiments—the 53rd and 56th—hesitated. Their officers, with entreaties and orders, kept them steady till the sun rose, and then, unfortunately, dismissed them to their tents. Here they were quickly corrupted by their comrades, who had returned laden with booty from the plundered Treasury.

But before they had actually broken into mutiny, while they were yet swaying to and fro in agitated groups, by some blunder a gun from Wheeler's entrenchments opened on the Sepoys' lines. The argument of the flying grape was final! The men broke, and—a tumultuous mob—made for the city. Even then, however, some eighty Sepoys kept their fidelity, and actually joined the British within their defences, and fought bravely side by side with them for nearly twenty desperate days.

For a few wild hours murder raged through the streets of Cawnpore. Then the mutineers turned their faces towards Delhi. Had no malign influence arrested their march the great tragedy might have been escaped, and the word "Cawnpore" would not be to-day the most tragical cluster of syllables in British history. But at this point the subtle and evil genius of Nana Sahib interposed with dire effect.

Nana Sahib—or, to give his proper name, Seereek Dhoondoo Punth—was a Hindu of low birth, who had been adopted by the Peishwa of Poonah, the last representative of a great Mahratta dynasty, a prince who had been dethroned, but assigned a royal pension by the East India Company. Nana Sahib on the Peishwa's death, inherited his private fortune, a sum computed at £4,000,000 sterling; but he also claimed the great pension which the Peishwa enjoyed. The Company rejected that claim, and henceforth Nana Sahib was a man consumed with hate of the British name and power. He concealed that hate, however, beneath a smiling mask of courteous hospitality. His agent had seen the wasted British lines round Sebastopol, and reported to his master that the British strength was broken. Nana Sahib, too, who understood the Hindu character, saw that the Sepoy regiments in Bengal were drunk with arrogance, and inflamed to the verge of mere lunacy, with fanatical suspicions, while a British garrison was almost non-existent.

Here, then, were the elements of a great outbreak, and Nana Sahib believed that the British raj was about to perish. He threw in his lot with the mutineers, but he had no idea of following them to Delhi, and being merged in the crowd that plotted and wrangled in the royal palace there. He would build up a great power for himself round Cawnpore. He might make himself, he dreamed, the despot of Northern India. He might even, by-and-by, march as a conqueror down the valley of the Ganges, fight a new Plassey, very different from the last, and, to quote Trevelyan, "renew the Black Hole of Calcutta, under happier auspices and on a more generous scale, and so teach those Christian dogs what it was to flout a Mahratta!"

But, as a preliminary to all this, the great company of Christian people within Wheeler's lines must be stamped out of existence. "The wolves, with their mates and whelps, had been hounded into their den, and now or never was the time to smoke them out and knock on the head the whole of that formidable brood." So, with bribes, and promises, and threats, Nana brought back the Sepoys, who had begun their Delhi march, to Cawnpore.

On June 6, with an odd touch of official formality, Nana sent in notice to General Wheeler that he was about to attack his position. Sunday, June 7, was spent in hunting from their various places of concealment in Cawnpore all the unhappy Europeans who lingered there. One trembling family was discovered lurking under a bridge, another concealed in some native huts. They were dragged out with shouts of triumph and despatched. One Englishman, who had taken refuge in a native house, held it against the Sepoys till his last cartridge was expended, then walked out and bade them cut his throat—a request promptly complied with. When the safe and delightful luxury of hunting out solitary Europeans was exhausted, then began the attack on the British entrenchments.

The odds were tremendous! In the centre of Wheeler's entrenchment stood two single-storeyed barracks, built of thin brickwork, with verandas, and one of them roofed with straw. The mud wall, which formed the defence of the position, was four feet high, so thin that a rifle-ball could pierce it, with rough gaps made for the ten light pieces which formed the artillery of the garrison. On the north side of the entrenchment was a little triangular outwork, which the British called the Redan. On its left front, some four hundred yards distant, was a row of unfinished barracks, part of which was held by the British, part by the Sepoys, and which became the scene of the most bloody fighting of the siege. Behind these slender bulwarks was gathered a company of perhaps a thousand souls, of whom more than half were women and children.

At first the barracks gave to the non-combatants a brief shelter; but the 24-pounders of the Sepoys pierced them as though they had been built of cheese, and before many hours they were shattered into wreck, and the besieged were practically without any shelter, not merely from the rain of lead, but from the consuming heat of Indian suns and the heavy dews of Indian nights.

Sometimes, indeed, the men dug holes in the earth, into which their wives and children might creep and be sheltered by a few planks from the intolerable glare of the sun, and the incessant flight of hostile bullets. Quite as commonly, however, a British officer or civilian, as he crouched behind the poor wall of earth, loaded musket in hand, saw the white faces of his children as they slept or moaned, in the ditch by his side, while the wasted figure of his wife bent over them. There was no privacy, or shelter, or rest. The supply of food quickly failed. There was not water enough to satisfy the little children who cried from thirst, or to bathe the shattered limbs of the wounded. The men had the fierce excitement of fighting; but who shall paint the anguish of English ladies—wives and mothers—who could not find water for their children's fevered lips, or shelter them from sun and bullet.

The imagination lingers pitifully over those groups of British ladies sitting or crouching in the ditches under the earthworks: "Unshod, unkempt, ragged and squalid, haggard and emaciated, parched with drought and faint with hunger, they sat waiting to hear that they were widows. Woe was it in those days unto them that were with child. There were infants born during the terrible three weeks—infants with no future."

There were two wells in the encampment; one which, to quote Trevelyan, "yielded nothing then, which will yield nothing till the sea, too, gives up her dead." It was some two hundred yards from the rampart, and lay open to the fire of the Sepoys' batteries. It was turned into a sepulchre. Thither, night by night, the besieged carried their dead, and cast them into its depths with brief and whispered prayer; while the guns of the Sepoys thundered their requiem. Within three weeks 250 English people were cast by English hands into that strange grave. The other well lay also directly under hostile fire, and on it the Sepoy gunners, trained by British science, concentrated their fire night and day. Every drop of water drawn from it may be said to have been reddened with blood.

Over this handful of British people, faint with hunger, fevered with thirst, wasted by sickness, half mad with the sun's heat, roared day and night a tempest of hostile shot. Never before, perhaps, was such a fire concentrated on one poor patch of soil. The Sepoys could mount as many guns as they chose, and almost of whatever calibre they pleased. And they could fire, within a distance ranging from 300 to 800 yards, from under almost shot-proof shelter. From roof and window of all the buildings commanding the entrenchments streamed, with scarcely a moment's pause, showers of musketry bullets. At night the Sepoys crept within pistol-shot, and fired without cessation. Wheeler's entrenchments were literally girdled with fire; they were whipped, day and night, with incessant volleys.

By the third day every window and door in the poor barracks which served as shelter to the sick, and to the women and children, had been beaten in; and shell and ball ranged at will through the rooms. One who saw the building after the siege wrote: "The walls are riddled with cannon-shot like the cells of a honeycomb. The doors are knocked into shapeless openings. Of the verandas only a few splintered rafters remain. At some of the angles the walls are knocked entirely away, and large chasms gape blackly at you."

Never was a position more desperate; and never was there one held with a valour more obstinate. Wheeler's men had everything that was most dear to them at their backs, and everything that was most hateful in their front; and under these conditions how they fought may be imagined. In the scanty garrison, too, were over a hundred officers of the regiments in mutiny, fighters of the finest quality. It was a *corps d'élite*; a garrison of officers!

Indian life, it may be added, develops all that is proudest and most manly in the British character. The Englishman there feels that he is a member of an imperial and conquering race. To rule men is his daily business. To hunt the fiercest game in the world is his amusement. The men who knelt behind Wheeler's mud walls, had faced tigers in the jungle, had speared the wild boar in the plains, had heard the scream of a charging elephant. They were steady of nerve, quick of eye, deadly of aim, proud of their blood and race. They were standing at bay over their wives and little ones, playing a game in which the stake was a thousand British lives. And never before, or since, perhaps, was more gallant fighting done than behind Wheeler's entrenchments.

The natural leaders of the garrison emerged in such a crisis, and their names ought to awaken to-day in British ears emotions of pride as lofty as that which Greeks knew when, in the rolling and sonorous cadences of Homer's great epic, they heard the names of the heroes who fought and died round classic Troy. One of the most heroic figures in the siege is that of Captain Moore, of the 32nd, in charge of the cluster of invalids belonging to that regiment in Cawnpore. Moore was an Irishman, though with the fair hair and blue eyes proper to Saxon blood. To say that he was fearless is a very inadequate description of his temper. He delighted in the rapture and glow of battle. His courage had in it a certain cool and smiling quality that made flurry or anxiety impossible. Moore, in fact, carried about with him a sort of radiance, so that, as Trevelyan puts it, "wherever he had passed he left men something more courageous, and women something less unhappy." This fair-haired Irishman was a born king of men, of unfailing resource and "dare-devil" courage. He was wounded early in the siege, and carried his arm in a sling, but he walked to and fro calmly amid a tempest of bullets, and the men would follow his cheerful leading against any odds.

The tiny little Redan on the north face of the entrenchment was held by Major Vibart, of the 2nd Cavalry. A dreadful cross-fire searched and raked this little triangle of earth, and the handful of heroes that held it had to be renewed again and again. But the Redan kept up its splutter of answering fire day and night for three weeks, and Vibart himself survived the siege, to perish under Sepoy bullets on the river. Ashe was a young artillery officer of great promise; he commanded a battery of three guns at the north-east corner of the entrenchments, and seldom were guns better aimed and better fought. Ashe had first to invent his gunners, and next to improvise his shot, firing 6-pound balls, for example, from a 9-pound muzzle. But his cool science and sleepless activity made his battery the terror of the Sepoys.

Delafosse, of the 53rd, one of the four men who actually survived the siege, was an officer as daring and almost as skilled as Ashe. He had charge of three 9-pounder guns at the south-east angle. On one occasion the carriage of a gun in his battery took fire, and the wood, made as inflammable as tinder by the fierce Indian sun, named and crackled. There was powder—and the peril of explosion—on every side. The Sepoys, noting the dancing flame, turned all their guns on the spot. Delafosse crawled beneath the burning carriage, turned on his back, and with his naked hands pulled down the red splinters, and scattered earth on the flames, fighting them in this desperate fashion till two soldiers ran up to his help, and the fire was put out.

Perhaps the most obstinate and bloody fighting during the siege took place in the line of unfinished barracks which crossed the S.W. angle of the entrenchments. The Sepoys held the northern half of this line of buildings. Of the three buildings to the south—which completely commanded the entrenchment—what was called "No. 4," was held by a party of amateur soldiers—civil engineers employed on the East Indian railroads. There were a dozen of them, young fellows more familiar with theodolites than with rifles; but a cluster of English Lifeguards could not have fought with cooler bravery. And the civil engineers had a keenness of wit and a fertility of mechanical resource which veteran soldiers might easily have lacked.

Vainly the Sepoys pelted "No. 4" with 24-pounder shot, scourged it with musketry fire, or made wild rushes upon it. The gallant railway men devised new barriers for the doors, and new shields for the windows, and shot with cool and deadly aim, before which the Sepoys fell like rabbits. "No. 4," like Hougoumont at Waterloo, might be battered into wreck, but could not be captured. In the Memorial Church at Cawnpore to-day, not the least touching tablet is one upon which is inscribed:—

> To the memory of the Engineers of the East India Railway, who died and were killed in the great insurrection of 1857. Erected in affectionate remembrance by their brother Engineers in the North-Western Provinces.

Barrack No. 2 was a microscopic fortress, as fiercely attacked, and as valiantly defended as Barrack No. 4. It was first held by Lieutenant Glanville and a party of fourteen officers. Glanville was desperately wounded, and three-fourths of his heroic garrison killed; then the barrack was put in charge of Mowbray Thomson, of the 56th Native Infantry, one of the two officers who survived Cawnpore. Only sixteen men could find standing and fighting room in the barrack. The sixteen under Mowbray Thomson consisted of Ensign Henderson, a mere boy, half-a-dozen

Madras Fusileers, two plate-layers from the railway works, and seven men of the 84th. As the garrison dwindled under the ever-scorching fire that played on the building, it was fed with new recruits. "Sometimes," says Mowbray Thomson, "a civilian, sometimes a soldier came." But soldier and civilian alike plied his rifle with a grim and silent courage that never grew flurried, and that never knew fear.

Mowbray Thomson, who was of an ingenious turn, contrived a perch in the topmost angle of the barrack wall, and planted there an officer named Stirling, who was at an age when other lads are playing at cricket with their schoolmates, but who was a quick and most deadly shot, and who "bagged" Sepoys as a sportsman, with a breech-loading shot-gun, might bag pheasants in a populous cover. Sometimes, on an agreed signal, the garrisons from No. 2 and No. 4 would dash out together, a little knot of ragged, unwashed, smoke-blackened Sahibs, counting about thirty in all, and running without regular order, but with that expression on their faces which the Sepoys knew meant tragical business; and, with musket and bayonet or hog-spear, they would sweep the line of barracks from end to end.

Nor was courage confined to the fighting men. In one fierce sally, at an early stage of the siege, eleven mutineers were captured. A desperate fight was raging at the moment, and every man was required at the front. A rope was hastily passed round the wrists of the eleven captured Sepoys, and they were put into the charge of the wife of a private of the 32nd, named Bridget Widdowson. Drawn sword in hand, this soldier's wife, who had little children of her own in the beleaguered entrenchments, stood over the eleven mutineers, while they squatted nervously on their hams before her; and so business-like was the nourish of her weapon, so keen the sparkle in her eye, that not one man of the eleven dared to move. It was only when a guard of the stronger sex took Bridget's place that the eleven, somehow, contrived to escape. Later on in the siege the supply of cartridges failed, and all the ladies were requisitioned for their stockings, to be used in the construction of new cartridges. When before, or since, did war claim for its service such strange material!

The Sepoys, at intervals, made furious assaults on the mud walls, but these were lined by shots too deadly, and held by hands too strong, to make success possible. Had the British, indeed, been the attacking force, they would have swept over the poor earthen barrier, not four feet high, with a single charge, before the siege was a dozen hours old. But, during the whole three weeks of their attack, though the Sepoys, counting fighting men, outnumbered their foes by, perhaps, thirty to one, they never succeeded in even reaching the irregular line of earth behind which the British stood.

Their best chance occurred when, on the eighth night of the bombardment, the thatch on the barrack used as a hospital, took fire. The whole building was quickly in flames, and in their red light the entrenchment, in every part, was as visible as at noonday. The barrack was used as a sleeping-place for the women and children of the 32nd. These fled from the burning building, but not all the sick and wounded could be rescued; some perished in the smoke and flame. That was, indeed, a night of horror. "The roar of the flames," says Trevelyan, "lost every ten seconds in the peal of the rebel artillery; the whistle of the great shot; the shrieks of the sufferers, who forgot their pain in the helpless anticipation of a sudden and agonising death; the group of crying women and children huddled together in the ditch; the stream of men running to and fro between the houses, laden with sacks of provisions, and kegs of ammunition, and living burdens more precious still; the guards crouching silent and watchful, finger on trigger, each at his station along the external wall; the forms of countless foes, revealed now and again by the fitful glare, prowling around through the outer gloom"—all this made up a strangely terrible scene.

It is a proof of the quality of Moore's daring that, by way of proving to the Sepoys that this calamity had not lowered the spirits of the garrison, he organised on the following night a sally, and, with fifty picked men, dashed out on the rebel lines, swept them for many hundreds of yards, spiked a number of 24-pounder guns, and slew their gunners.

But the burning of the barracks was the fatal turning-point of the siege. It destroyed the last shelter of the sick and the women and children. The whole stock of medicines and of surgical appliances was consumed, and the wounded could no longer have their injuries dressed. The eighty odd Sepoys who formed part of the garrison had been lodged in the building now burned. It was deemed imprudent to allow them to mix with the garrison generally, and they were told to provide for themselves, and were allowed to steal out of the entrenchment and escape.

The deaths amongst the British multiplied fast. The fire of the Sepoys grew more furious. "The round shot crashed and spun through the windows, raked the earthworks, and skipped about the open ground in every corner of our position. The bullets cut the air, and pattered on the wall like hail. The great shells rolled hissing along the floors and down the trenches, and, bursting, spread around them a circle of wreck and mutilation and promiscuous destruction."

How fast the poor besieged wretches perished under this deadly hail may be imagined. A bomb, for example, fell into a cluster of seven ladies and slew them all in a breath. A soldier's wife, carrying a twin child on each shoulder, with her husband by her side, was crossing a fire-raked angle of the entrenchment. The same ball slew the husband, shattered both elbows of the wife, and tore asunder the body of one of the little twins. General Wheeler's son was lying wounded. His mother and two sisters were busy tending him, his father looking on, when a cannon-ball tore through the wall of the room and smashed the wounded lad's head literally to fragments.

One well had been turned into a sepulchre; to-day it is built over, and on the monument above it is written this inscription:—

> In a well under this enclosure were laid by the hands of their fellows in suffering the bodies of men, women, and children who died hard by during the heroic defence of Wheeler's entrenchment, when beleaguered by the rebel Nana.

Then follows a verse from Psalm cxli:—

> "Our bones are scattered at the grave's mouth, as when one cutteth and cleaveth wood upon the earth. But mine eyes are unto Thee,

O God the Lord."

The scanty supplies of water for that thirst-wasted crowd had to be drawn from the other well, and on it the Sepoys, day and night, concentrated their fire. To draw from it was a literal service of death. One brave-hearted civilian, named John MacKillop, described himself as "no fighting man," but claimed to be appointed "captain of the well," and devoted himself to the business of drawing water, the most dangerous task of the whole entrenchment. He kept to his task for nearly a week, and then, while drawing a vessel of water, was shot.

He staggered a few paces, mortally wounded, then fell, but held up with his dying hands the vessel filled with the precious fluid, and begged one who ran to his help to carry it to the lady to whom he had promised it. Bayard, dying on the banks of the Secia, and handing the water for which he himself thirsted to another dying soldier, has not a better title to be remembered than simple-minded John MacKillop, the "captain" of the Cawnpore well.

On June 24—when for nineteen days the wretched garrison had been under gun-fire—Wheeler writes to Lawrence, "All our carriages more or less disabled, ammunition short.... We have no instruments, no medicine: the British spirit alone remains; but it cannot last for ever.... Surely we are not left to die like rats in a cage." Lawrence writes back on June 27, giving what encouragement he can, and warning him not to accept any terms. "You cannot rely on the Nana's promises. *Il a tué beaucoup de prisonniers.*"

By the twenty-first day of the siege the position of the British was hopeless. Food had almost completely failed. Their guns had become unserviceable. The unconquerable garrison was fast dwindling. "At rare intervals behind the earth-work they stood—gaunt and feeble likenesses of men—clutching with muffled fingers the barrels of their muskets, which glowed with heat intolerable to the naked hand, so fierce was the blaze of the mid-day sun." They might have sallied out and cut their way through their enemies, or died fighting amongst them; and they would have done so fifty times over but for one consideration. They could not take their women and children with them; they could not abandon them. There was the certainty, too, that the Indian rains, long delayed, must soon burst upon them. Then their firearms would be rendered useless; the holes in which the women and children crouched would be flooded; their wall of mud would be washed away.

No sign of help came from without. Wheeler's last despatch, dated June 24, ended with the words, "We want aid, aid, aid." But not merely no aid, no whisper even from the outer world reached the unhappy garrison.

The Sepoys, on their part, were growing weary of the siege. Their losses were enormous. They might batter the entrenchments into dust, but they could not capture an inch of the blackened area these shot-wrecked lines of earth girdled. These Sahibs were fiercer than wounded tigers. They were, indeed, perplexingly and disquietingly aggressive. They were perpetually making fierce little sallies, whose track was marked by slaughtered Sepoys. Nana Sahib felt there was real danger that his allies might abandon their desperate task. He therefore undertook to accomplish by craft what the Sepoys could not do with cannon and bayonet.

Nana Sahib unearthed from some gloomy room in the building which formed his headquarters a captive Englishwoman waiting to be slaughtered, and sent her as a messenger to the entrenchments on the morning of June 24. "All those," ran the brief note, "who are in no way connected with the acts of Lord Dalhousie, and are willing to lay down their arms, shall receive a safe passage to Allahabad."

Wheeler, with a soldier's pride, was unwilling to give up the patch of ground he held for the Queen. The younger men, with the flame of battle in their blood, were eager to fight to the bitter end. To trust to the faith of mutineers, or to the humanity of a Hindu of Nana Sahib's tiger-like nature, they argued, was a sadly desperate venture. Yet that way there might lie a chance of life for the women and children. Death was certain if the siege lasted. It might be less certain if they capitulated.

The 25th was spent in negotiations. Moore and two others met the Nana's representatives at a spot 200 yards outside the entrenchments. They offered to surrender on condition that they were allowed to march out under arms, with sixty rounds of ammunition to each man; that carriages were provided for the wounded, the ladies, and the children; and that boats, duly stocked with food, were supplied to carry them to Allahabad. In the afternoon the Nana sent in a verbal message saying that he accepted the terms, and the British must march out that night. They refused to do this, as they needed to make some preparations. On this, the Nana sent an insolent message announcing that he must have his will; that if they delayed he would open on them with all his guns; and, as they were perishing fast from mere hunger, a few hours would leave not one of them alive.

Whiting, a gallant soldier, met the insolent threat with high courage. Let the Nana's soldiers, if they liked, he answered, try to carry the entrenchments. They had tried in vain for three weeks to do so. "If pushed to the last extremity," Whiting added, "they had powder enough in the magazine to blow both armies into the Ganges!"

Then the Nana changed his tone, and grew effusively polite. His emissaries condoled with Wheeler for the sufferings he had gone through. But, thanks to Allah, the Ever-Merciful, all was ended now! The sahibs and the memsahibs had nothing before them but a pleasant river voyage to their friends! A committee of British officers, under a guard of rebel cavalry, inspected the boats gathered at the landing-place, scarcely a mile distant from the entrenchments; at their request temporary floors of bamboos were laid down in the boats, and roofs of thatch stretched over them.

Nana Sahib, as a matter of fact, meant murder; murder, sudden, bloody, and all-embracing. But he enjoyed, so to speak, toying with his unconscious victims beforehand. Over the gorgon-like visage of murder he hung a smiling and dainty mask, and with soft-voiced courtesy he consented to all arrangements for the "comfort" of his victims!

That night at Cawnpore there were two busy spots, a mile distant from each other. In the entrenchments the poor survivors were preparing for their march, a march—though they knew it not—to the grave. Mothers were collecting the garments of their little ones. Some paid a last sad visit to the fatal well, where their dead were lying. Others were packing their scanty possessions, intending to carry them with them. Soldiers were cleaning their muskets and storing their cartridges. And a mile distant, Tantia Topee, the Nana's general, was planting his cannon and arranging his Sepoys so as to pour upon the boats at a given signal a fire which should slay the whole unhappy company they carried.

CHAPTER V

CAWNPORE: THE MURDER GHAUT

It was a company of some 450 persons—old and young, sick and wounded, men, women, and children—who filed out of Wheeler's entrenchments on the morning of June 27, in that sad pilgrimage.

Trevelyan describes the scene:—

> First came the men of the 32nd Regiment, their dauntless captain at their head; thinking little as ever of the past, but much of the future; and so marching unconscious towards the death which he had often courted. Then moved on the throng of native bearers, groaning in monotonous cadence beneath the weight of the palanquins, through whose sliding panels might be discerned the pallid forms of the wounded; their limbs rudely bandaged with shirt-sleeves and old stockings and strips of gown and petticoat. And next, musket on shoulder and revolver in belt, followed they who could still walk and fight. Step was not kept in those ranks. Little was there of martial array, or soldier-like gait and attitude. In discoloured flannel and tattered nankeen, mute and in pensive mood, tramped by the remnant of the immortal garrison. These men had finished their toil, and had fought their battle, and now, if hope was all but dead within them, there survived at least no residue of fear.

Vibart, in his single person, constituted the rearguard. A wounded man lying in a bed carried by four native bearers, an English lady walking by his side, came out of the entrenchment shortly after the rest had left. It was Colonel Ewart, of the 34th, with his faithful wife. The little group could not overtake the main body, and when it had passed out of sight round a bend in the road a crowd of the colonel's own Sepoys stopped the poor wife and her wounded husband. The porters were ordered to lay the bed down, and with brutal jests the Sepoys mocked their dying colonel. "Is not this a fine parade?" they asked, with shouts of laughter.

Then, mirth giving place to murder, they suddenly fell upon Ewart, and literally hewed him to pieces under the eyes of his agonised wife. They told her to go in peace, as they would not kill a woman, and by way of comment on the statement one of them stepped back to give himself room for the stroke, and slew her with a single blow.

The road to the Ganges, a little over a mile in length, crossed a little wooden bridge painted white, and swung to the right down a ravine to the river. "A vast multitude," says Trevelyan, "speechless and motionless as spectres, watched their descent into that valley of the shadow of death." Directly the last Englishman had crossed the bridge and turned down the lane, a double line of Sepoys was drawn across the entrance to the Ghaut, and slowly the great company made its way down to the river's edge. Some forty boats were lying there—eight-oared country budgerows, clumsy structures, with thatched roofs, and looking not unlike floating hay-stacks. They lay in the shallow water a few yards from the bank.

A moment's pause took place when the crowd of sahibs and memsahibs, with their wounded and the little ones, reached the water's edge. There were no planks by which they could reach the boats, none of the boatmen spoke a word, or made a movement. They sat silent, like spectators at a tragedy.

Then the crowd splashed into the water. The wounded were lifted into the boats; women with their children clambered on board; the men were finding their places; the officers, standing knee-deep in the river, were helping the last and feeblest to embark. It was nine o'clock in the morning.

Suddenly, in the hot morning air, a bugle screamed shrill and menacing, somewhere up the ravine. It was the signal! Out of the forty boats the native boatmen leaped, and splashed through the water to the bank. Into the straw roofs of many of the boats they thrust, almost in the act of leaping, red-hot embers, and nearly a score of boats were almost instantly red-crested with flames.

A little white Hindu temple high up on the bank overlooked the whole scene. Here sat Tantia Topee, the Nana's general, with a cluster of Sepoy officers. He controlled the whole drama from this point of vantage like a stage-manager; and, on his signal, from the lines of Sepoys who were lying concealed in the undergrowth, from guns perched high on the river-bank, and from both sides of the river at once, there broke upon the forty boats, with their flaming roofs and hapless crowds of white-faced passengers, a terrific storm of shot.

Those slain by the sudden bullet were many, and were happy in their fate. The wounded perished under the burning flakes and strangling smoke of the flaming straw roofs. Many leaped into the river, and, crouching chin-deep under the sides of the boats, tried to shelter themselves from the cruel tempest of shot. Some swam out into the stream till they sank in the reddened water under the leisurely aim of the Sepoys. Others, leaping into the water, tried to push off the stranded boats. Some of yet sterner temper, kneeling under the roofs of burning thatch, or standing waist-deep in the Ganges, fired back on the Sepoys, who by this time lined the river's edge.

General Wheeler, according to one report, perished beneath the stroke of a Sepoy's sword as he stepped out of his palkee. His daughters were slain with him, save one, the youngest, who, less happy, was carried off by a native trooper to die later. In the official evidence taken long afterwards is the account given by a half-caste Christian woman. "General Wheeler," she said, "came last in a palkee. They carried him into the water near the boat. I stood close by. He said, 'Carry me a little farther towards the boat.' But a trooper said, 'No; get out here.' As the general got out of the palkee head foremost, the trooper gave him a cut with his sword through the neck, and he fell into the water. My son was killed near him. I saw it, alas! alas! Some were stabbed with bayonets; others cut down. Little infants were torn in pieces. We saw it, we did! and tell you only what we saw. Other children were stabbed and thrown into the river. The school-girls were burnt to death. I saw their clothes and hair catch fire."

Presently the fire of the Sepoys ceased, and the wretched survivors of the massacre—125 in number—were dragged ashore. They came stumbling up the slope of the bank, a bedraggled company, their clothing dripping with the water of the Ganges, or soiled with its mud. They crept up the ravine down which, a brief hour before, they had walked with Hope shining before them. Now Grief kept pace with them; Despair went before them; Death followed after. They had left their dead in the river behind them; they were walking to a yet more cruel fate in front. "I saw that many of the ladies were wounded," said one witness afterwards; "their clothes had blood on them. Some had their dresses torn, but all had clothes. I saw one or two children without clothes. There were no men in the party, but only some boys of twelve or thirteen years of age."

The sad company was marched back to the old cantonment, where the Nana himself came out to exult over his victims. Lady Canning, in her journal, writes: "There were fifteen young ladies in Cawnpore, and at first they wrote such happy letters, saying time had never been so pleasant; it was every day like a picnic, and they hoped they would not be sent away; they said a regiment would come, and they felt quite safe. Poor, poor things; not one of them was saved." How many of that girlish band of fifteen perished, with flaming hair and dress, in the boats? Or did they strand shivering in the icy chill of terror, amongst the captives over whom the tiger glance of Nana Sahib wandered in triumph? After being duly inspected, these poor captives were thrust into a couple of rooms in the Savada-house, and left to what reflections may be imagined.

Three boats out of the forty, meanwhile, had actually got away. Two drifted to the Oude shore, and were overtaken by instant massacre. One boat, however, had for the moment a happier fate. It caught the mid-current of the Ganges, and went drifting downwards; and that solitary drifting boat, without oars or rudder, bearing up in its crazy planks above the dark waters of the Ganges the sole survivors of the heroic garrison of Cawnpore, started on a wilder, stranger voyage than is recorded elsewhere in all history.

It was Vibart's boat; and by a curious chance it included in its passengers the most heroic spirits in the garrison. Moore was there, and Ashe, and Delafosse; Mowbray Thomson swam out to it from his own boat, and with him Murphy, a private of the 32nd—two of the four who finally survived out of the whole garrison. The boat was intended to carry only fifty, but nearly a hundred fugitives were crowded within its crazy sides.

A cannon-shot smashed its rudder. It had no oars nor food. From either bank a hail of shot pursued it. Every now and again the clumsy boat would ground on some shallow; then, while the Sepoys shot fast and furiously, a group of officers would jump overboard, and push the clumsy craft afloat again.

Moore, pushing at the boat in this fashion, with broken collar-bone, was shot through the heart. Ashe and Bowden and Glanville shared the same fate. Soon the dying and the dead on the deck of this shot-pelted boat were as many as the living. "We had no food in the boat," wrote Mowbray Thomson afterwards; "the water of the Ganges was all that passed our lips. The wounded and the dead were often entangled together in the bottom of the boat."

When evening came the boat ran heavily aground. Under the screen of darkness the women and children were landed, and the boat, with great effort, floated again; the Sepoys accompanying the operation with volleys of musketry, flights of burning arrows, and even a clumsy attempt at a fire-ship. "No one slept that night, and no one ate, for food there was none on board."

When day broke the tragical voyage was continued, still to an accompaniment of musketry bullets. At two o'clock the boat stranded again. "Major Vibart," says Mowbray Thomson, "had been shot through one arm on the preceding day. Nevertheless, he got out, and, while helping to push off the boat, was shot through the other arm. Captain Turner had both his legs smashed, Captain Whiting was killed, Lieutenant Harrison was shot dead." These are sample records from that strange log.

Towards evening a boat, manned by some sixty Sepoys, appeared in pursuit, but it, too, ran upon a sand-bank, and this gave the sahibs an opportunity at which they leaped with fierce joy. From the sorely battered boat, which had been pelted for nearly two days and nights with bullets, a score of haggard and ragged figures tumbled, and came splashing, with stern purpose, through the shallows. And then, for some twenty breathless minutes, the Sepoys, by way of change, instead of being hunters, became the hunted, and only some half-dozen, who were good swimmers, escaped to tell their comrades what the experience was like. Mowbray Thomson tells the story in disappointingly bald prose. "Instead of waiting for them to attack us," he says, "eighteen or twenty of us charged them, and few of their number escaped to tell the story."

Night fell black and stormy, and through falling rain and the sighing darkness the boat, with its freight of dead and dying, drifted on. It recalls the ship of which Tennyson sang, with its "dark freight, a vanished life." In the morning it was found that the boat had drifted into some backwater whence escape was impossible. The Sepoys lined the bank and fired heavily. Vibart, who was dying, but still remained the master spirit of the little company, ordered a sally. "Whilst there was a sound arm among them that could load and fire, or thrust with the bayonet," says Kaye, "still the great game of the English was to go to the front and smite the enemy, as a race that seldom waited to be smitten."

Mowbray Thomson and Delafosse, with some twelve men of the 82nd and 34th, clambered over the side of the boat, waded ashore, and charged the Sepoys, who fled before them. They pressed eagerly on, shooting and stabbing, but presently found new crowds of the enemy gathering in their rear. The gallant fourteen faced about, and fought their way back to where they had left the boat. Alas! it had vanished.

They commenced to march along the river-bank in the direction of Allahabad, with an interval of twenty paces between each man, so as to make the fire of their pursuers less deadly. Shoeless, faint with hunger, bareheaded, they fought their way for some miles. Their pursuers grew rapidly in numbers and daring. One Englishman had fallen; the others wheeled suddenly round, and seized a small Hindu temple, determined to make a last stand there. There was just room enough for the thirteen to stand upright in the little shrine. Their pursuers, after a few minutes' anxious pause, tried to rush the door; but, as the historian of the fight puts it, "there was no room for any of them inside"—though, as it turned out, a good deal of room was required outside for the dead bodies of those who had made the attempt.

An effort was made to smoke out, and then to burn out, the unconquerable sahibs. When these devices failed, gunpowder was brought up, and arrangements made for blowing the entire shrine, with its indomitable garrison, into space. Seeing these preparations, the British charged out. Seven of them, who could swim, stripped themselves, and headed the sally, intending to break through to the river.

Seven naked sahibs, charging through smoke and flame, with levelled bayonets, would naturally be a somewhat disquieting apparition, and the seven had no difficulty in breaking through their enemies, and reaching the Ganges. The other six, who could not swim, ran full into the Sepoy mass, and died mute and fighting.

Then commenced the pursuit of the swimmers. Two were soon shot and sank; a third, swimming on his back, and not seeing where he was going, struck a sand-spit, where some natives were waiting to beat out his brains at leisure. There remained four—Mowbray Thomson, Delafosse, and two privates, a pair of strong-limbed and brave-hearted Irishmen, named Murphy and Sullivan. This heroic and much-enduring four, diving like wild ducks at the flash of hostile muskets, outswam and out-tired their pursuers. When at last they landed, they had between them "a flannel shirt, a strip of linen cloth, and five severe wounds"! They found refuge with a friendly landowner, and reached the British lines, though Sullivan died within a fortnight of reaching the place of safety.

Meanwhile, what had happened to the boat after the gallant fourteen left it? Its crew consisted of little else than wounded men, dead bodies, and exhausted women and children. Upon these swooped down a great crowd of enemies. The boat was captured, and its stem promptly turned back towards Cawnpore. On the morning of June 30, the boat lay again at the entrance of the fatal ghaut.

In the evidence taken long afterwards, there were brought back, according to one native witness, sixty sahibs, twenty-five memsahibs, and four children. "The Nana ordered the sahibs to be separated from the memsahibs, and shot. So the sahibs were seated on the ground, and two companies of the Nadiree Regiment stood ready to fire. Then said one of the memsahibs, the doctor's wife (What doctor? How should I know?) 'I will not leave my husband. If he must die, I will die with him.' So she ran and sat down behind her husband, clasping him round the waist. Directly she said this, the other memsahibs said, 'We also will die with our husbands,' and they all sat down, each with her husband. Then their husbands said, 'Go back,' but they would not. Whereupon the Nana ordered his soldiers; and they, going in, pulled them away forcibly. But they could not pull away the doctor's wife."

Captain Seppings asked leave to read prayers before they died. His hands were untied; one arm hung broken, but, standing up, he groped in his pocket for a little prayer-book, and commenced to read—but what prayer or psalm, none now can tell. "After he had read," as the witness tells the story, "he shut the book, and the sahibs shook hands all round. Then the Sepoys fired. One sahib rolled one way, one another as they sat. But they were not dead, only wounded. So they went in and finished them off with swords." When all was over, the twenty-four mem-sahibs, with their four children, were sent to swell the little crowd of captives in Savada-house. Some seventeen days of weeping life yet intervened between them and the fatal Well.

The story of the final act in the great tragedy at Cawnpore cannot be told without some account of events outside Cawnpore itself. A relieving force had been organised at Calcutta, of which Neill's Fusileers at Allahabad were the advance guard; but a leader was wanted, and on June 17 Sir Patrick Grant brought Havelock, "the dust of Persia still in the crevices of his sword-handle," to the Governor-General, saying, "Your Excellency, I have brought you the man."

Havelock was sixty-two years of age when the great chance of his life came to him. A little man, prim, erect, alert, quick-footed, stern-featured, with snow-white moustache and beard. Havelock, no doubt, had his limitations. A strain of severity ran through his character. "He was always," says one who served under him, "as sour as if he had swallowed a pint of vinegar, except when he was being shot at, and then he was as blithe as a schoolboy out for a holiday." There is a touch of burlesque, of course, in that sentence; but Havelock was, no doubt, austere of temper, impatient of fools, and had a will that moved to its end with something of the fiery haste and scorn of obstacles proper to a cannon-ball. He was fond, too, of making Napoleonic orations to his men, and had a high-pitched, carrying voice, which could make itself audible to a regiment. And the British soldier in fighting mood is rather apt to be impatient of oratory.

But Havelock was a trained and scientific soldier, audacious and resolute in the highest degree; a deeply religious man, with a sense of duty of the antique sort, that scorned ease, and reckoned life, when weighed against honour, as a mere grain of wind-blown dust. And Havelock, somehow, inspired in his men a touch of that sternness of valour we associate with Cromwell's Ironsides.

It is curious, in view of Havelock's achievements and after-fame, to read in the current literature of the moment, the impression he made upon hasty critics in Calcutta and elsewhere. The *Friend of India*, the leading Calcutta journal, described him as a "fossil general"! Lady Canning, in her journal, writes: "General Havelock is not in fashion. No doubt he is fussy and tiresome; but his little, old, stiff figure looks as active and fit for use as if he were made of steel." She again and again refers to "dear little old Havelock, with his fussiness"—"fussiness" being in this case, little more than the impatience of a strong will set to a great task, and fretted by threads of red tape. Lord Hardinge had said, "If India is ever in danger, let Havelock be put in command of an army, and it will be saved." And Havelock's after-history amply justified that prediction.

Havelock had about the tiniest force that ever set forth to the task of saving an empire. It never was able to put on the actual battlefield 1500 men. There were 76 men of the Royal Artillery; less than 400 of the Madras Fusileers; less than 300 of the 78th Highlanders; 435 men of the 64th, and 190 of the 84th, with 450 Sikhs of somewhat doubtful loyalty, and 50 native irregular horse, whose disloyalty was not in the least doubtful. Havelock's reliable cavalry consisted of 20 volunteers, amateurs mostly, under Barrow.

Measured against the scale of modern armies, Havelock's force seems little more than a corporal's guard. But the fighting value of this little army was not to be measured by counting its files. "Better soldiers," says Archibald Forbes, "have never trod this earth." They commenced their march from Allahabad on July 7; they marched, and fought, and conquered under the intolerable heat of an Indian midsummer, and against overwhelming odds; until when, on September 19—little more than eight weeks afterwards—Outram and Havelock crossed the Ganges in their advance on Lucknow, only 250 of Havelock's "Ironsides" were left to take part in that advance. In the whole history of the war, men have seldom dared, and endured, and achieved more than did Havelock's column in the gallant but vain struggle to relieve Cawnpore.

Maude commanded its tiny battery; Hamilton led the Highlanders; Stirling the 64th; the gallant, ill-fated Renaud, the Fusileers. Stuart Beatson was Havelock's assistant adjutant-general; Fraser Tytler was his assistant quartermaster—general. Of the Highlanders—the Ross-shire Buff's—Forbes says, "It was a remarkable regiment; Scottish to the backbone; Highland to the core of its heart. Its ranks were filled with Mackenzies, Macdonalds, Tullochs, Macnabs, Rosses, Gunns, and Mackays. The Christian name of half the Grenadier company was Donald. It could glow with the Highland fervour; it could be sullen with the Highland dourness; and it may be added, it could charge with the stern and irresistible valour of the North."

When the little force began its march for Cawnpore, the soil was swampy with the first furious showers of the rainy season, and in the intervals of the rain, the skies were white with the glare of an Indian sun in July. "For the first three days," says Maude, "they waded in a sea of slush, knee-deep now, and now breast-high, while the flood of tropical rain beat down from overhead. As far to right and left as eye could pierce extended one vast morass." After these three days' toil through rain and mud, the rains vanished; the sky above them became like white flame, and, till they reached Cawnpore, Havelock's troops had to march and fight under a sun that was well-nigh as deadly as the enemy's bullets.

On July 11 Havelock marched fifteen miles under the intolerable heat to Arrapore. Camping for a few hours, he started again at midnight, picked up Renaud's men while the stars were yet glittering in the heaven, pushed steadily on, and at seven o'clock, after a march of sixteen miles, camped at Belinda, four miles out of Futtehpore. The men had outmarched the tents and baggage, and were almost exhausted. They had fallen out, and were scattered under the trees, "some rubbing melted fat on their blistered feet, others cooling their chafes in the pools; many more too dead-beaten to do anything but lie still." It was Sunday morning.

Suddenly there broke above the groups of tired soldiery the roar of cannon. Grape-shot swept over the camp. Over the crest and down the opposite slopes rode, with shouts and brandished tulwars, a huge mass of rebel cavalry. It was a genuine surprise! But the bugles rang out shrilly over the scattered clusters of Havelock's men. They fell instantly into formation; skirmishers ran to the front, and the enemy's cavalry came to an abrupt halt. It was a surprise for them, too. They had expected to see only Renaud's composite force—a mere handful; what they beheld instead, was Havelock's steady and workmanlike front.

Havelock did not attack immediately. His cool judgment warned him that his over-wearied soldiers needed rest before being flung into the fight, and orders were given for the men to lie down in rank. Presently the rebel cavalry wheeled aside, and revealed a long front of infantry, with batteries of artillery, and the rebel general, finding the British motionless, actually began a movement to turn their flank.

Then Havelock struck, and struck swiftly and hard. Maude's battery was sent forward. He took his pieces at a run to within 200 yards of the enemy's front, wheeled round, and opened fire. The British infantry, covered by a spray of skirmishers armed with Enfield rifles, swept steadily forward. The rebel general, conspicuous on a gorgeously adorned elephant, was busy directing the movements of his force; and Maude tells the story of how Stuart Beatson, who stood near his guns, asked him to "knock over that chap on the elephant." "I dismounted," says Maude, "and laid the gun myself, a 9-pounder, at 'line of metal' (700 yards) range, and my first shot went in under the beast's tail, and came out at his chest, rolling it over and giving its rider a bad fall."

Its rider, as it happened, was Tantia Topee, the Nana's general; and had that 9-pound ball struck him, instead of his elephant, it might have saved the lives of the women and children in Cawnpore.

Meanwhile, the 64th and the Highlanders in one resolute charge had swept over the rebel guns. Renaud, with his Fusileers, had crumpled up their flank, and the Nana's troops, a torrent of fugitives, were in full flight to Futtehpore. The battle was practically won in ten minutes, all the rebel guns being captured—so fierce and swift was the British advance.

The rebel Sepoys knew the fighting quality of the sahibs; but now they found a quite new fierceness in it. Havelock's soldiers were on fire to avenge a thousand murders. And, flying fast, as Trevelyan puts it, the Nana's troops "told everywhere that the sahibs had come back in strange guise; some draped like women to remind them what manner of wrong they were sworn to requite; others, conspicuous by tall blue caps, who hit their mark without being seen to fire—the native description of the Enfield rifle with which the Madras Fusileers were armed."

The fight at Futtehpore is memorable as being the first occasion on which British troops and the rebel Sepoys met in open battle. The Nana had shortly before issued a proclamation announcing that the British had "all been destroyed and sent to hell by the pious and sagacious troops who were firm to their religion"; and, as "no trace of them was left, it became the duty of all the subjects of the Government to rejoice at the delightful intelligence." But Futtehpore showed that "all the yellow-faced and narrow-minded people" had not been "sent to hell." They had reappeared, indeed, with uncomfortable energy, and a disagreeable determination to despatch every Sepoy they could capture somewhere in that direction!

Havelock's men had marched nineteen miles, and fought and won a great battle, without a particle of food, and so dreadful was the heat that twelve men died of sunstroke. Havelock camped on July 13 to give his men rest, resumed his march on the 14th, and on the morning of the 15th found the Sepoys drawn up in great strength in front of a village called Aong, twenty-two miles south of Cawnpore. Renaud led his Fusileers straight at the village, and carried it with a furious bayonet charge, but the gallant leader of the "blue caps" fell, mortally wounded, in the charge. Maude's guns smashed the enemy's artillery, and when the Highlanders and the 64th were seen coming on, the Sepoys again fled.

Havelock pressed steadily on, and found the Sepoys had rallied and were drawn up in a strong position, covered by a rivulet, swollen bank-high with recent rains, known as Pandoo Nuddee. A fine stone bridge crossed the river; it was guarded by a 24-pound gun, a 25-pound carronade, and a strong force of infantry. Havelock quickly developed his plan of attack. Maude raced forward with his guns, and placed them at three different points, so as to bring a concentric fire to bear on the bridge. Maude's first blast of spherical case-shell broke the sponge staves of the heavy guns in the rebel battery, and rendered them useless.

The Sepoys tried to blow up the bridge. But Maude's fire was hot; Stephenson, with his "blue caps," was coming up at the double, and the Sepoys got flurried. They had mined the bridge, and the mine was fired prematurely. The explosion shattered the parapet of the bridge, but through the white smoke came the Fusileers, their bayonets sparkling vengefully. The Highlanders followed eagerly in support. The bridge was carried, the guns taken, the rebel gunners bayoneted, the rebel centre pierced and broken, and the rebel army itself swept northwards, with infinite dust and noise, in a mere tumult of panic-stricken flight.

The British camped for the night on the battlefield. At three o'clock in the morning, with the stars sparkling keenly over their heads, and a full moon flooding the camp with its white light, Havelock formed up his men. He told them he had learned there were some 200 women and children still held as prisoners in Cawnpore, the survivors of the massacre of June 27. "Think of our women and the little ones," he said, "in the power of those devils incarnate." The men answered with a shout, and, without waiting for the word of command, went "fours right," and took the road.

It was a march of twenty miles. The sun rose and scorched the silent and panting ranks of the British with its pitiless heat. The Highlanders suffered most;

they were wholly unprepared for a summer campaign, and were actually wearing the heavy woollen doublets intended for winter use; but their stubborn Northern blood sustained them. Every now and again, indeed, some poor fellow in the ranks dropped as though shot through the head, literally killed with the heat. Nana Sahib himself held the approach to Cawnpore, with 7000 troops and a powerful artillery, and his position was found to be of great strength.

Havelock studied it a few minutes with keen and soldierly glance, and formed his plans. He had the genius which can use rules, but which also, on occasion, can dispense with rules. He violated all the accepted canons of war in his attack upon the Nana's position. He amused the enemy's front with the fire of a company of the Fusileers, and the manœuvres of Barrow's twenty volunteer sabres, while with his whole force he himself swept round to the right to turn the Nana's flank. Havelock, that is, risked his baggage and his communications, to strike a daring blow for victory.

As Havelock's men pressed grimly forward, screened by a small grove, they heard the bands of the Sepoy regiments playing "Auld lang syne" and "Cheer, boys, cheer," and the sound made the men clutch their muskets with a little touch of added fury. The Sepoys discovered Havelock's strategy rather late, and swung their guns round to meet it. Their fire smote the flank of Havelock's column cruelly, but the British never paused nor faltered. When Havelock judged his turning movement was sufficiently advanced, he wheeled the column into line. His light guns were insufficient to beat down the fire of the heavy pieces worked by the rebels, and he launched his Highlanders at the battery. They moved dourly forward under a heavy fire, till within eighty yards of the guns. Then the bayonets came down to the charge, and with heads bent low and kilts flying in the wind, the Highlanders went in with a run. The charge was in perfect silence, not a shot nor a shout being heard; but it was so furious that mound and guns were carried in an instant, and the village itself swept through. As Forbes describes it, "Mad with the ardour of battle, every drop of Highland blood afire in every vein, the Ross-shire men crashed right through the village, and cleared it before they dropped out of the double." They had crushed the enemy's left, taken its guns, and sent a great mass of Sepoys whirling to the rear.

But the moment they emerged from the village, the great howitzer in the Nana's centre opened fire upon the Highlanders, and once more the unequal duel between bayonet and cannon had to be renewed. Havelock himself galloped up to where the Highlanders were reforming after the confusion and rapture of their rush, and, pointing with his sword to the great howitzer, pouring its red torrent of flame upon them, cried: "Now, Highlanders! another charge like that wins the day."

The Gaelic blood was still on fire. The officers could hardly restrain their men till they were roughly formed. In another moment the kilts and bonnets and bayonets of the 78th were pouring in a torrent over the big gun, and the rebel centre was broken! Meanwhile the 64th and 84th had thrust roughly back Nana Sahib's right wing; but, fighting bravely, the Sepoys clung with unusual courage to a village about a mile to the rear of the position they first held, and their guns, drawn up in its front, fired fast and with deadly effect.

The Highlanders, pressing on from the centre, found themselves shoulder to shoulder with the 64th, advancing from the left. Maude's guns, with the teams utterly exhausted, were a mile to the rear. Men were dropping fast in the British ranks, worn out with marching and charging under heat so cruel. In the smoke-blackened lines men were stumbling from very fatigue as they advanced on the quick red flashes and eddying smoke of the battery which covered the village. But Havelock, riding with the leading files, knew the soldier's nature "from the crown of his shako down to his ammunition boots." "Who," he cried, "is to take that village—the Highlanders or the 64th?" Both regiments had Northern blood in them—the 64th is now known as the North Staffordshire—and that sudden appeal, that pitted regiment against regiment, sent the stout Midlanders of the 64th and the hot-blooded Gaels from the clachans and glens and loch sides of Ross-shire, forward in one racing charge that carried guns and village without a check.

The battle seemed won, and Havelock, reforming his column, moved steadily forward. But the Nana was playing his last card, and his generals at least showed desperate courage. They made a third stand athwart the Cawnpore road, and within a short distance of Cawnpore itself. A 24-pounder, flanked on either side by guns of lighter calibre, covered the Nana's front, and his infantry, a solid mass, was drawn up behind the guns. Havelock's men had marched twenty miles, and made a dozen desperate charges. Their guns were far in the rear. Yet to halt was to be destroyed.

Havelock allowed his men to fling themselves panting on the ground for a few minutes; then, riding to the front, and turning his back to the enemy's guns, so as to face the men, he cried in his keen, high-pitched voice, "The longer you look at it, men, the less you will like it! The brigade will advance—left battalion leading."

The left battalion was the 64th. Major Stirling promptly brought forward his leading files, and Havelock's son and aide-de-camp galloped down, and, riding beside Stirling, shared with him the leadership of the charge—a circumstance for which the 64th, as a matter of fact, scarcely forgave him, as they wanted no better leadership than that of their own major. There was less of *élan* and dash about this charge than in the earlier charges of the day; but in steady valour it was unsurpassed.

On came the 64th, silently and coolly. Havelock himself, in a letter to his wife, wrote with a father's pride about his son. "I never saw so brave a youth," he wrote, "as the boy Harry: he placed himself opposite the muzzle of a gun that was scattering death into the ranks of the 64th Queen's, and led on the regiment under a shower of grape to its capture. This finished the fight. The grape was deadly, but he calm, as if telling George stories about India."

When the steady but shot-tormented line of the 64th found itself so near the battery that through the whirling smoke they could see the toiling gunners and the gleam of Sepoy bayonets beyond them, then the British soldiers made their leap. With a shout they charged on and over the guns, and through the lines behind, and Nana Sahib's force was utterly and finally crushed. Havelock had not a sabre to launch on the flying foe; but his tired infantry, who had marched twenty miles, and fought without pause for four hours, kept up the pursuit till the outer edge of Cawnpore was reached. Then Havelock halted them; and, piling arms, the exhausted soldiers dropped in sections where they stood, falling asleep on the bare ground, careless of food or tents.

They were aroused long before daybreak, and through their ranks ran in whispers the story, grim and terrible, of the massacre which, by only a few hours, had cheated their splendid valour of its reward.

How great was the valour, how stubborn the endurance, shown thus far by Havelock's men is not easily realised. In nine days—betwixt July 7-16—they had, to quote their commander's words "marched under the Indian sun of July 126 miles, and fought four actions." What better proof of hardihood, valour, and discipline could be imagined? But the British soldier is a queer compound, with very sudden and surprising alternations of virtue. When Cawnpore was won and plundered, immense stores of beer and spirits fell into the hands of the soldiers, and for a time it seemed as if Havelock's band of heroes would dissolve into a mere ignoble gang of drunkards. Havelock promptly ordered every drinkable thing in Cawnpore to be bought or seized. "If I had not done this," he wrote, "it would have required one half my force to keep the other half sober, and I should not have had a soldier in camp!"

Whether the terror of Havelock's advance on Cawnpore actually caused the massacre of the English captives there may be doubted; it certainly hastened it. Nana Sahib, to whom murder was a luxury, would no more have spared the women and the children than a tiger would spare a lamb lying under its paw. But even a tiger has its lazy moods, and, say, immediately after a full meal, is temporarily careless about fresh slaughter. Nana Sahib had supped full of cruelty, and was disposed, for a brief period at all events, to allow his captives to live. Moreover, some of the women in his own harem sent him word they would slay themselves and their children if he murdered the memsahibs and their little ones. But on the night of July 15 the fugitives from Pandoo Nuddee reached Cawnpore, amongst them being Bala Rao, the Nana's brother and general, who brought from the fight a bullet in his shoulder, and a new argument for murder in his heart.

In a council held between the Nana and his chief officials that night, the fate of the captives was discussed. Teeka Sing understood British nature so ill that he argued Havelock's men would be robbed of their only motive for continuing their advance on Cawnpore if the captives were slain. They might, he urged, risk the perils of a new battle for the sake of rescuing the captives, but not for the mere pleasure of burying them. That they might have the passion to avenge them did not enter into Teeka Sing's somewhat limited intelligence. Other chiefs argued, again, that if the captives were allowed to live, they might prove very inconvenient witnesses against a good many people.

It is probable that the strongest argument on the side of murder was the mere joy of killing somebody with a white face. Havelock's Fusileers and Highlanders declined to allow themselves to be killed; they were, in fact, slaying the Nana's Sepoys with disconcerting fury and despatch. But the heroes who had fled again and again before a British force one-fifth their number, could revenge themselves in perfect security by slaying the helpless women and children imprisoned in the Bebeeghur. So the order for massacre went forth.

From July 1 the captives, 210 in number, had been crowded into a small building containing two rooms, each 20 ft. by 10 ft., and an open court some fifteen yards square. In that suffering and helpless crowd were five men, guessed to have been Colonels Smith and Goldie, Mr. Thornhill, the judge of Futteghur, and two others. They had neither furniture nor bedding, nor even straw, and were fed daily on a scanty ration of native bread and milk. Two of the ladies were taken across each morning to the Nana's stables, and made to grind corn at a hand-mill for hours together. This was done, not for the sake of the scanty store of flour the poor captives ground out, but by way of insult. To the Eastern imagination, when a dead enemy's womankind grind corn in the house of his slayer, captivity has reached its blackest depths. The English ladies, according to native testimony, did not object to do the work of slaves in this fashion, as it, at least, enabled them to carry back a handful of flour to their hungry little ones.

Sickness mercifully broke out amongst the captives, and in a week eighteen women and seven children died. A native doctor kept a list of these, and after Havelock captured Cawnpore the list was discovered. Months afterwards there was sad joy in many an English household when, on the evidence of this list, it was known that their loved ones had, in this way, anticipated and escaped the Nana's vengeance. One poor wife, in the sadness of that captivity, gave birth to a little one, and in the native doctor's list of deaths is the pathetic record—a tragedy in each syllable—"An infant two days old."

The evidence seems to show that during these terrible days the women were not exposed to outrage in the ordinary sense of that word, or to mutilation, but every indignity and horror which the Hindu imagination could plan short of that was emptied upon them, and some of the younger women, at least, were carried off to the harems of one or other of the Nana's generals. On the face of the earth there could have been at the time no other scene of anguish resembling that in the crowded and darkened rooms of the Bebeeghur, where so great a company of women and children, forsaken of hope, with the death of all their dearest behind them, sat waiting for death themselves.

Nana Sahib was an epicure in cruelty, and was disposed to take his murders in dainty and lingering instalments. At four o'clock on the afternoon of July 15 he sent over some of his officers to the Bebeeghur, and bade the Englishmen come forth. They came out, the two colonels, the judge, a merchant named Greenaway, and his son, and with them a sixth, an English boy, fourteen years of age, nameless now, but apparently willing to share the perilous responsibilities of "being a man." Poor lad! Motherless, his name all unknown, his father, perhaps, floating a disfigured corpse on the sliding current of the muddy Ganges, he appears for a moment, a slender, boyish figure, in the living frescoes of that grim tragedy, and then vanishes.

Under the cool shade of a lime tree sat Nana Sahib, dark of face, gaudy of dress, and round him a cluster of his kinsmen and officers, Bala Rao among them, whose wounded shoulder was now to be avenged. Brief ceremony was shown to this little cluster of haggard and ragged sahibs. A grim nod from the Nana, a disorderly line of Sepoys with levelled muskets and retracted lips, and the six were shot down and their bodies cast on the dusty roadside for every passer-by to spit at.

A little before five o'clock a woman from the Nana's household stepped inside the door of the Bebeeghur, and looked over the crowd of weary mothers and wan-faced children. A curious stillness fell on the little company, while, in careless accents, the woman gave the dreadful order: they were "all to be killed"! One English lady, with quiet courage, stepped up to the native officer who commanded the guard, and asked "if it was true they were all to be murdered." Even the Sepoys shrank from a crime so strange and wanton. The officer bade the Englishwomen not to be afraid, and the woman from the Nana's harem was told roughly by the soldiers that her orders would not be obeyed.

It seemed monstrous indeed that an order which was to send 200 helpless human beings to death should be brought, like a message about some domestic trifle, on a servant-woman's lips. The messenger vanished. The Sepoys on guard consulted together and agreed that with their own hands, at least, they would not slay the prisoners. According to one account they were ordered by a new messenger to fire through the windows upon the company of women and children, many now praying within. They obeyed the order to fire, and the sudden wave of flame and smoke, with the crash of twenty discharged muskets, swept over the heads of the captive crowd within. But the Sepoys, of design, fired high, and no one was wounded.

When Havelock's men afterwards entered those rooms, one little detail bore mute witness to the use to which some of the ladies had turned the few minutes which followed the volley of the Sepoys. They evidently tore strips from their dresses, and with them tried to tie the door fast; and still those broken strips of linen and silk were hanging from the door handles when Havelock's men, two days afterwards, entered Cawnpore.

Crime never wants instruments, and Nana Sahib soon found scoundrels willing to carry out his orders. It was a little after five o'clock—just when Stephenson's Fusileers and Hamilton's Highlanders were sweeping over the bridge at Pandoo Nuddee—that five men, each carrying a tulwar, walked to the door of the Bebeeghur. Two were rough peasants; two belonged to the butcher's caste; one wore the red uniform of the Nana's bodyguard. The five men entered, and the shuddering crowd of women and children was before them. The crowd, who watched as the door opened, saw standing erect on the threshold the English lady who had asked the native officer whether they were all to be killed. Then the door was closed, and over the scene that followed the horrified imagination refuses to linger.

Wailing, broken shrieks, the sound of running feet crept out on the shuddering air. Presently the door opened, and the man in the red uniform of the Nana's bodyguard came out with his sword broken short off at the hilt. There were 212 to be killed, and the strain on steel blades as well as on human muscles was severe!

He borrowed a fresh sword, and went back to his work, again carefully closing the door behind him. After a while he re-emerged once more with a broken blade, and, arming himself afresh, returned a third time to his dreadful business. It was dark when the five men—all alike now with reddened garments—came out and locked the door behind them, leaving that great company of wives and mothers and little children in the slaughter-house. The men had done their work but roughly, and all through the night, though no cry was heard in the Bebeeghur, yet sounds, as if sighs from dying lips, and the rustle as of struggling bodies, seemed to creep out into the darkness incessantly through its sullen windows and hard-shut doors.

At eight o'clock the next morning the five men returned, attended by a few sweepers. They opened the door, and commenced to drag the nearer bodies, by their long tresses of hair, across the courtyard to the fatal well, hard by. Then, amongst the bodies lying prone over all the floor, there was a sudden stir of living things. Were the dead coming back to life?

Native evidence, collected afterwards, reports that a few children and nearly a dozen women had contrived to escape death by hiding under the bodies of the slain. They had lain in that dreadful concealment all night, but when the five returned they crept out with pitiful cries. Some of these were slain without parley; some ran like hunted animals round the courtyard, and then threw themselves down the well. One by one the victims were dragged out, stripped, and, many of them yet living, were flung into that dreadful grave.

One native witness, quoted by Trevelyan, says, "There was a great crowd looking on; they were standing along the walls of the compound. They were principally city people and villagers. Yes, there were also Sepoys. Three boys were alive. They were fair children. The eldest, I think, must have been six or seven, and the youngest five years. They were running round the well (where else could they go to?), and there was none to save them. No, none said a word, or tried to save them." The youngest of these children, a tender little fellow, lunatic with terror, broke loose and ran like a hare across the courtyard. He was captured by an unsympathetic spectator, brought back, and flung down the well.

It was two days after this, on July 17, that three men of the 78th entered the court, for Havelock was now in possession of Cawnpore, and the Nana was a fugitive. The whispers and gestures of the natives drew their attention to the shut door of the bungalow. One of the Highlanders pushed open the door and stepped inside. "The next moment," to quote Archibald Forbes, "he came rushing out, his face ghastly, his hands working convulsively, his whole aspect, as he strove in vain to gasp out some articulate sounds, showing that he had seen some dreadful sight." No living thing was in the place; but the matting that covered the floor was one great sponge of blood, and he who had crossed it found himself, to borrow Burns's phrase, "red wat shod."

Little pools of blood filled up each inequality in the rough floor. It was strewn with pitiful relics, broken combs, pinafores, children's shoes, little hats, the leaves of books, fragments of letters. The plastered wall was hacked with sword-cuts, "not high up, as where men had fought, but low down and about the corners, as if a creature had crouched to avoid a blow." Long locks of hair were strewn about, severed, but not with scissors.

There were no inscriptions on the walls, but many a pitiful record upon the scattered papers on the floor. A few childish curls marked "Ned's hair, with love;" the fly-leaf of a Bible, with a loving inscription—giver and recipient now both dead; a prayer-book, pages splashed red where once praying eyes had lingered. The pages of one grimly appropriate book—Drelincourt's "Preparation for Death"—were scattered over the whole floor.

* * * * *

To write this story is a distress, to read it must be well-nigh an anguish. Yet we may well endure to know what our countrymen and countrywomen have suffered. Their sufferings are part of the price at which a great empire has been built.

Into what a passion of fury—half generous, half devilish—the soldiers who looked on these things were kindled may well be imagined. It will be remembered that Neill compelled some of the Sepoys captured at Cawnpore, and guilty of a share in this tragedy—high-caste Brahmins—to clean up, under the whip, a few square inches of the blood-stained floor, and then immediately hanged them, burying them in a ditch afterwards. These Brahmins, that is, were first ceremonially defiled, and then executed. That was an inhumanity unworthy of the English name, which Lord Clyde promptly forbade.

Nana Sahib had fled the palace. Principality, and power, and wealth, all had vanished. He was, like Cain, a fugitive on the face of the earth. In what disguises he hid himself, through what remote and lonely regions he wandered, where he died, or how, no man knows. His name has become an execration, his memory a horror.

The Bebeeghur has disappeared. The site where it once stood is now a beautiful garden. In the centre of the garden, circled with a fringe of ever-sighing cypresses, is a low mound, with fence of open stonework. The circular space within is sunken, and upon the centre of the sunken floor rises the figure—not too artistic, unhappily—of an angel in marble, with clasped hands and outspread wings. On the pedestal runs the inscription: "Sacred to the perpetual memory of the great company of Christian people, chiefly women and children, who, near this spot, were cruelly massacred by the followers of the rebel Nana Doondoo Punth, of Bithoor, and cast, the dying and the dead, into the well below, on the 15th day of July 1857."

CHAPTER VI

LUCKNOW AND SIR HENRY LAWRENCE

And ever upon the topmost roof our banner of England flew.

—TENNYSON.

On the night of May 30, 1857, the steps of the Residency at Lucknow witnessed a strange sight. On the uppermost steps stood a group of British officers in uniform. Sir Henry Lawrence was there, with his staff; Banks, the chief commissioner; Colonel Inglis, of the 32nd. The glare of a flaming house a hundred and fifty yards distant threw on the group a light as intense almost as noonday. Forty paces in front of the group stood a long line of Sepoys loading in swift silence. The light of the flames played redly on their dark faces, on their muskets brought quickly into position for capping. For weeks the great city had been trembling on the verge of revolt, and an officer of his staff had brought Lawrence news that gun-fire that night, nine o'clock, was to be the signal for the outbreak.

Lawrence had taken all human precautions, and was familiar with such warnings as that now brought to him, and he sat down with his staff to dinner with iron composure. At nine o'clock there rolled through the sultry darkness the sound of a gun, and silence fell for a moment on the dinner party. Nothing followed the roar of the gun. Lawrence leaned forward with a smile on his face, and said to the officer who brought the news, "Your friends are not punctual."

At that moment there rose in sharp succession on the still night air the crack of a dozen muskets. Then came the sound of running feet, the confused shouts of a crowd. The Mutiny had come!

Lawrence, without a change of countenance, ordered the horses, waiting ready saddled, to be brought round, and, followed by his staff, went out on to the Residency steps to wait for them. As they stood there red flames were breaking out at a score of points in the black mass of houses on which they looked. The air was full of tumult. An English bungalow only a hundred and fifty yards distant broke into flame, showing how near the mutineers were.

At that moment, with the tramp of disciplined feet, a body of Sepoys came running up at the double out of the darkness, and swung into line facing the Residency steps. It was the native officer bringing up the Residency guard; and, saluting Captain Wilson, Lawrence's aide-de-camp, he asked "if the men should load." These men were known to be disloyal; before the morning dawned, as a matter of fact, they were in open mutiny. Ought they to be treated as loyal, and permitted to load with the entire British staff of the city at the muzzles of their muskets? Wilson reported the native officer's question to Lawrence. "Yes," said he quietly, "let them load," and the group on the Residency steps quietly watched while ramrods rang sharply in the musket barrels, and the gun-nipples were capped. The sound of ramrods falling on the leaden bullets was perfectly audible in the hush; and, says Colonel Wilson, "I believe Sir Henry was the only man of all that group whose heart did not beat the quicker for it."

SIR HENRY LAWRENCE

Reproduced by permission of Sir Henry Waldemar Lawrence, *from a drawing in his possession*

Then there came a thrilling pause. These men had the entire British staff at Lucknow before them at point-blank distance! A single gesture, a shout, and that line of muskets would have poured its deadly fire upon the group on the Residency steps, and with the sound of that one volley Lucknow must have fallen, and perhaps the course of history been changed.

These brave men standing there under the very shadow of death knew this, and not a figure stirred! Had there been the least sign of agitation or fear, perhaps the Sepoys would have fired. But the cool, steadfast bearing of that group of Englishmen put a strange spell on the Sepoys. Another moment of intensest strain, and the native officer gave a sharp word of command. The magic of discipline prevailed: the men swung round and marched off into the darkness. But the fate of Lucknow and a thousand British lives hung on those few critical moments. It was the haughty, ice-cold courage of that heroic group on the Residency steps which, for the moment, averted a great disaster.

Sir Henry Lawrence is the hero of the earlier stages of the siege of Lucknow, and it is difficult to imagine a loftier or more gallant character. He came of that sturdy, strong-brained North of Ireland stock, which has given to the British Empire so many gallant soldiers and famous administrators, so many great engineers and captains of labour. Lawrence's face, with its long features, thin-flowing beard, deep-set, meditative, not to say dreamy eyes, and high cheek bones, was an odd compound of, say, Don Quixote and Abraham Lincoln. His valour was "a sword of Spain, the ice-brook's temper"; but he had better qualities than even valour of that fine edge. He was an administrator of the first order. His intellect had in it a curious penetrating quality, and perhaps his brain alone forecast, in its true scale, the great Mutiny which shook almost to its fall the British rule in India. His courtesy, his unselfishness, his passionate scorn of injustice, his generous pity for the oppressed, gave a strange charm to Lawrence's character, while his meditative piety added gravity and depth to it. The whole interval between the tragedy of Cawnpore and the glory of Lucknow is to be measured by the single personality of Henry Lawrence. That he was of a different type from Wheeler, explains how Lucknow escaped while Cawnpore perished.

The two cities are about forty-five miles distant from each other. Wheeler and Lawrence had each to face, practically, the same situation, and with resources not very unequal. Wheeler's credulous faith in his Sepoys flung away the last chance of the ill-fated British in Cawnpore. It was this which made him gather them within those thin lines of earth, shelterless from shot or sunstroke, and without supplies, where no fate except death or surrender was possible. Lawrence, with surer insight, measured the problem before him. He chose wisely the spot where the British must make their stand for existence. He gathered within the lines he selected all the treasure and warlike resources of the city, with supplies that a siege of five months did not exhaust. And his splendid foresight and energy saved Lucknow.

There is no space to tell here in detail the tale of the noble courage and energy with which Lawrence kept the seething and turbulent city from revolt through May and June. The mere garrison figures of Lucknow show Lawrence's position. He had 700 Europeans on whom he could rely. There were 7000 Sepoys, all potential, and highly probable mutineers. Beyond this was a great turbulent and fanatical city, with a population of, say, 700,000, a magazine waiting to explode at the touch of a match.

The peril was certain in its character, but was uncertain in scale, and time, and form. Lawrence had to arm himself against that vague, formless, yet terrific peril, without letting those who watched him closely and keenly discover that he was conscious of its existence. He had to hide an anxious brain behind a cheerful face; to prepare minutely for swift-coming and desperate war, while wearing the dress, and talking the language of peace; to turn a hospitable Residency into a fortress; and yet keep open doors and an open table. And he did it all! When, the morning after Chinhut, the Residency was closely and furiously besieged, it was found to be provisioned, organised, and armed for a stern and obstinate and, in the end, successful defence!

Lawrence read the whole position of affairs so truly that his forecast of events has in it a gleam of something like prophecy, or of magic. "He told me," says Colonel Wilson, "that nearly the whole army would go, but not, he thought, the Sikhs; that in every native regiment there was a residuum of loyal Sepoys, and he meant, if possible, to retain these—as he actually did. If Cawnpore held out, Lucknow would be unassailed; but if Cawnpore fell, Lucknow would be hard pressed, and no succour could reach the city before the middle of August; that the outbreak would remain a revolt of the Sepoys, and not a rising of the people."

Lawrence's own policy, meanwhile, was to fight for time. Every hour the Mutiny could be postponed lessened its chances of success. "Time," he writes in his diary on May 18, "is everything just now; time, firmness, promptness, conciliation, prudence." But Lawrence had many difficulties in carrying out that wise policy, some of them created by the divided judgments of his own staff. Mr. Gubbins, the financial commissioner, in particular, vehemently mistrusted Lawrence's mild handling of the Sepoys. Gubbins was clever, audacious, quick-witted, fatally over-quick, perhaps, in judgment, with a gift for giving advice in confident—not to say imperious—accents, which his official superiors found somewhat trying. He valued his own advice, too, so highly that he could not forgive the dulness in his superiors which failed to discern its excellence, or the hesitation which lingered in putting it into practice. He was perpetually urging Lawrence to disarm and expel all the native troops in Lucknow. Yet Lawrence's milder policy was justified by events. Some seven hundred Sepoys remained true to their salt, and served through the great siege with a devotion and a courage beyond praise. "Neither temptation nor threats from their comrades without," says Fayrer, "or hardships and privation within, could induce them to desert. There is nothing in the history of the Sepoy army more creditable or honourable than their behaviour."

Lawrence had other troubles with the Europeans in Lucknow. An indiscreet editor in Lucknow published some alarmist articles of a singularly mischievous character, and Lawrence sent for him, and warned him that, if he continued to write in a fashion calculated to provoke mutiny, he would suppress his paper. But Lawrence knew human nature too well to believe that mere threats would keep a foolish editor from committing folly. A few days afterwards, happening to ride by the newspaper office, he suddenly drew rein, and said to his staff, "Let us go in and edit the paper for Mr. ——." He entered, said to the astonished editor, "Mr. ——, to show you I bear no ill-will, I am come to write you a leading article;" and, sitting down, dashed off an article expounding the resources of the Government for meeting and putting down a revolt. The article acted as a tonic on native and European opinion in the city; but it also captured the editor.

Lawrence had not a very keen sense of humour, but occasionally humour—of a grim sort—broke out from him. A Hindu of some rank advised that a number of monkeys should be collected in the Residency, and be attended and fed by high-caste Brahmins. This would ensure the favour of all the Hindu divinities, and would make the English popular. Lawrence listened gravely, then said, "Your advice is good. Come," he said, rising and taking his hat, "I will show you my monkeys." He led the way to a battery which had just been completed; and laying his hand on an 18-pounder gun, said, "See! here is one of my monkeys. That"—pointing to a pile of shot—"is his food, and this"—laying his hand on the shoulder of a sentry of the 32nd, who stood at attention close by—"is the man who feeds them. Now go and tell your friends of my monkeys!"

The serene quality of Lawrence's courage is shown by a letter he writes to Raikes on May 30: "We are pretty jolly ... but we are in a funny position.... We are virtually besieging four regiments—in a quiet way—with 300 Europeans. I ... reside in cantonments guarded by the gentlemen we are besieging." That very night, as it happened, the outbreak came!

On the last day of June the disastrous fight at Chinhut brought affairs at Lucknow to a crisis. The revolted regiments from Eastern Oude were marching on Lucknow, and Lawrence, acting on the one principle of British war in India—of striking and never waiting to be struck—marched out to crush the approaching mutinous regiments. His little force consisted of 300 of the 32nd, 230 more or less loyal Sepoys, 36 British volunteers on horseback, 120 native cavalry, and 10 guns, of which six were manned by Sepoys. There was grave doubt as to how the native artillery would behave; but Lawrence said, "We must try and 'blood' them."

As it happened, Lawrence was completely deceived as to the strength of the enemy. He reckoned they might number 5000; they were nearer 15,000, with not less than thirty guns. By some accident, too, the 32nd were marched out without having broken their fast, and, marching eight miles under the glare of an Indian sun, were exhausted before they fired a shot.

The day at Chinhut, in brief, was one of blunders and disasters. "Everything," says Fayrer, "was against us." The force started late, and without adequate preparation. The supplies of food and water never came up. The men of the 32nd had to attack when exhausted by heat, thirst, and fatigue, and want of food. The native artillerymen deserted; the Sikh cavalry fled. The one formidable gun the British had, an 8-inch howitzer, was thrown out of action owing to the elephant that drew it taking fright. The British, in addition, were badly armed. Many of their muskets would not go off. In the confusion of the retreat an officer called on a private of the 32nd by name to turn round and fire on the enemy. "I will do so, sir, if you wish," said the man, "but it's no use! I have snapped six caps already and the piece won't go off." The Sepoys, as it happened, were armed with new and clean muskets.

The enormous number of the Sepoys enabled them to outflank the scanty British force, and nothing remained but retreat. There were many individual acts of gallantry; but, in broken, desperately fighting clusters, the 32nd had to fall back, many of the men dropping from exhaustion or sunstroke while they tried to fight. An officer in the battle has described the huge mass of the Sepoys as it pressed on the flank of the retreating British. "The plain," he says, "was one moving mass of men. Regiment after regiment of the Sepoys poured steadily towards us, the flanks covered with a foam of skirmishers. They came on in quarter-distance columns, the standards waving in their places, and everything performed as steadily as possible. A field-day on parade could not have been better." Under the terrific fire poured on their flank the gallant 32nd simply melted away. Their colonel, Case, a splendid soldier, fell desperately wounded, and one of the officers ran to assist him. "Your place," Case told him, "is with your men. Never mind me. Leave me to die, but stand by your men."

Lawrence rode, hat in hand, wherever the fire was fiercest, cheering the men; but again and again he wrung his hands, and was heard to say, "My God! I have brought them to this!" A great body of native cavalry was about to charge down on the clusters of broken red-coats, when the thirty-six volunteers on horseback rode at them with such fury that the whole hostile mass was broken, and, with its two guns and sea of glittering sabres, was actually driven off in flight! The retreating column had reached the iron bridge; the Sepoys, outnumbering them by hundreds to one, were pressing on, when Lawrence saved them by a flash of warlike genius.

The British gun ammunition was exhausted, but Lawrence ordered the empty guns to be planted across the bridge, and the gunners to stand beside them with lighted port-fires, and before the menace of those unloaded guns the Sepoy pursuit was arrested! Out of his little European force no fewer than 112 men and five officers of the 32nd were slain. The memory of those gallant men poisoned Henry Lawrence's dying moments. He blamed himself because, as he said, he "had been moved by the fear of man to undertake so hazardous an enterprise."

How darkly that night settled down on Lucknow may be imagined. The scene when the broken troops, blackened with dust, staggering with exhaustion, bloody from wounds, came streaming into the Residency, was one of the wildest confusion. It seemed as if everything was lost. The victorious Sepoys might carry the Residency with one breathless rush. "The end of all things seemed to have come," says Dr. Fayrer—who was busy dressing wounds amid all the tumult. "The poor ladies," he adds, "who, like others, were anticipating immediate death, were perfectly calm, and showed great fortitude." Lady Inglis has told how she "watched our poor soldiers returning—the most mournful sight. They were straggling in by twos and threes; some riding, some on guns, some supported by their comrades." "Almost every other cavalry volunteer," says another eye-witness, "was encumbered with two, three, or even four foot-soldiers; one perhaps holding his hand, another laying fast hold on the crupper, or the tail of the horse, or the stirrup, or on all together."

Lady Inglis tells the story of how the news of Colonel Case's death was brought to his wife. "Mrs. Case came up to me and said, 'Oh, Mrs. Inglis, go to bed. I have just heard that your husband and mine are both safe.' I said, 'Why, I did not know Colonel Case went out.' Just then John (Colonel Inglis) came in. He was crying, and after kissing me turned to Mrs. Case and said, 'Poor Case!' Never shall I forget the cry of agony from the poor widow."

It was at a crisis like this that the gallant and masterful spirit of Henry Lawrence shone out. The Sepoys had a saying that "when Lawrence Sahib had looked once down to the ground, and once up to the sky, and stroked his beard, he knew what to do." He had, that is, in an unrivalled degree, the faculty of seeing into the heart of a difficulty, and the twin faculty of swift decision. The disaster of Chinhut had changed the whole situation. Lawrence had armed and garrisoned a cluster of castellated buildings, called the Mutchee Bhawan, about a thousand yards from the Residency, for the purpose of over-awing the city. But his losses at Chinhut made it difficult to hold the Residency, and impossible to hold both the Residency and the Mutchee Bhawan; and on the morning of July 1, from a rough semaphore on the roof of the Residency, a message was signalled to the Mutchee Bhawan, "Retire to-night at twelve. Blow up well."

Colonel Palmer, of the 48th Native Infantry, was in command at the Mutchee Bhawan; he called his officers together, and laid his plans with perfect skill and coolness. There was a magazine consisting of 250 barrels of gunpowder and nearly 1,000,000 cartridges; these were put together in a huge pile; every gun that could not be carried off was spiked, and at midnight the garrison filed silently out, and the fuse was lighted. The garrison reached the Residency gate without meeting an enemy, and just as the last man entered, with a shock as of an earthquake and a flame that for a moment lit up half the city, Mutchee Bhawan blew up. It turned out that a private of the 32nd was left drunk and sound asleep in the building. He was blown up, of course, but the next morning was standing, stark naked, hammering at the Residency gate, shouting, "Arrah, then, open your —— gates!"

Lawrence had thus concentrated all his force within the lines of that scanty patch of soil which was to witness a defence as heroic and stubborn as that of Saragossa against the French, or of Jerusalem against the Romans; and which for the next eighty-eight days—till Havelock's Highlanders, that is, with blackened faces and crimsoned bayonets came streaming through the Bailey Guard—was to be ringed with the fire of hostile guns.

What was called the Residency was really an irregular cluster of houses and gardens, covering an area of about thirty-three acres, looking down from a slight ridge upon the river Goomtee. In the centre stood the Residency itself, a lofty three-storeyed building with many windows and wide-circling verandahs: a spacious and comfortable residence, but singularly ill adapted for the purposes of war. The houses and gardens around it had been woven together with trenches and earthworks, with light batteries sprinkled at regular intervals on each front, and the external walls of the houses along the outer fronts were pierced with loopholes. But in the whole position there was not a defence anywhere that could resist artillery fire.

The whole position formed a rough, irregular pentagon. What may be called the northern front looked down a gentle slope, and across a line of native shops called the Captan Bazaar, to the river, the north-western angle being prolonged, like the horn of a rhinoceros, to include a little point of rising ground occupied by a residence known as Innes's house.

The exterior defence was divided into seventeen posts, each post having its commandant and its tiny garrison of soldiers or of civilians, or of the few Sepoys still faithful to their salt. And each post had to fight, like Hal o' the Wynd, for "its ain hand"; to dig its own trenches, drive its own mines, make sorties on its own account, and repel assaults with its own muskets and bayonets as best it could. One man from each post was detailed to fetch each morning provisions for the day, but, for the rest, the little cluster of smoke-blackened heroes held their post with desperate valour on their own account, and without communication with any other post. There were no reliefs. Every man was on continuous duty day and night, and if he cast himself down for a brief and broken slumber, it was with his musket by his side, and without undressing.

Innes's post, at the extreme north-west angle, was commanded by Lieutenant Loughnan with a little garrison of clerks and men of the 32nd. Next came a stretch of earthworks called the North Curtain, under Colonel Palmer. The Redan, a projecting battery of three guns, was held by Lieutenant Lawrence, of the 32nd, with a few men of his regiment. The hospital, an unsheltered post, was held by Lieutenant Langmore; the Bailey Guard adjoining it by Lieutenant Aitken, with some Sepoys of the 13th Native Infantry. The post was armed with two 9-pounders and a howitzer, and the Sepoys regarded the tiny battery entrusted to them with peculiar pride.

Following down the east face, Dr. Fayrer's house was held by Captain Weston, with some Sepoy pensioners; Sago's house was in charge of Lieutenant Clery, of the 32nd, with some men of that regiment. The Financial Commissioner's office was held by Captain Saunders, with a mixed garrison of uncovenanted clerks and men of the 32nd; the Judicial Commissioner's office, or Germon's post, as it was called, was in charge of Captain Germon, and a batch of Sepoys and clerks. Anderson's garrison—a two-storeyed house at the south-east angle of the position—was held by Captain Anderson and a cluster of the 32nd, and some volunteers.

The Cawnpore battery formed the extreme east of the southern face. This was armed with three light guns, and was so completely under the enemy's fire that, when that fire was in full blast, no man could live beneath it, and the commander of this post was changed every day. The Sikhs' square formed the western angle of the south front, and was held by Captain Harding, with some Sikh cavalry. Gubbins' battery formed the southern extremity of the west front; it had a mixed garrison of Sepoy pensioners, some men of the 32nd, and some native levies raised by Mr. Gubbins. The Racket-court, the Slaughterhouse, the Sheep-pen, and the Church formed the defences of the west front, and were held chiefly by men of the commissariat department. The Residency itself was held by a company of the 84th, under Captain Lowe, as a reserve, though only once during the siege was it called out.

Above the Residency flew, in haughty challenge to the whole world, the flag of England. That flag provoked in a quite curious degree the wrath of the mutineers. Every gun that could be brought to bear on it pelted it with shot, and again and again the staff was carried away. But the damage was instantly repaired, and through the whole of that desperate siege, while the tumult of the fight raged on every face of the entrenchments—

"Ever aloft on the palace roof the old banner of England blew!"

Upon this patch of soil, a little over thirty acres in extent, ringed with trenches and palisades, with loopholed house-walls and low earthworks, were gathered some 3000 human beings. Of these, more than 600 were European women and children; nearly 700 were native servants, non-combatants; another 700 were Sepoys, of somewhat dubious loyalty. The real fighting strength of the garrison consisted of 535 men of the 32nd, 50 of the 84th, 89 artillerymen, 100 British officers—mainly escapees from revolted regiments—and 153 civilians, mostly clerks, who now suddenly had to exchange the pen for the musket and bayonet.

About 900 British, that is, constituted the true fighting force of Lucknow, and these 900 had to be distributed amongst seventeen "posts," or batteries, and round the 2500 yards, or thereabouts, of constantly threatened front. This gave an average of, roughly, fifty men to each post, a number, of course, which grew less every day.

The position had one remarkable feature. The Residency resembled nothing so much as a low island, set in a sea of native houses. Lawrence, with wise prevision, had attempted to clear each front of the Residency, and from June 12 he had some 600 workmen employed on this task. Nawabs' palaces and coolies' huts alike were attacked with pickaxe and gunpowder; but the undertaking was stupendous, and practically only the upper storeys of these houses were destroyed, so that they could not sweep the British entrenchments with their fire. But the lower walls were left standing, and these afforded perfect cover to the Sepoys, and enabled them to carry on their mining operations undetected.

Along the eastern face these houses were at distances from the British entrenchments ranging from twenty-five to fifty yards; on the southern face they came up to within thirteen yards of the Residency front, an interval, say, as wide as a city lane! So close were the two hostile lines for those eighty-eight desperate days, that the British could easily overhear the talk of the Sepoys; and when bullets ceased to fly across the narrow space between, expletives—couched in shrill Hindu or in rough Anglo-Saxon—naturally took their place!

The strength of the mutineers was a varying and uncertain quantity. Sometimes it was wildly guessed to have risen to 100,000, at other times to have sunk to 30,000. Colonel Inglis, in his official report of the siege, after speaking of "the terrific and incessant fire day and night," says "there could not have been less than 8000 men firing at one time into our position." This describes the common experience of eighty-eight days. And yet this great host, with all their constant tempest of fire, their repeated assaults, their innumerable mines, never gained a single foot of that ground above which flew the flag of England!

Sir Henry Lawrence's keen and forecasting intellect made the triumphant defence of Lucknow possible, but in that defence he himself took the briefest share. The siege practically began on July 1. Lawrence had taken up his quarters in a room in the Residency, which gave him a complete view of the enemy, but was also peculiarly open to their fire. On that first day the Sepoys threw an 8-inch shell into the room where Lawrence was sitting, but he escaped without injury. He was entreated to change his quarters, but answered, with a laugh, he did not think the enemy had a gunner good enough to put a second shot through that same window! He was still pressed, however, to change, and at last he consented to do so "when he had arranged for moving his papers."

At 8 P.M. on July 2 Lawrence was lying on his bed in this room, with Colonel Wilson sitting beside him writing down some instructions from his lips. Lawrence's nephew, George, was reclining on a bed a few feet distant from his uncle; a coolie sat on the floor pulling the punkah. Suddenly, with a terrific rush, a second shell from that fatal howitzer broke into the room and exploded there. As George Lawrence describes it, "There was an instant's darkness, and a kind of red glare, and a blast as of thunder. I found myself uninjured, though covered with bricks from top to toe." The very clothes were torn off Wilson's body, but he, too, was uninjured. Lawrence was the only member of the group struck by the exploding shell, and he was mortally wounded, the whole of the lower part of his body being shattered.

Colonel Wilson tells graphically the story of the exploding shell, the sheet of flame, the blast of sound, the dust, the thick darkness, the strangling smoke. He was himself thrown on the floor, and lay for a few moments stunned. Staggering to his feet, he cried, "Sir Henry, are you hurt?" "Twice I thus called without any answer; the third time he said, in a low tone, 'I am killed.'" When the dust cleared away, it was seen that the coverlet on Lawrence's bed, a moment before white, was now crimsoned with his blood. He died on the morning of July 4, and the story of the thirty-six hours between his wound and his death is strangely pathetic.

Fayrer, who was the resident surgeon, was brought hurriedly in, and Lawrence in a whisper asked him how long he had to live. A fragment of the shell had struck the hip and comminuted the upper part of the thigh-bone. The wound was plainly fatal; and as the walls of the room in which Lawrence lay were shaking continually to the stroke of the enemy's round-shot, the dying man was carried to the verandah of Dr. Fayrer's house, and there lay through the night, while life ebbed away. The Sepoys, somehow, got to know that Lawrence was lying under this particular verandah, and they turned on it what Fayrer describes as a "most fiendish fire of round-shot and musketry." Through it all Lawrence kept the most perfect composure. He named his successor, Major Banks, and dictated exact and most luminous instructions as to the conduct of the siege. No finer proof of his clear, tenacious, forecasting intellect can be imagined than is supplied by the counsels which, whispered with dying breath, he gave to those on whom the responsibility of the defence must rest. Lawrence thought of everything and foresaw everything. The whole tactics of defence—how to keep the English members of the garrison in health, how to use the Sepoys, how to economise the provisions. "Entrench, entrench," was the burden of his whispered counsels, urged with dying lips. "Let every man," he said, "die at his post, but never make terms." Only when he mentioned his wife's name did his iron composure fail, and he wept those rare, reluctant tears which strong men know. He wished to partake of the Sacrament of the Lord's Supper. The service was held in the open verandah, the sound of the chaplain's voice being broken by the incessant crackle of hostile muskets and the crash of cannon-ball. Brave men knelt with unshamed tears by Lawrence's bedside, and partook of the Sacrament with him.

After it was over the dying man begged them to kiss him. The whole story, indeed, recalls that scene in the cockpit of the *Victory*, and the dying Nelson's "Kiss me, Hardy!" "Bury me," said Lawrence, "without any fuss, and in the same grave with any men of the garrison who may die at that time." Then, records his biographer, "speaking rather to himself than to those about him," he framed his own immortal epitaph, a sentence which deserves to be remembered as long as Nelson's great signal itself, and which, indeed, has the same key-word: "Here lies Henry Lawrence, who tried to do his duty. May God have mercy on him." It is not so well known that Lawrence wished a verse of Scripture should be added to his epitaph. To the chaplain, Harris, he said, "This text I should like, 'To the Lord our God belong mercies and forgivenesses, though we have rebelled against Him.'" "It was," he added, with a sudden touch of loving memory, "on my dear wife's tomb."

He was buried at nightfall. The combat was raging fiercely along each front of the Residency's defences, and not an officer could follow the general to his grave. Four men of the 32nd were detailed to carry his body to its last rough resting-place. Before they lifted the couch on which it lay, one soldier drew down the sheet, and stooping, kissed with rough and quivering lips the dead man's forehead, and each man of the party followed his example. What better sign of soldierly honour could be imagined? Lawrence's burial curiously recalls that of Sir John Moore at Corunna. He, too, was buried, according to somewhat inaccurate tradition, "darkly, at the dead of night," and had for his requiem the thunder of the foeman's guns.

The story of the siege is, in the main, one of personal combats; of the duels of hostile sharpshooters; of desperate fighting underground in the mines; of sorties by the few against the many; of the assaults of thousands repulsed by scores. As a type of the long-enduring courage with which individual "posts" were held may be taken the single fact that Captain Anderson, whose residence formed what was called "Anderson's post," and who had a garrison of only twenty men, held his position for five months, though a battery of nine 9-pounder guns was playing upon it almost day and night!

The standing orders were, "Keep under cover, be always on the alert, and never fire a shot unless you can see your man." But it was very difficult to enforce the first clause of those instructions, at least. Lady Inglis tells how she once personally remonstrated with a too daring private of the 32nd for exposing himself too rashly, and reminded him of the "instructions." "Yes," he said, "but it's not the way of Englishmen to fight behind walls!"

As a matter of fact, the sorties were incessant and most daring, and were commonly got up by small independent parties, who wished to clear out a house held by the enemy, or silence a gun that proved too tormenting. "The local sorties," says Innes, "were made generally by parties of not more than half-a-dozen men." They would choose their own leader, creep out close to the site of some hostile gun or picket, dash on it, spike the gun, kill a few of the enemy, send the others flying, and return in triumph!

In the more regular sorties an engineer officer and a sergeant leading would run out, carrying a bag of gunpowder or a couple of hand grenades. If the door of the attacked house was open, grenades were thrown in. If it were shut they drove in a bayonet, or screwed a gimlet in its wood, suspended a bag of powder to it, and lit the fuse. The moment the crash came the stormers charged into the building, bayoneted the Sepoys holding it, placed another bag of gunpowder on the floor, lit the fuse, and fell back, the house five minutes afterwards flying up in fragments into the air. So expert did the men become in these house attacks that they learned the art of always going to the right, not the left, of a doorway or passage, so that they could fire into it without exposing the whole body.

This sort of fighting naturally brought the more gallant spirits to the front. A private of the 32nd, called Cooney, played a great part in these independent combats. With a single comrade he charged into an enemy's battery, shouting, as he leaped over the ridge of earth, "Right and left, extend!" so that the Sepoys imagined a strong body was following, and fled precipitately, leaving the ingenious Cooney and his comrade to spike the guns at leisure!

Captain Birch says: "Cooney's exploits were marvellous. He was backed by a Sepoy named Kandiel, who simply adored him. Single-handed, and without any orders, Cooney would go outside our position, and he knew more about the enemy's movements than anybody else. Over and over again he was put into the guard-room for 'disobedience of orders,' and as often let out when there was fighting to be done. On one occasion, he surprised one of the enemy's batteries into which he crawled, followed by his faithful Sepoy, bayoneting four men, and spiking the guns. He was often wounded, and several times left his bed to volunteer for a sortie." Cooney was an Irishman, and loved fighting for its own sake. He fell in a sortie made after Havelock's relief.

Fayrer, the Residency surgeon, combined with equal energy the somewhat contradictory duties of inflicting wounds and of healing them. He worked with tireless energy, attending to the sick and wounded in the Residency itself. But he records, "I have constant opportunity of using my guns and rifles from the roof of my house, or from the platform in front of it." And when this indefatigable doctor was not going his round among the sick and dying, he was to be found on his house-roof bringing down Sepoys with the deadly skill he had learned in the jungle against tigers and deer.

The best shot on the British side was Lieutenant Sewell, who, happy in the possession of a double-barrelled Enfield rifle, from a loophole on the top of the brigade mess, which commanded a thoroughfare through the Sepoy position, bagged his men as a good sportsman might bag pheasants in a crowded cover.

But the Sepoys, too, had their marksmen, whose accuracy was deadly, and whose exploits won from the British garrison the nicknames of "Jim the Rifleman" and "Bob the Nailer." "Bob the Nailer," from his perch high up in what was called Johannes' house, wrought deadly mischief. The British at last paid him the compliment of levelling a howitzer at him, and dropping a shell into his eyrie. But shells were vain. It was discovered afterwards that "Bob the Nailer," when he saw that the gun was about to fire, dropped down into a sheltered room, to emerge, as soon as the shell had exploded, with his fatal rifle once more.

Once a dash was made at Johannes' house, and its garrison slaughtered, but "Bob the Nailer" escaped, and there was not time to blow up the house. Later in the siege a mine was run under his perch, and Johannes' house, crowded with Sepoys, with "Bob the Nailer" at its summit, was blown into space.

There were moments in the siege when, naturally, the spirits of many in the garrison sank. The children were dying from want of air, of exercise, of wholesome food. They shrank into mere wizen-faced old men—tiny skeletons with tightened, parchment-like skin, instead of round, cherub-like faces. Scurvy tainted the blood of the unfortunate garrison. Sleeplessness and the ever-present atmosphere of danger shook their nerves. Men stole out day after day, at the risk of their lives, to gather the leaves of a cruciferous plant, whose green leaves, unscorched by the flame of powder, could be seen amongst the ruins. A rank and dreadful stench of decaying bodies hung over the shot-tormented Residency, and poisoned the very air. Lady Inglis tells how the ladies held rueful debate among themselves as to the lawfulness of taking their own lives if the Residency fell.

Amongst the Sepoys within the Residency, again, as the few weeks grew into months and no relief came, there spread a conviction that the fate of the sahibs was sealed, and there were many desertions. Sixteen went off in a body one night, headed by a Eurasian with the very British name of "Jones." They left the post they held open to the enemy, and scribbled on the walls in several places the explanation, "Because we have no opium." Jones and his fellow-deserters, it is not unsatisfactory to know, were shot by the Sepoys.

One of the ugly features of the siege was that several European renegades—amongst them at least one Englishman—were fighting on the side of the mutineers. Rees says that at the battle of Chinhut a European—"a handsome-looking man, well built, fair, about twenty-five years of age, with light moustache, and wearing the undress uniform of a European cavalry officer"—headed a cavalry charge on the men of the 32nd. He might have been a Russian, but was vehemently suspected of being an Englishman, who had forsaken both his faith and his race. His name was even whispered, and Rees adds that he was of good family. Two of his cousins were fighting valiantly in the Residency against the rebels, a third was wounded at Agra, a fourth held a high military appointment. Yet this apostate was recognised laying a gun against the Residency! His shrift would have been particularly short had he fallen into British hands. The British privates in the Residency, too, were kindled to a yet higher temperature of wrath by hearing the bands of the Sepoy regiments playing—as if in irony—"God save the Queen" under the shelter of the ruined buildings that came almost up to the line of the British entrenchments.

But on the whole the average Briton is apt to be grimly cheerful when a good fight is in progress, and even this dreadful siege was not without its humours. Thus Rees tells how, on the night of July 26, the men of his post were spreading themselves out in the chorus of "Cheer, Boys, cheer," with the utmost strength of their voices, when an alarm was given at the front. They dashed out, and, with the unfinished syllables of that chorus yet on their lips, found themselves in the tumult and fury of a desperate assault. After the fight was over they returned and finished their interrupted song!

Innes, again, relates how, when a long mine of the enemy had been seized, and two officers were exploring its darkness, they heard the earth fall in behind them. One of the two, famous for his resonant laugh, shouted with a burst of merriment, "What fun! They are cutting us off," and turned round gaily to charge on his foes!

Danger, in a word, had become an inspiring jest to these brave spirits. "Sam" Lawrence, who commanded the Redan, was famous for the cheerful view he always took of affairs. It was known that the Sepoys had several mines converging on the projecting horn of the Redan, and Lawrence, as unconquerably jolly as Mark Tapley himself, expressed his view of the situation to his brigadier by saying, with a laugh, that "he and his men expected very shortly to be up amongst the little birds!"

On June 14, Fayrer records, "If we can believe our enemies, we are the last Englishmen in the country." This might or might not be the case; but the garrison determined grimly that, if they were the last of their race, they would not disgrace it. In the vernacular of the camp, they had agreed to "blow the whole —— thing into the air" rather than surrender. "I was quite determined," says Fayrer, "that they should not take me alive, and I would kill as many of them as I could before they took me.... Some men asked me to give them poison for their wives, if the enemy should get in. But this I absolutely refused to do."

Courage, when high-strung, sometimes evolves an almost uncanny cheerfulness. The Sepoys brought a mortar into action that dropped shell after shell on one particular house. "We got the ladies up out of the Tyekhana," records Fayrer, and they amused themselves by trying to be cheerful and singing part-songs in the portico, to the rushing of shells and the whistling of musket-balls. When before were such songs attempted to such an accompaniment? But the women of the Residency showed throughout a courage quite as high as that of the men. During the great assault on July 20, when, on the explosion of a mine, the Sepoys attempted to storm the Residency at half-a-dozen points, "every one," says Fayrer, "was at his post, and poured shot, shell, grape, and musketry into them as hard as possible. The noise was frightful, the enemy shouting and urging each other on. It certainly seemed to me as if our time had come. But all the poor ladies were patiently awaiting the result in the Tyekhana."

"During the whole siege," says Gubbins, "I never heard of a man among the Europeans who played the coward. Some croaked, no doubt, many were despondent, yet others grew grimly desperate during those terrible days." Gubbins relates how he was one evening taken aside by an officer, who explained that he had arranged with his wife that, if the Sepoys forced their way in, he would shoot her. "She had declared herself content to die by a pistol-ball from his hand." He offered to do the same friendly service for Gubbins's wife, if necessary, and wanted Gubbins to undertake a like desperate office for his wife, if required. To such desperate straits were civilised and Christian men driven!

The courage shown by the women was uniform and wonderful. Dr. Fayrer relates how a shell broke in the bedroom where his wife was lying. It shattered the room and set fire to the bedclothes with its explosion. Fayrer ran in; and, he says, "My wife immediately spoke to me out of the smoke, and said she was not hurt. She was perfectly composed and tranquil, though a 9-pound bombshell had just burst by the side of her bed."

There were three great all-round attacks, on July 20, August 10, and September 5. The most desperate, perhaps, was that on the Cawnpore battery, the most nearly successful that on the Sikh square. The attack on the Sikh square was preceded by the explosion of a mine which made a breach thirty feet wide in the British defences, and buried seven of its defenders under the ruins. There was good cover for the enemy close up to the breach, and no reason why they should not have swarmed in, except the argument of the smoke-blackened, grim-looking sahibs who suddenly appeared, musket in hand, to guard the great gap.

A rush was, indeed, made by the Sepoys, and a native officer of the Irregular Cavalry, who headed the rush gallantly enough, actually crossed the line of the entrenchments—the only mutineer who, during the long siege, succeeded in putting his foot on the soil held by the British. He was instantly shot, and so cruel and swift was the fire poured in upon the Sepoys that they fell back in confusion, and under Inglis's orders planks and doors were brought quickly up, and arranged, one overlapping the other, till the whole gap was covered, and a pile of sand-bags built behind it.

Gubbins describes one critical moment in the siege. On July 21st it was discovered the Sepoys had dug through an adjoining wall and found their way into a narrow lane which skirted the compound; and, literally, only a canvas screen parted them from the British position! Gubbins ran to the single loophole which commanded the lane, and, with his rifle, shot down every Sepoy who attempted to cross it while the gap in the British defences was being hurriedly built up. "At this moment," he says, "I heard the voice of a European behind me, and, without turning my head, begged that the wall in the rear of the mutineers might be loopholed and musketry opened upon them. The person behind me, it seems, was Major Banks. He approached my post to get a sight of the enemy, and while looking out incautiously received a bullet through the temples. I heard the heavy fall, and turned for a second. He was dead. He never moved, and I resumed my guard over the enemy." For two stern hours Gubbins guarded the gap. Then assistance came, the Sepoys were driven from their point of vantage, and the gap in the defences built up.

Later on in the siege the fighting was carried on beneath the surface of the earth. The Sepoys had amongst them many men belonging to a caste famous for skill with the spade, and from more than a score of separate points they drove mines towards the entrenchments. Spade had to fight spade; and, as in the 32nd were many Cornishmen familiar with mining work, these were employed to countermine the enemy. The Sepoys undertook 37 separate mines, and of these 36 were failures, only one—that directed against the Sikh square—proving successful.

One of the most heroic figures in the immortal garrison was Captain Fulton, the garrison engineer, who, on the death of Major Anderson, took charge of all engineering operations. Fulton was a superb engineer, and all the stories of the siege do justice to the part he played in the defence. Gubbins says he was "the life and soul of everything that was persevering, chivalrous, and daring," and declares that he deserved to be called "the Defender of Lucknow." Mr. Fulton, of Melbourne, a relation of this brave man, still preserves the journal of the siege kept by his kinsman. It is a document of real historical value, and gives a graphic picture of the great struggle from day to day. He tells again and again how he met the enemy's mines by countermines, how he broke in upon them, swept them from their drive like flying rabbits, and blew the whole affair up, as he puts it, "with great enjoyment of the fun and excitement!"

Fulton once found that they had driven a mine close up to the wall of a house that formed part of the British defence, and he could hear the sound of pick and shovel distinctly. "I thought this very impudent," he writes; "they could be so easily met; but it seemed a bore to begin to counter. So I just put my head over the wall and called out in Hindustanee a trifle of abuse and 'Bagho! bagho!'—'Fly! fly!'—when such a scuffle and bolt took place I could not leave for half-an-hour for laughing. They dropped it for good—that was the best of the joke."

Fulton took his full part in the general fighting. Thus, in the assault on the Cawnpore battery, he relates that he "found the enemy led by a man in pink, whom I had noticed several times directing them as they came up. I put a rifle-ball through him, and then sent Tulloch to order hand-grenades, the second of which, well thrown, cleared the ditch." Here is a picture, again, of one of Fulton's many sorties to destroy houses by which the British were annoyed:

> We sneaked out of our lines into a house. I had only a penknife, slow match, and port-fire in my hand, and was followed close by two Europeans, and supported by a dozen more. We expected to find the house empty, but George Hutchinson, who was first, suddenly startled us by firing his revolver and calling out "Here are twenty of them!" The two Europeans—indeed, all of them—fell back a pace or two; but I seized a musket from one, and ran forward. They followed, and I put them in position to guard doors, while I twitted the enemy with not showing their faces, as I did, in front of the door, but standing with only their firelocks showing. The chaff had the effect, for one dashed out and fired at me, but I shot him instanter. They then bolted as I gave the word "Charge!" and we blew up the house. Great fun and excitement in a small way!

Fulton detected a mine the enemy had driven a certain distance; he ran a short countermine to meet it, and then sat patiently, revolver in hand, waiting for the unconscious enemy to break through. "Some one," he relates, "looking for me, asked one of the Europeans if I was in the mine. 'Yes, sir!' said the sergeant, 'there he has been for the last two hours, like a terrier at a rat-hole, and not likely to leave it either all day!'" It was to the energy, skill, and daring of this gallant officer that the complete defeat of the enemy's mines was due.

The last entry in his journal is dated September 11; on September 13 he was killed. Says Captain Birch, "The death of this brilliant officer was occasioned by one of the most curious of wounds. He had been inspecting a new battery in an earthwork opposite Mr. Gubbins's house. He was lying at full length in one of the embrasures, with a telescope in his hand. He turned his face, with a smile on it, and said: 'They are just going to fire,' and sure enough they did! The shot took away the whole of the back of Captain Fulton's head, leaving his face like a mask still on his neck. When he was laid out on his back on a bed, we could not see how he had been killed. His was the most important loss we had sustained after that of Sir Henry Lawrence."

MAJOR-GENERAL SIR HENRY HAVELOCK, K.C.B.

From an engraving

CHAPTER VII

LUCKNOW AND HAVELOCK

Lucknow is only forty-five miles from Cawnpore. On July 25, Havelock, at the head of his tiny but gallant force, by this time tempered in the flame of battle to the quality of mere steel, crossed the Ganges in a tempest of rain, and started to rescue the beleaguered garrison of Lucknow from the fate of Cawnpore. But it was not until September 25 that Outram and Havelock clambered through the shot-battered gun embrasure in the low wall beside the Bailey Guard at Lucknow, and brought relief to the hard-pressed garrison. And the story of those nine weeks is scribbled over with records of daring and of achievement unsurpassed in the history of war.

Havelock left 300 men under Neill to hold Cawnpore, where rough but adequate entrenchments had been thrown up. Furious rains had swollen the Ganges, and it took him four days to transport his little force across its turbid and far-extended waters. He had under his command Neill's "blue-caps," the 64th, the 84th, the 78th, and Brasyer's Sikhs, a force not quite 1500 strong—of which only 1200 were British—with ten small field-pieces and a troop of sixty horsemen. And with this mere handful of men a dozen strong positions had to be carried, a great river crossed, and a huge city, swarming with enemies, pierced!

The village of Onao barred the road, some nine miles from the banks of the Ganges. Every house was held by Oude irregulars, a stubborn and hard-fighting race; the rain-water, lying deep on both flanks of the village, made a turning movement impossible. The infantry had outmarched the guns, and Havelock wished to keep them back till his artillery came up.

But the men were fiercely impatient, and could hardly be restrained. "Pray, sir," urged Colonel Hamilton, of the 78th, "let them go at the place and have done with it." Havelock nodded, and in an instant Highlanders and Fusileers, vehemently racing against each other, went at a run into the village. Every house was a loopholed fortress, and the fighting was stubborn and deadly. House after house broke into flames, while clusters of Highlanders and Fusileers broke through doors and windows. The Oude men, to quote Forbes's phrase, "fought like wild cats while they roasted." The 64th next came up at the double, and the village was carried.

Beyond the village the flying guns of the enemy halted, and drew up across the narrow causeway, barring it with a fiery hedge of shot and flame; but the "blue-caps," their officers leading, swept like a human whirlwind down on the guns, and the stubborn Oude gunners, to a man, were bayoneted at their pieces.

Six miles further the walled town of Bussarat Gunj crossed the road, its gateway spanning the whole width of the causeway. Havelock took his guns within short range of the gateway, and commenced to batter it, whilst he despatched the 64th to turn the town and cut off the retreat of the enemy. It was clever strategy, but the 78th and the Fusileers were too quick, the 64th too slow. Highlanders and "blue-caps" carried trench, gateway, and battery with one sustained and angry rush, and as they came storming through the gateway with bent heads and bayonets at the charge, the enemy were driven, a jumble of flying horsemen, galloping artillery, and wrecked infantry, through the town beyond it. The 64th, it is said, marched reluctantly on their turning movement. The men were eager to share the straight rush at the gate.

Young Havelock, mistaking the men's temper, galloped up to the regiment with a message from his impatient father that lost nothing in carrying—"If you don't go at the village I'll send men that will go, and put an everlasting disgrace on you!" Brave men do not lightly endure the whip of a message like that, and Forbes relates how a private named Paddy Cavanagh leaped from the ranks, ran single-handed in on the enemy, "cursing his comrades with bitter Irish malisons as he sped, and was literally hacked to pieces, fighting like a wild cat in the ranks of his enemies"! How the 64th followed where valiant Paddy Cavanagh had led may be imagined; but the late arrival of the 64th had spoiled Havelock's combination, and he was too much given to vehement rhetoric to spare the heavy-footed 64th a lash of the whip. "Some of you," he said in his order of the day next morning, "fought yesterday as if the cholera had seized your mind as well as your bodies!"

Havelock had by this time marched fifteen miles, fought two battles, used up one-third of his ammunition, and lost by bullet or cholera about one-sixth of his force. At this rate of progress he would reach Lucknow with powderless guns and 600 bayonets! Cawnpore itself, too, was threatened, and at Dinapore, a vital point in the long water-line between Calcutta and Allahabad, three regiments of Sepoys had broken into mutiny, and threatened Havelock's communications with the capital.

Havelock consulted with Tytler, his quartermaster-general, his chief engineer, and his son. Young Havelock, with the effervescing and heady valour of youth, was for "pushing on at all hazards"; the older men declared this meant the entire destruction of the force, and perhaps the loss of Lucknow, and Havelock was too good a soldier not to agree with this view. It was an act of nobler courage to fall back than to advance, but Havelock's fine-tempered valour was equal to the feat, and he turned the faces of his reluctant soldiers back to Cawnpore.

Neill, fierce and vehement by nature, when he heard the news, despatched an amazing letter to his chief.

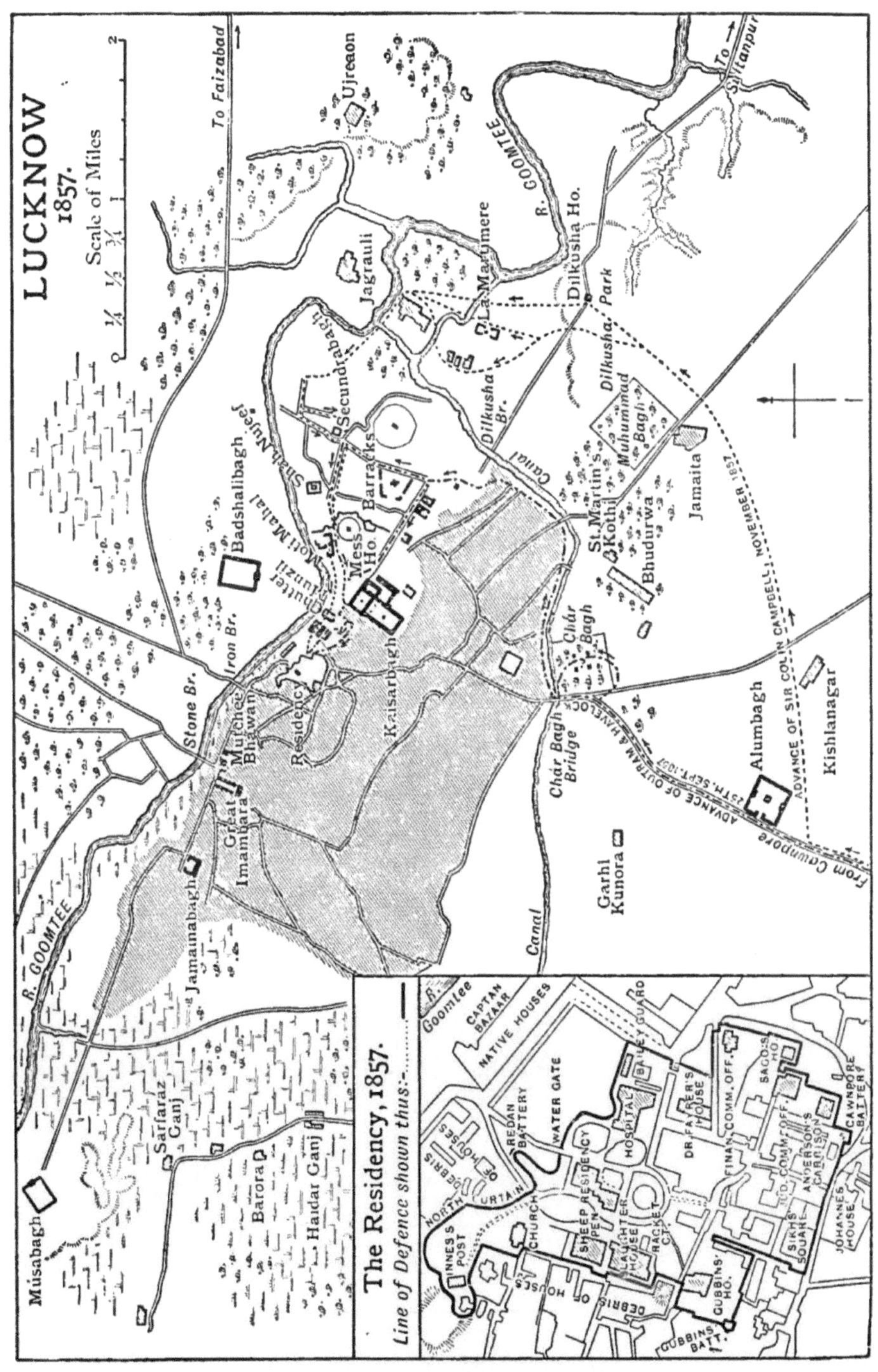

LUCKNOW, 1857.

Walker & Cockerell sc.

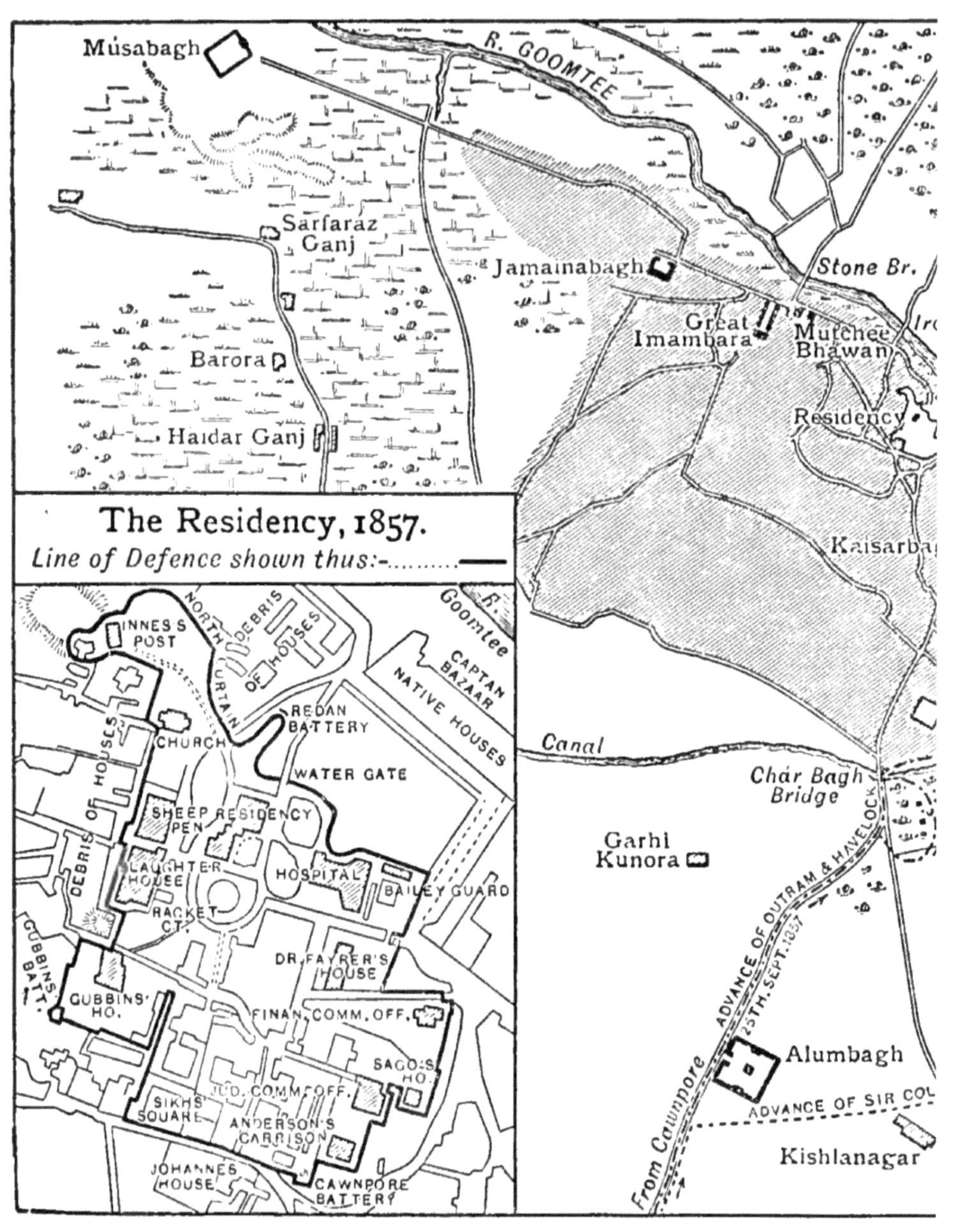

Lucknow, 1857 (*Enlarged - Left*)

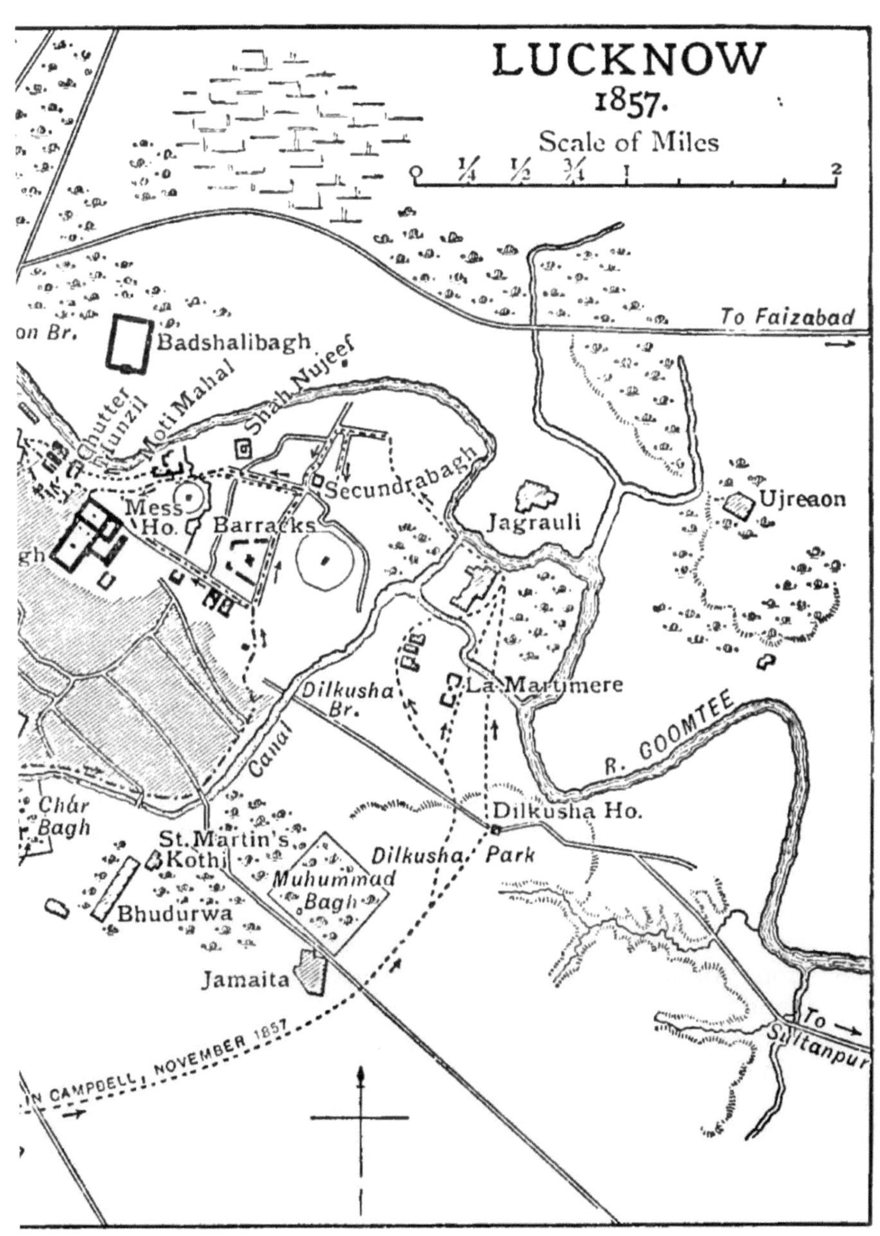

Lucknow, 1857 (*Enlarged - Right*)

"You ought not to remain a day where you are," he wrote. "You talk of advancing as soon as reinforcements reach you. You ought to advance again, and not halt until you have rescued, if possible, the garrison of Lucknow." Havelock, with that note of shrill temper which ran through his character, was the last man to endure exhortations of this peremptory quality from a subordinate. "There must be an end," he wrote back, "to these proceedings at once." Nothing, he said, but the possible injury to the public service prevented him from putting Neill under immediate arrest! "But," he added, "you now stand warned. Attempt no further dictation!"

The truth is, both men were splendid soldiers, but of a type so different that neither could understand the other. Neill was of the silent, dour type; Havelock was too shrill and vocal for him. Havelock, on the other hand, often felt Neill's stern silence to be an unsyllabled reproof, and he more than suspected Neill of the desire to overbear him. When Neill joined him at Cawnpore, Havelock's first words to him were, "Now, General Neill, let us understand each other. You have no power or authority here whilst I am here, and you are not to issue a single order here." There were the elements of a very pretty quarrel betwixt the two soldiers who were upholding the flag of England at the heart of the Mutiny; and yet, so essentially noble were both men, and so fine was their common standard of soldierly duty, that they laid aside their personal quarrel absolutely, and stood by each other with flawless loyalty till, under the fatal archway at the Kaisarbagh, Neill fell, shot through the head.

Havelock telegraphed to Calcutta that he could not resume his march to Lucknow till he had been reinforced by 1000 infantry and Olpherts' battery complete. Yet on August 4, when he had been reinforced by merely a single company and two guns, he started afresh for Lucknow, won another costly victory at Bussarat Gunj, and then fell back once more on Cawnpore, with cholera raging amongst his men. Almost every fourth British soldier under his command was disabled either by sickness or wounds. Havelock had simply to wait till reinforcements came up; but he relieved his feelings while he waited by marching out and destroying Bithoor, Nana Sahib's palace.

The days crept past leaden-footed; reinforcements trickled in, so to speak, drop by drop. Not till September 16 was Havelock ready for the final march to Lucknow. And then Outram arrived to supersede him! It was, in a sense, a cruel stroke to Havelock. But he and Outram were tried comrades, knitted to each other by a friendship woven of the memories and companionship of many years, and Outram was himself one of the most chivalrous and self-effacing men that ever lived. The story of how he refused to take the command out of Havelock's hands, confined himself to his civil office as commissioner, and put himself, as a mere volunteer, under Havelock's orders, is an oft-told and most noble tale.

On September 19 Havelock crossed the Ganges, by this time bridged, with a force numbering 3000 men of all arms. The Madras Fusileers, the 5 th Fusileers, the 84th, and two companies of the 64th, under Neill, formed the first brigade. The second brigade, under Colonel Hamilton, consisted of the 78th Highlanders, the 90th, and Brasyer's Sikhs. The artillery consisted of three batteries, under Maude,

Olpherts, and Eyre respectively; and no guns that ever burned powder did more gallant and desperate service than these. The pieces, indeed, might well have been stored, as heroic relics, in some great museum. The cavalry was made up of 109 volunteers and 59 native horsemen, under Barrow.

The rain fell as though another Noachian deluge was imminent. The rice-fields on either side of the road were either lakes or quagmires. The column, however, pushed on with eager and cheerful, if wet-footed, courage. The Sepoys held the village of Mungulwagh strongly. Havelock smote them in front with his artillery, turned their flank with his infantry, marching—or rather splashing—through the swamps, and when the Sepoys had been, in this manner, hustled out of the town, he launched his little squadron of cavalry upon them. Outram rode among the troopers armed with nothing but a gold-mounted cane, with which he thumped the heads and shoulders of the flying enemy.

Here some mutineers, stained with special crimes, fell into Havelock's hands, and Maude, in his "Memories of the Mutiny," tells how Havelock asked him "if he knew how to blow a man from a gun." This art does not form part of the curriculum at Woolwich, but Maude could only touch his cap and say he "would try." Here is a grim picture of the doings of that stern time:—

> When we halted for the night, I moved one of my guns on to the causeway, unlimbered it, and brought it into "action front." The evening was just beginning to grow dusk, and the enemy were still in sight, on the crest of some rising ground a few hundred yards distant. The remainder of my guns were "parked" in a nice mango-tope to the right of the road.... The first man led out was a fine-looking young Sepoy, with good features, and a bold, resolute expression. He begged that he might not be bound, but this could not be allowed, and I had his wrists tied tightly each to the upper part of a wheel of the gun. Then I depressed the muzzle, until it pointed to the pit of his stomach, just below the sternum. We put no shot in, and I only kept one gunner (besides the "firing" number) near the gun, standing myself about 10 ft. to the left rear. The young Sepoy looked undauntedly at us during the whole process of pinioning; indeed, he never flinched for a moment. Then I ordered the port-fire to be lighted, and gave the word "Fire!" There was a considerable recoil from the gun, and a thick cloud of smoke hung over us. As this cleared away, we saw two legs lying in front of the gun, but no other sign of what had, just before, been a human being and a brave man. At this moment, perhaps from six to eight seconds after the explosion, down fell the man's head among us, slightly blackened, but otherwise scarcely changed. It must have gone straight up into the air, probably about 200 feet.

This was stern, uncanny occupation for a humane-minded British officer! But the times were stern, the crisis supreme.

On the evening of the second day's march the air was full of a faint, far-off, vibrating sound. It was the distant roar of the enemy's cannon breaking like some angry and dreadful sea on the besieged Residency! When the camp was pitched Havelock fired a royal salute, hoping the sound would reach the ears of the beleaguered garrison, and tell them rescue was coming; but the faint wind failed to carry the sound to the Residency. When the soldiers began their march on September 23, Lucknow was only sixteen miles distant, and by noon the Alumbagh was in sight, held by a force of some 12,000 men.

Havelock turned the enemy's right with his second brigade, while he engaged the enemy's guns with Eyre's battery in front. Olpherts, with his guns, was sent to assist the turning movement. Here is a stirring battle picture drawn by Forbes:—

> At a stretching gallop, with some volunteer cavalry in front of it, the horse battery dashed up the road past the halted first brigade, which cheered loudly as the cannon swept by, Neill waving his cap and leading the cheering. On the left of the road there was a great deep trench full of water, which had somehow to be crossed. Led by Barrow, the cavalry escort plunged in, and scrambled through, and then halted to watch how Olpherts would conquer the obstacle. "Hell-fire Jack" was quite equal to the occasion, and his men were as reckless as himself. With no abatement of speed the guns were galloped into the great trough. For a moment there was chaos—a wild medley of detachments, drivers, guns, struggling horses, and splashing water; and then the guns were out on the further side, nobody and nothing the worse for the scramble, all hands on the alert to obey Olpherts' stentorian shout, "Forward at a gallop!"

Hamilton's men marched and fought knee-deep in water; but the enemy's right was smashed, his centre tumbled into ruin, and the men of the 78th and the Fusileers actually carried the Alumbagh in ten minutes! To tumble 12,000 men into flight, and carry the Alumbagh in this fashion, and in a space so brief, was a great feat; and while the men were in the exultation of victory, a messenger came riding in with the news—unhappily not true—that Delhi had fallen!

On the 24th the little force rested, while its leaders matured their plans for the advance to the Residency. Before them ran the great canal, the road crossing it by what was called the Charbagh bridge. Havelock's plan was to bridge the Goomtee, the river into which the canal ran, march along its further bank, round the city to its north-west angle, and re-cross by the iron bridge immediately in front of the Residency, and in this way avoid the necessity of forcing his way, with desperate and bloody street-fighting, through the interlaced and tangled lanes of the city.

But the soil between the canal and the river was little better than a marsh, and it was determined to force the Charbagh bridge, advance on a lane which skirted the left bank of the canal, then turn sharply to the left, and fight a way across the city to the Residency.

Three hundred footsore and sick men were left to hold the Alumbagh. In the grey dawn of September 25, Havelock's men, scanty in number, worn with marching, and hardened with a score of fights, were falling into line for the final march, which was to relieve Lucknow. "The sergeants of companies," says an eye-witness, "acting on their orders, were shouting 'Fall out, all you men that are footsore or sick;' but many added the taunt, 'and all you fellows whose heart isn't good as well!'" But no man fell out of the ranks that grey September morning on that coward's plea! At half-past eight the bugles sang out the advance, and with a cheer, and a quick step which the officers could scarcely restrain from breaking into the double, the men moved off for the last act in this great adventure.

Maude's guns moved first, covered by two companies of the 5th (Northumberland) Fusileers. Outram rode by Maude's side with the leading gun. Instantly, from a wide front, a cruel and deadly fire smote the head of the little column. From the enemy's batteries on either flank, carefully laid and admirably served, from the cornfields, from the garden walls, from the house-roofs, a terrific fire of musketry and cannon-shot lashed, as with a scourge of flame, the causeway on which the English guns were moving. Maude's guns were halted, and opened fiercely in answer to this fire. The men fell fast. A musket-ball passed through Outram's arm, but, says Maude, "he only smiled, and asked one of us to tie his handkerchief tightly above the wound." The cluster of British guns, with their gallant gunners, stood in the very centre of a tempest of shot. Here is a picture, drawn by Maude, of the carnage in his battery:—

> Almost at the same moment the finest soldier in our battery, and the best artilleryman I have ever known, Sergeant-Major Alexander Lamont, had the whole of his stomach carried away by a round shot. He looked up to me for a moment with a piteous expression, but had only strength to utter two words, "Oh! God!" when he sank dead on the road. Just then another round shot took off the leg, high up the thigh, of the next senior sergeant, John Kiernan. He was afterwards carried back to the Alumbagh, but soon died from the shock. Kiernan was an excellent specimen of a Roman Catholic North of Ireland soldier. He was as true as steel. Another tragic sight on that road was the death of a fine young gunner, the only one, I believe, who wore an artillery jacket that day. A round shot took his head clean off, and for about a second the body stood straight up, surmounted by the red collar, and then fell flat on the road. But as fast as the men of the leading gun detachments were swept away by the enemy's fire I replaced them by volunteers from other guns. Several times I turned to the calm, cool, grim general standing near, and asked him to allow us to advance, as we could not possibly do any good by halting there. He agreed with me, but did not like to take the responsibility of ordering us to go on.

At last the order to move on came, and Charbagh bridge was reached. It was defended on the further side by a solid earthen rampart 7ft. high, but with a narrow slit in the middle through which one man at a time could pass. It was armed with six guns, two of them 24-pounders. Tall houses, crowded with musketrymen, covered the bridge with their fire, and solid battalions were drawn up in its rear. Maude was planted with two of his guns in the open, and within short range of the enemy's battery, and commenced a valiant duel with it. Outram led the 5th Fusileers by a detour for the purpose of smiting the battery at the bridge-head with a flank-fire. Maude's two guns were fighting six, at a distance of 150 yards, and his gunners fell fast.

Again and again he had to call for volunteers to work his guns from the Madras Fusileers lying down under cover near him. The guns were of an ancient pattern, and carried a large leathern pouch full of loose powder for priming uses. "As the lane was very narrow," says Maude, "the two guns were exceedingly close to one another, and when in their recoil they passed each other, amid a shower of sparks and smoke, they frequently set fire to the loose powder in the priming pouches, and blew the poor gunners up!" Yet Maude's gallant lads worked their guns unflinchingly.

Neill stood in a bay of a garden wall close by, with his "blue-caps" lying down under cover, waiting till Outram's flanking movement should tell on the enemy's battery; and Maude, with his artillerymen almost all shot down, said to young Havelock, "Do something, in the name of Heaven!" Havelock rode through the tempest of shot to Neill, and urged an immediate rush on the bridge; but Neill, with soldierly coolness, declared he would not move without orders. Then young Havelock played a boyish and gallant trick. He rode quietly off, turned round a bend in the road, and a moment after came back at a gallop, gave a smart salute to Neill as he pulled up his horse on its haunches, and said, as though bringing an order from his father, "You are to carry the bridge at once, sir!"

At the word, Arnold, who commanded the "blue-caps," leaped to his feet and raced on to the bridge, his men rising with a shout and following him. Havelock and Tytler overtook him at a gallop, and the bridge in a moment was covered with a mass of charging soldiers.

But a blast of shots from the guns at its head—the deep bellow of the 24-pounders sounding high above the tumult—swept the bridge for a moment clear. Arnold had fallen with both legs smashed, Tytler's horse had gone down with its brave rider; only young Havelock and a corporal of the Fusileers, named Jakes, stood unhurt. Havelock rode coolly up to the rampart of earth, and, waving his sword, called to the Fusileers to "come on"; and Corporal Jakes, as he busily plied his musket, shouted to Havelock, soothingly, "Never fear, sir! We'll soon have the beggars out of that!" All this took but a few seconds of time; the Sepoys were toiling with frantic energy to reload their guns. Then through the white smoke came the rush of the Madras Fusileers—an officer leading. Over the bridge, up the seven-foot rampart, through the intervals betwixt the guns as with a single impulse, came the levelled bayonets and fierce faces of the charging British, and the bridge was won!

The entire British force came swiftly over, the 78th was left to hold the bridge and form the rearguard, while the British column swung round to the right and pushed on through the narrow lane that bordered the canal.

The 78th, while guarding the bridge, had a very trying experience. A great force of the enemy came down the Cawnpore road with banners flying and loud beating of drums, and flung itself with wild courage on the Highlanders. A little stone temple stood a hundred yards up the road, commanding the bridge; the Sepoys took possession of this, and from it galled the Highlanders cruelly with their fire. Hastings, of the 78th, stepped out to the front, and called for volunteers to storm the temple. There was an angry rush of Highlanders up the road; the temple was carried at the point of the bayonet, and then held as a sort of outwork to the bridge.

The Sepoys next brought up three brass guns, and lashed temple and road alike with their fire. Webster, an officer of the 78th, famous for his swordsmanship and strength, called out, "Who's for these infernal guns?" and ran out, sword in hand. His Highlanders followed him, but could not overtake Webster, who sprang upon the guns, and slew a gunner, just in the act of putting his linstock to the touch-hole, with a stroke so mighty that it clove the Sepoy through skull and jaws almost to the collar-bone! The guns were captured, dragged with a triumphant skirl of the pipes to the canal, and flung in, and the Highlanders set off to follow the column.

They did not follow in its immediate track, but made a wide sweep to the right, and both sections of the column, with much stern fighting, reached what was called the Chutter Munzil Palace. "Here," says Forbes, "were the chiefs of the little army. On his big 'waler' sat Outram, a splash of blood across his face, and one arm in a sling, the Malacca cane, which formed his sole weapon in battle, still grasped in the hand of the sound limb. Havelock, on foot, was walking up and down on Outram's near side, with short steps. All around them, at a little distance, were officers, and outside of the circle so formed were soldiers, guns, wounded men, bullocks, camels"—all the tumult, in a word, of the battle.

Outram and Havelock disagreed as to the next step to be taken. Outram—the cooler brain of the two—wished to halt for the night, and then to push their way in the morning through the successive courts of the palaces right up to the Residency. Havelock was eager to complete the day's work, and reach the Residency with a final and desperate rush.

A long, winding, and narrow street stretched before them up to the Bailey Guard Gate, the entrance to the Residency. It was true that every cross street that broke its length was swept by the fire of the enemy's guns, that the houses were loopholed and crowded with Sepoys, and from the flat roofs of the houses above a tempest of fire would be poured upon the British. But Havelock was full of warlike impatience. "There is the street," said he; "we see the worst. We shall be slated, but we can push through, and get it over." Outram acknowledged afterwards that he ought to have said, "Havelock, we have virtually reached the Residency. I now take the command;" but he added to the confession, "My temper got a little the better of me, and I said, 'In God's name, then, let us go on.'"

The Highlanders led, Havelock and Outram riding with their leading files.

Brasyer's Sikhs followed. It was, as Forbes says, "a true *via dolorosa*." From house-roof, from door, from window, from every cross lane poured a tempest of shot, and through it the British could only push with dogged, all-enduring courage, seldom halting to fire back. And this experience stretched over more than three-quarters of a mile! Here is a little battle vignette taken from Forbes:—

> In the foremost company of the Highland regiment were two staunch comrades, named Glandell and M'Donough, Irishmen and Catholics among the Scots and Presbyterians. In this street of death M'Donough's leg was shattered by a bullet. He fell, but was not left to die. His stalwart chum raised the wounded man, took him on his back, and trudged on with his heavy burden. Nor did the hale man, thus encumbered, permit himself to be a non-combatant. When a chance offered him to fire a shot, Glandell propped his wounded comrade up against some wall, and would betake himself to his rifle, while it could be of service. Then he would pick M'Donough up again, and stagger cheerily onward, till the well-deserved goal of safety was reached.

The road at one point ran under an archway, and here Neill met with his death-shot. He drew up his horse by the arch quite coolly, and was steadying the soldiers as they swept through it. A Sepoy leaned forward from a window above the arch, with his musket almost touching Neill's head. Neill sat with his face turned to his shoulder, watching a gun going through the archway, when the Sepoy fired. His bullet struck the side of Neill's head above the ear, and killed him instantly. Out of the tumult and passion of the fight thus dropped, in a moment, this most gallant of soldiers.

Still the fierce fight raged. Still, beaten with a tempest of shot, the tormented column pushed on its dogged way. Suddenly from the head of the column rose a mighty shout. It was not the cry of soldiers at the charge, full of the wrath of battle. It was a great cry of exultation and triumph. Through the grey twilight, dark with eddying smoke, the leading files of the British had seen the battered archway of the Bailey Guard. The goal was reached.

The beleaguered garrison had listened, with what eagerness may be imagined, to the tumult of the fight as it crept nearer them. Its smoke was blowing over their defences. Those who watched the advance from the Residency could measure the approach of the relieving force by the attitudes and gestures of the Sepoys on the house-tops, as they fired furiously down on the gallant column forcing its way along the streets beneath them. The storm of sound grew louder, clearer, deeper. Suddenly, through the smoke and twilight, they caught a glimpse of figures on horseback, the gleam of bayonets, the white faces and red uniforms of British soldiers. An earthwork blocked the Bailey Gate itself, but the handful of men acting as the garrison of the gate, pulled hurriedly back from its ragged embrasure in the wall, to the left of the entrance, one of the guns, and through that embrasure—Outram, on his big Australian horse, leading—came the Highlanders, with Havelock and his staff; then the Sikhs; then the Fusileers. The Residency was reached!

How the shout of exultation ran round the seventeen shot-battered posts of the long-besieged entrenchments can be imagined. The women, the children, the very sick in the hospital, lent their voices to that shout. The Highlanders, who came first, poured their Celtic exclamations and blessings on the men and women they had rescued. "We expected to have found only your bones," said one. That the children were still alive filled the gallant but soft-hearted Highlanders with amazed joy. "The big, rough-bearded soldiers," wrote one of the rescued ladies, "were seizing the little children out of our arms, kissing them with tears running down their cheeks, and thanking God that they had come in time to save them from the fate of those at Cawnpore."

Let it be remembered that for more than eighty days the garrison had lived under the shadow of death. No message, no whisper of news, from the outside world had reached them. Their rescuers were men of the same name and blood, who had fought their way as if through the flames of the Pit to reach and save them! And into what a mood of passionate joy amongst the delivered, and of passionate exultation and triumph amongst the deliverers, the crowd which thronged the Residency that night was lifted may be more easily imagined than described. It was a night worth living for; almost worth dying for.

Lady Inglis has told how she listened to the tremendous cheering that welcomed the British across the Residency lines, and how her husband brought up "a short, quiet-looking, grey-haired man," who she guessed at once was Havelock. It was a great triumph, but a great price was paid for it. The relieving column, out of its 3000 men, lost in killed or wounded more than 700, nearly one in every four of its whole number!

One unfortunate incident marked the relief. As the Highlanders approached the Bailey Guard Gate they took Aitken's men of the 13th for the enemy, and leaped upon them with gleaming and angry bayonets, and slew some before their blunder was discovered. It was never imagined that the very outpost of the heroic garrison would be found to consist of Sepoys, fighting with such long-enduring loyalty against their own countrymen. It was a very cruel fate for these faithful Sepoys to perish under the bayonets of the relieving force.

Still another remarkable incident may be described. A cluster of doolies, with wounded officers and men, lost its way in the tangled streets and was cut off. Nine men of the escort, with five wounded, took refuge in a small building which formed one side of the gateway where Neill had been shot; and for a whole day and night they defended themselves against overwhelming numbers. Dr. Home, of the 90th, was one of the party, and has left a graphic account of what is perhaps the most brilliant little incident in the whole history of the siege.

The Sepoys kept up a bitter and tireless fire on the single doorway of the room held by the nine. One of the British, a Fusileer named M'Manus, stood outside the doorway, sheltering himself behind a pillar, and shot down man after man of the enemy. So cool and quick and deadly was his fire that the Sepoys feared to make a rush. At last their leader, to encourage them, shouted there were but three sahibs in the house, whereupon the whole fourteen, wounded included, joined in a loud cheer to undeceive them. Captain Arnold, of the Fusileers, lay wounded in one of the abandoned doolies visible through the doorway. Two gallant privates, Ryan and M'Manus, charged out through the fire and carried their officer into the house. They ran out a second time and brought in a wounded private; but in each case the comrade they carried was mortally wounded while in their arms.

Again and again some leader of the Sepoys ran out, heading a charge on the doorway; but each time the leader was shot, and the Sepoys fell back. The sorely beleaguered party was rescued the next morning. Just when hope seemed to have abandoned them, a new blast of musketry volleys was heard at a little distance, and one of the Fusileers recognised the regular sound. He jumped up, shouting, "Oh, boys, them's our own chaps!"

CHAPTER VIII

LUCKNOW AND SIR COLIN CAMPBELL

Havelock fought his way through blood and fire into the Residency, but he shrank from leading a great procession of women and children and wounded men along that *via dolorosa*—that pathway of blood—by which, at so grim a cost, he had himself reached the beleaguered garrison. The Residency, it was clear, must be held, since the great company of helpless women and children it sheltered could not be carried off. So what Havelock and Outram really accomplished was not so much a Relief as a Reinforcement.

Outram assumed the command, and for six weeks the greatly-strengthened garrison held its own with comparative ease against the revolted swarms, reckoned—uncertainly—at no less than 60,000 strong, who still maintained a sullen blockade of the Residency.

Early in November reinforcements were pouring in from England, and a new actor appeared on the scene. The crisis of the Mutiny called to the post of commander-in-chief in India the best soldier Great Britain possessed. Colin Campbell was not, perhaps, a great general, in the sense in which Sir John Moore, or Wellington, or Sir Charles Napier were generals. But he was a tough, hard-fighting, much-experienced soldier, with that combination of wariness and fire which marks the Scotch genius for battle. What he did not know of the details of a soldier's business might almost be described as not worth knowing. He had served his apprenticeship to war in the perils and hardships of Moore's retreat to Corunna. A list of the battles and sieges in which he took part would cover almost the entire military history of Great Britain between Corunna and the Crimea. His cool skill and daring as a soldier are picturesquely illustrated by the famous "thin red line" incident at Balaclava; where, disdaining to throw his troops into square, he received a charge of Russian cavalry on a thin extended front, and smote the assailing squadron into fragments with a single blast of musketry.

Colin Campbell was sixty-five years of age, and regarded his military career as over; but on July 11, when the news of General Anson's death reached England, Lord Panmure offered Campbell the chief command in India, and with characteristic promptitude the Scottish veteran offered to start for India the same afternoon! Campbell landed at Calcutta on August 13, spent some weeks there in "organising victory"—or, rather, in reorganising the whole shattered military system of the Presidency—and on October 27 hurried to the seat of war. He reached Cawnpore on November 3, and on the 9th set out to relieve Lucknow. "Our friends in Lucknow," he wrote to his sister, "have food only for five or six days." This was a mistake that cost the lives of many brave men. Lawrence had provisioned the Residency better than was imagined. But the delusion of imminent starvation, which made Havelock fight his way at such desperate speed and cost into Lucknow, still prevailed, and governed British strategy. Delhi had fallen by September 20—a story yet to be told—and part of its besieging force was thus available for a new march on Lucknow.

On the afternoon of November 11 Campbell reviewed the relieving force at Buntera. It was modest in numbers—counting only about 4700 men. But war-hardened, and full of fiery yet disciplined daring, it was as efficient for all the purposes of battle as Napoleon's Old Guard or Wellington's famous Light Division. The cavalry brigade included two squadrons of the 9th Lancers, Hodson's Horse, and three squadrons of native cavalry. The Naval Brigade was under Peel, the third son of the great Prime Minister of England, one of the most daring yet gentle spirits that ever fought and died for England. Evelyn Wood, who served under him as middy in the Crimea, describes him as "the bravest of the brave," and yet "an ideal English gentleman." "His dark brown wavy hair was carefully brushed back, disclosing a perfectly oval face, a high square forehead, and deep blue-grey eyes, which flashed when he was talking eagerly, as he often did." The Artillery Brigade consisted of five batteries. The infantry was made up of detachments from the 4th, the 5th, the 23rd Fusileers, a wing of the 53rd, part of the 82nd, and the full strength of the 93rd Highlanders, with some Sikh regiments.

The 93rd was 1000 strong, and 700 men in the ranks carried the Crimean medal on their breasts. It has been described as "the most Scotch of all the Highland regiments," and a strong religious—as well as a rich Celtic—strain ran through its ranks. Forbes-Mitchell, indeed, who marched in its ranks, says the regiment constituted a sort of military Highland parish, ministers and elders complete. The elders were selected from among the men of all ranks, two sergeants, two corporals, and two privates. It had a regular service of communion plate, and the communion was administered to the whole regiment by its chaplain twice a year.

The 93rd was drawn up in quarter-distance column on the extreme left of the line as Colin Campbell rode down to review his forces that November afternoon. It was in full Highland costume, with kilts and bonnets and wind-blown plumes. Campbell's Celtic blood kindled when he reached the Highlanders. "Ninety-third!" he said, "you are my own lads; I rely on you to do the work." And a voice from the ranks in broadest Doric answered, "Ay, ay, Sir Colin, ye ken us and we ken you; we'll bring the women and children out of Lucknow or die wi' you in the attempt." And then from the steady ranks of the Highlanders there broke a shout, sudden and deep and stern, the shout of valiant men—the men of the hardy North—pledging themselves to valiant deeds.

Here is the description given by an eye-witness of the little army, less than 5000 strong, but of such magnificent fighting quality, down whose ranks Colin Campbell rode as the November sun was going down:—

> The field-guns from Delhi looked blackened and service-worn;

> but the horses were in good condition, and the harness in perfect repair; the gunners bronzed, stalwart, and in perfect fighting case. The 9th Lancers, with their gallant bearing, their flagless lances, and their lean but hardy horses, looked the perfection of regular cavalry on active service. Wild and bold was the bearing of the Sikh horsemen, clad in loose fawn-coloured dress, with long boots, blue or red turbans and sashes; and armed with carbine and tulwar. Next to them were the worn and wasted remains of the 8th and 75th Queen's, who, with wearied air, stood grouped under their colours. Then came the two regiments of Punjab infantry, tall of stature, with fierce eager eyes under their huge turbans—men swift in the march, forward in the fight, and eager for the pillage. On the left of the line, in massive serried ranks, a waving sea of plumes and tartan, stood the 93rd Highlanders, who with loud and rapturous cheers welcomed the veteran commander whom they knew so well and loved so warmly.

On November 12 Campbell had reached the Alumbagh, and, halting there, decided on the line of his advance to the Residency. Instead of advancing direct on the city, and fighting his way through loopholed and narrow lanes, each one a mere valley of death, he proposed to swing round to the right, march in a wide curve through the open ground, and seize what was known as the Dilkusha Park, a great enclosed garden, surrounded by a wall 20 feet high, a little over two miles to the east of the Residency. Using this as his base, he would next move round to the north of the city, forcing his way through a series of strong posts, the most formidable of which were the Secundrabagh and the Shah Nujeef, and so reach the Residency. And the story of the fighting at those two points makes up the tragedy and glory of the Relief of Lucknow.

Outram, of course, was not the man to lie inertly within his defences while Campbell was moving to his relief. He had already sent plans of the city and its approaches, with suggestions as to the best route, to Campbell by means of a spy, and he was prepared to break out on the line by which the relieving force was to advance. But if Campbell could be supplied with a guide, who knew the city as he knew the palm of his own hand, this would be an enormous advantage; and exactly such a guide at this moment presented himself. A civilian named Kavanagh offered to undertake this desperate mission.

Kavanagh was an Irishman, a clerk in one of the civil offices, and apparently possessed a hundred disqualifications for the business of making his way, disguised as a native, through the dark-faced hordes that kept sleepless watch round the Residency, and through the busy streets of Lucknow beyond. He was a big-limbed, fair man, with aggressively red hair, and uncompromisingly blue eyes! By what histrionic art could he be "translated," in Shakespeare's sense, into a spindle-shanked, narrow-shouldered, dusky-skinned Oude peasant? But Kavanagh was a man of quenchless courage, with a more than Irish delight in deeds of daring, and he had a perfect knowledge of native dialect and character. He has left a narrative of his adventure.

A spy had come in from Campbell, and was to return that night, and Kavanagh conceived the idea of going out with him, and acting as guide to the relieving force. Outram hesitated to permit the attempt to be made, declaring it to be too dangerous; but Kavanagh's eagerness for the adventure prevailed. He hid the whole scheme from his wife, and, at half-past seven o'clock that evening, when he entered Outram's headquarters, he was so perfectly disguised that nobody recognised him. He had blackened his face, neck, and arms with lamp-black, mixed with a little oil. His red hair, which even lamp-black and oil could hardly subdue to a colder tint, was concealed beneath a huge turban. His dress was that of a budmash, or irregular native soldier, with sword and shield, tight trousers, a yellow-coloured chintz sheet thrown over the shoulders, and a white cummerbund.

A little after eight o'clock Kavanagh, with his native guide, crept to the bank of the Goomtee, which ran to the north of the Residency entrenchment. The river was a hundred yards wide, and between four feet and five feet deep. Both men stripped, crept down the bank, and slipped, as silently as otters, into the stream. Here for a moment, as Kavanagh in his narrative confesses, his courage failed him. The shadowy bank beyond the black river was held by some 60,000 merciless enemies. He had to pass through their camps and guards, and through miles of city streets beyond. If detected, he would certainly perish by torture. "If my guide had been within my reach," he says, "I should perhaps have pulled him back and abandoned the enterprise." But the guide was already vanishing, a sort of crouching shadow, into the blackness of the further bank; and, hardening his heart, Kavanagh stole on through the sliding gloom of the river.

Both men crept up a ditch that pierced the river-bank to a cluster of trees, and there dressed; and then, with his tulwar on his shoulder and the swagger of a budmash, Kavanagh went boldly forward with his guide. A matchlock man first met the adventurous pair and peered suspiciously at them from under his turban. Kavanagh in a loud voice volunteered the remark that "the night was cold," and passed on. They had to cross the iron bridge which spanned the Goomtee, and the officer on guard challenged them lazily from the balcony of a two-storeyed house. Kavanagh himself hung back in the shade, while his guide went forward and told the story of how they belonged to a village some miles distant, and were going to the city from their homes.

They were allowed to pass, ran the gauntlet of many troops of Sepoys, recrossed the Goomtee by what was called the stone bridge, and passed unsuspected along the principal street of Lucknow, jostling their way through the crowds, and so reached the open fields beyond the city. "I had not been in green fields," writes Kavanagh, "for five months. Everything around us smelt sweet, and a carrot I took from the roadside was the most delicious thing I had ever tasted!" But it was difficult to find their way in the night. They wandered into the Dilkusha Park, and stumbled upon a battery of guns, which Kavanagh, to the terror of his guide, insisted upon inspecting.

They next blundered into the canal, but still wandered on, till they fell into the hands of a guard of twenty-five Sepoys, and Kavanagh's guide, in his terror, dropped in the dust of the road the letter he was carrying from Outram to Campbell. Kavanagh, however, kept his coolness, and after some parleying he and his guide were allowed to pass on. The much-enduring pair next found themselves entangled in a swamp, and, waist-deep in its slime and weeds, they struggled on for two hours, when they reached solid ground again. Kavanagh insisted on lying down to rest for a time. Next they crept between some Sepoy pickets which, with true native carelessness, had thrown out no sentries, and finally, just as the eastern sky was growing white with the coming day, the two adventurers heard the challenge, "Who comes there?" from under the shadow of a great tree!

It was a British cavalry picket, and Kavanagh had soon the happiness of pouring into Sir Colin Campbell's ears the messages and information he brought, while a flag, hoisted at twelve o'clock on the summit of the Alumbagh, told Outram that his messenger had succeeded, and that both the garrison and the relieving force had now a common plan. It is difficult to imagine a higher example of human courage than that supplied by "Lucknow" Kavanagh, as he was afterwards called, and never was the Victoria Cross better won.

On the afternoon of the 15th Campbell made an elaborate reconnaissance on his extreme left, and all night he thundered in that direction with his guns, and the enemy gathered in full strength on that line, persuaded that the British would advance on it. But by daybreak on the 16th Campbell was moving off, light-footed and swift, by his right, exactly where the enemy did not expect him! He had little over 3000 bayonets in his force, but he was strong in artillery, counting in all thirty-nine guns, six mortars, and two rocket-tubes, and he hoped to smash by the weight of his fire every obstacle that stood in his path to the Residency. Yet, be it remembered, he was moving on the arc of a great fortified central position, held by a hostile force not less than 60,000 strong, or more than fifteen times more numerous than his own.

Blunt's guns and a company of the 53rd formed Campbell's advance-guard. They crossed the canal, followed for a mile the river-bank, and then swung sharply to the left by a road which ran parallel to the rear of the Secundrabagh. This was a great garden, 150 yards on each face, with walls twenty feet high, and a circular bastion at each angle, and from its rear face, as the head of the British column came in sight, broke an angry tempest of musket-shot, a fire which, it must be remembered, smote the advancing British column on the flank. Cavalry and infantry were helpless in the narrow lane, and something like a "jam" took place. Blunt, however, an officer of great daring, with an enthusiastic belief that British guns could go anywhere and do anything, cut the knot of the difficulty. The bank of the lane was so steep that it seemed impossible that horses and guns could climb it, but Blunt, with cool decision, put the guns in motion, swung the horses' heads sharply round, and, with whip and spur and shout, his gunners drove the snorting, panting horses up the bank into the open space under the fire of the Secundrabagh.

Travers, with two of his 18-pounders, came stumbling and struggling up the steep bank after Blunt. The guns were swung round, and, within musket-shot distance of the crowded walls and under a tempest of bullets, they opened a breaching fire on the face of the Secundrabagh. The British infantry meanwhile, lying down under the bank of the lane, waited for the moment of assault. Forbes-Mitchell gives a very realistic picture of the march up the lane, and the waiting under the shelter of a low mud-wall while the breach was being made, through which they must charge. Campbell himself, before the men moved up, had given amusingly prosaic instructions as to how they were to fight. When they swept into the Secundrabagh they were to "keep together in clusters of threes, and rely on nothing but the bayonet." The central man of each group of three was to attack, and his comrades, right and left, guard him with their bayonets, &c.

As the 93rd moved up the lane, Forbes-Mitchell relates how they saw sitting on the roadside a naked Hindu, with shaven head and face streaked with white and red paint, busy counting his rosary, and unmoved by the tumult of battle. A Highlander said to a young staff-officer who was just passing, "I would like to try my bayonet on the hide of that painted scoundrel, sir; he looks a murderer." "Don't touch him," answered the staff-officer, "he is a harmless Hindu mendicant; it is the Mohammedans who are to blame for the horrors of the Mutiny." Scarcely had he spoken the words when the Hindu stopped counting his beads, slipped his hands under the mat on which he sat, and, with a single movement, drew out a short bell-mouthed blunderbuss and fired into the unfortunate staff-officer's breast, killing him instantly, and himself dying a moment afterwards, under the reddened bayonets of half-a-dozen furious Highlanders.

Sir Colin Campbell himself stood by the guns, watching the balls tearing away flakes from the stubborn bricks which formed the immense thickness of the wall. Every now and then he repressed the eagerness of the Highlanders or Sikhs, waiting to make their rush. "Lie down, 93rd!" he said. "Lie down! Every man of you is worth his weight in gold to England to-day." For nearly three-quarters of an hour that strange scene lasted, the British guns battering the tough brick wall, while from hundreds of loopholes a tempest of bullets scourged the toiling gunners. Twice over the detachments at the guns had to be renewed before the breach could be made.

The crouching infantry meanwhile could hardly be restrained. A sergeant of the 53rd, a Welshman named Dobbin, called out, "Let the infantry storm, Sir Colin! Let the two Thirds at them"—meaning the 53rd and 93rd—"and we'll soon make short work of the murdering villains." Campbell, always good-tempered when the bullets were flying, recognised the man, and asked, "Do you think the breach is wide enough, Dobbin?"

The three regiments waiting for the rush were the 53rd, the 93rd, and a Sikh regiment—the 4th Rifles; and suddenly they leaped up and joined in one eager dash at the slowly widening breach. Whether the signal to advance was given at all is doubtful, and which regiment led, and which brave soldier was first through the breach, are all equally doubtful points.

Malleson says the rush on the Secundrabagh was "the most wonderful scene witnessed in the war." No order was given; but suddenly the Sikhs and the Highlanders were seen racing for the breach at full speed, bonneted Highlander and brown-faced Sikh straining every nerve to reach it first. A Sikh of the 4th Rifles, he adds, outran the leading Highlander, leaped through the breach, and was shot dead as he sprang. An ensign of the 93rd, named Cooper, was a good second, and, leaping feet first through the hole like a gymnast, got safely through.

Hope Grant says that "before the order was given a native Sikh officer started forward, sword in hand, followed by his men." The 93rd determined not to let the Sikhs outcharge them, and instantly ran forward. The Sikhs had a few yards' start, but "a sergeant of the 93rd, Sergeant-Major Murray, a fine active fellow, outstripped them, jumped through the opening like a harlequin, and, as he landed on the other side, was shot through the breast and fell dead." Archibald Forbes says the first man through the breach was an Irishman, Lance-Corporal Donnelly, of the 93rd, killed as he jumped through the breach; the second was a Sikh, the third a Scotchman, Sergeant-Major Murray, also killed. Who shall decide when there is such a conflict of testimony betwixt the very actors in the great scene!

Roberts confirms Hope Grant in the statement that a Highlander was the first to reach the goal, and was shot dead as he reached the enclosure; and he adds one curiously pathetic detail. A drummer-boy of the 93rd, he says, "must have been one of the first to pass that grim boundary between life and death; for when I got in I found him just inside the breach, lying on his back, quite dead, a pretty, innocent-looking, fair-haired lad, not more than fourteen years old." What daring must have burned in that lad's Scottish blood when he thus took his place in the very van of the wild rush of veterans into the Secundrabagh!

Forbes-Mitchell, who actually took part in the charge, gives yet another account. The order to charge, he says, was given, and the Sikhs, who caught it first, leaped over the mud-wall, behind which they were lying, shouting their war-cry, and, led by their two British officers, ran eagerly towards the breach. Both their officers were shot before they had run many yards, and at that the Sikhs halted. "As soon as Sir Colin saw them waver, he turned to the 93rd, and said, 'Colonel Ewart, bring on the tartan! Let my own lads at them.'" Before the command could be repeated, or the buglers had time to sound the advance, "the whole seven companies like one man leaped over the wall with such a yell of pent-up rage as I never heard before nor since. It was not a cheer, but a concentrated yell of rage and ferocity, that made the echoes ring again; and it must have struck terror into the defenders, for they actually ceased firing, and we could see them through the breach rushing from the outside wall to take shelter in the two-storeyed building in the centre of the garden, the gate and doors of which they firmly barred."

The Secundrabagh, it must be remembered, was held by four strong Sepoy regiments, numbering in all from 2000 to 3000 men, many of them veteran soldiers, wearing the medals they had won in British service, and they fought with desperate courage. The human jet of stormers through the gap in the wall was a mere tiny squirt, but the main body of the 93rd blew in the lock of the great gate with their bullets, and came sweeping in.

Lord Roberts gives another version of this incident. The Sepoys, he says, were driven out of the earthwork which covered the gateway, and were swept back into the Secundrabagh, and the heavy doors of the great gateway were being hurriedly shut in the face of the stormers. A subahdar of the 4th Punjab Infantry reached the gate in time enough to thrust his left arm, on which was carried a shield, between the closing doors. His hand was slashed across by a tulwar from within, whereupon he drew it out, instantly thrusting in the other arm, when his right hand, in turn, was all but severed from the wrist! But he kept the gates from being shut, and in another minute the men of the 93rd, of the 53rd, and of the gallant Punjabee's own regiment went storming in.

The men of the 53rd again tried, with success, another device. They lifted their caps on the tips of their bayonets to a line of iron-barred windows above their heads, and thus drew the fire of their defenders. Then they leaped up, tore away the bars, and, clambering on each other's shoulders, broke through. Forbes-Mitchell was the fifth or sixth man through the breach, and was immediately fired upon point-blank by a Sepoy lying in the grass half-a-dozen yards distant. The bullet struck the thick brass buckle on his belt, and such was the force of the blow that it tumbled him head over heels. Colonel Ewart came next to Forbes-Mitchell, who heard his colonel say, as he rushed past him, "Poor fellow! he is done for." Ewart, a gallant Highlander, of commanding stature, played a great part in the struggle within the Secundrabagh. His bonnet was shot or struck off his head, and, bareheaded, amidst the push and sway and madness of the fight, he bore himself like a knight of old.

The fight within the walls of the Secundrabagh raged for nearly two hours, and the sounds that floated up from it as the Sepoys, "fighting like devils"—to quote an actor in the scene,—were driven from floor to floor of the building, or across the green turf of the garden, were appalling. The fighting passion amongst the combatants often took queer shapes. Thus one man, known amongst the 93rd as "the Quaker," from his great quietness, charged into the Secundrabagh like a kilted and male Fury, and, according to Forbes-Mitchell, quoting a verse of the Scottish psalm with every thrust of his bayonet or shot from his rifle:—

"I'll of salvation take the cup,
On God's name will I call;
I'll pay my vows now to the Lord
Before His people all."

Scottish psalm, punctuated with bayonet thrusts: this surely is the strangest battle-hymn ever heard!

Ewart found that two native officers had carried the regimental flag into a narrow and dark room, and were defending themselves like wild cats. Ewart leaped single-handed into the room, and captured the colours, slaying both officers. The fight within the Secundrabagh was by this time practically over, and Ewart ran outside, and bareheaded, with blood-stained uniform and smoke-blackened face, ran up to Sir Colin as he sat on his grey horse, and cried, "We are in possession, sir! I have killed the last two of the enemy with my own hand, and here is one of their colours." "D—— your colours, sir!" was the wrathful response of Sir Colin. "It's not your place to be taking colours. Go back to your regiment this instant, sir." Sir Colin had a Celtic shortness of temper; the strain of waiting while the madness of the fight raged within the great walls had told on his nerves. He was eager to get his 93rd into regimental shape again; and, as Forbes-Mitchell argues, believed, from his appearance and bearing, that Ewart was drunk! So he was: but it was with the passion of battle!

The officers of Sir Colin's staff read Ewart's condition more truly, and as this ragged, blood-stained figure, carrying the captured flag, came running out from the furnace of the great fight, they cheered vehemently. Later in the day Sir Colin himself apologised to Ewart for his brusqueness.

In the whole record of war there are not many scenes of slaughter to be compared with that which took place within the walls of the Secundrabagh. The 53rd held the north side of the great quadrangle, the Sikhs and the 93rd the east side, and a mixed force, composed of several regiments, held the south; on the west there was no escape. The great mass of Sepoys in the centre of the quadrangle was thus pelted with lead and fire from the three fronts. "We fired volley after volley into the dense multitude," says Jones-Parry, "until nothing was left but a moving mass, like mites in a cheese!"

Of the 2000 or 2500 Sepoys who formed the garrison of the Secundrabagh not one man escaped. Its whole area, when the fight was over, was red with blood and strewn with the bodies of slain men. Four whole regiments of mutineers were simply blotted out. Many of the slain Sepoys wore Punjab medals on their breasts; many, too, were found to have leave certificates, signed by former commanding officers, in their pockets, showing they had been on leave when the regiment mutinied, and had rejoined their regiment to fight against the British. The walls of the Secundrabagh still stand, a long, low mound along one side showing where the great company of slain Sepoys were buried. What other patch of the earth's surface, of equal size, has ever witnessed more of human valour and of human despair than those few square yards of turf that lie within the shot-battered walls of this ancient Indian pleasure-garden!

The British losses, curiously enough, were comparatively light, except amongst the officers. The 93rd had nine officers killed and wounded. The 4th Punjab infantry went into the fight with four British officers; two were killed, one was desperately wounded, and the regiment was brought out of the fight by the sole surviving officer, Lieut. Willoughby, himself only a lad. He was recommended for the V.C., but did not live to wear that much-coveted decoration, as he was slain in fight shortly afterwards.

But the strongest post held by the rebels, in the track along which the British were moving towards the Residency, was the Shah Nujeef, a great and massively-built mosque, girdled with a high loopholed wall, and screened by trees and enclosures of various kinds. Campbell brought up Peel, with his Naval Brigade, to make a breach in the massive walls of the Shah Nujeef, and that gallant sailor ran his guns up within twenty yards of the loopholed walls of the great mosque, and, swinging them round, opened fire, while the gunners were shot down in quick succession as they toiled to load and discharge their pieces. "It was an action," said Sir Colin in his despatch afterwards, "almost unexampled in war." Peel, in a word, behaved very much as if he were laying the *Shannon* alongside an enemy's frigate!

As the men ran up their guns to the walls of the Shah Nujeef, Forbes-Mitchell says he saw a sailor lad, just in front of him, who had his leg carried clean off by a round shot, which struck him above the knee. "He sat bolt upright on the grass, with the blood spouting from the stump of his leg like water from the hose of a fire-engine, and shouted, 'Here goes a shilling a day, a shilling a day! Remember Cawnpore, 93rd; remember Cawnpore! Go at them, my hearties;' and then sank down and died."

But the defence of the Shah Nujeef was stubborn, and for three hours Peel worked his guns under a double cross-fire, and still his 18-pounders failed to pierce the solid walls of the great mosque. The 93rd were brought up, and, lying down under what shelter they could secure, tried to keep down the musketry fire from the walls, and many of them were shot down by bullets or arrows from the summit of the mosque. The external masonry had flaked off, leaving a rough, irregular face, up which an active cat might possibly have scrambled; and at this a battalion of detachments—in which clusters from a dozen regiments were combined—under the command of Major Branston, was launched. The men ran forward with utmost daring, but the wall was twenty feet high; there were no scaling-ladders. It was impossible to climb the broken face of the masonry. Branston fell, shot, and his second in command, the present Lord Wolseley, kept up the attack, making desperate attempts to escalade.

A tree stood at an angle of the Shah Nujeef, close to the wall, and giving the chance of firing over it. Peel offered the Victoria Cross to any of his men who would climb it. Two lieutenants and a leading seaman named Harrison in a moment, with seamanlike activity, clambered up the tree, and opened a deadly fire on the enemy. Each man of the three was in turn shot, but not till they had accomplished the task they had undertaken.

Nightfall was coming on. It was impossible to turn back; it seemed equally impossible to carry the Shah Nujeef. Peel's guns, firing for nearly three hours at point-blank range, had failed to tear the stubborn masonry to pieces. The answering fire, both of cannon and musketry, from either flank, which covered the face of the great mosque being assailed, grew heavier every moment. Campbell then called upon the 93rd, and told them he would lead them himself, as the place must be carried. The lives of the women and children inside the Residency were at stake. A dozen voices from the ranks called out that they would carry the place, right enough, but Sir Colin must not expose his own life. "We can lead ourselves," cried one after another. Whether even the 93rd could have clambered over the lofty and unbroken walls of the Shah Nujeef may be doubted, but at this moment the wit and daring of a Scotch soldier saved the situation.

There are conflicting versions of the incident, but Forbes-Mitchell shall tell the story:—

> Just at that moment Sergeant John Paton, of my company, came running down the ravine at the moment the battalion of detachments had been ordered to storm. He had discovered a

> breach in the north-east corner of the rampart, next to the river Goomtee. It appears that our shot and shell had gone over the first breach, and had blown out the wall on the other side in this particular spot. Paton told how he had climbed up to the top of the ramparts without difficulty, and seen right inside the place, as the whole defending force had been called forward to repulse the assault in front. Captain Dawson and his company were at once called out, and while the others opened fire on the breach in front of them, we dashed down the ravine, Sergeant Paton showing the way. As soon as the enemy saw that the breach behind had been discovered, and their well-defended position was no longer tenable, they fled like sheep through the back gate next to the Goomtee, and another in the direction of the Mootee Munzil. If No. 7 company had got in behind them and cut off their retreat by the back gate, it would have been Secundrabagh over again.

Paton received the Victoria Cross for that signal service. He was a soldier of the finest type, took part in more than thirty engagements, and passed through them all without so much as a scratch. Paton emigrated in 1861 to Melbourne; a little later he entered the service of the New South Wales Government, and became Governor of Goulburn Gaol, retiring on a pension in February 1896.

A quiet night followed a day so fierce. The troops were exhausted. Their rifles, in addition, had become so foul with four days' heavy work that it was almost impossible to load them. The next day, however, the advance was continued, and position after position was carried, the last being what was known as the Mess-house. This was carried by a wing of the 53rd, led by Captain Hopkins—"one of the bravest men that ever lived," says Malleson; "a man who literally revelled in danger." From the summit of the Mess-house the Union Jack was hoisted as a signal to the Residency, but on the flag the exasperated Sepoys concentrated their fire, and twice in succession it was shot down. Forbes-Mitchell says that a previous and successful attempt to signal to the Residency had been made from the Shah Nujeef. The adjutant of the 93rd, Lieutenant M'Bean, a sergeant, and a little drummer-boy, twelve years old, named Ross, and tiny for his age, climbed to the summit of the dome of the Shah Nujeef, put a Highland bonnet on the tip of the staff, waved the regimental colour of the 93rd, while the boy sounded the regimental call shrilly on his bugle.

The signal was seen and answered from the Residency, its flag being raised and lowered three times; but every Sepoy battery within range instantly opened on the three figures on the summit of the dome. They quickly descended, but little Ross turned, ran up the ladder again like a monkey, and, holding on to the spire of the dome with his left hand, blew the call known as "The Cock of the North" as a blast of defiance to the enemy!

Outram meanwhile was pushing cautiously on in the direction of Campbell's attack, occupying building after building; and late in the afternoon Outram and Havelock and Campbell had clasped hands on the sloping ground in front of the Mess-house. A hole had to be broken through the western wall of the Pearl Palace enclosure to let the chiefs of the beleaguered garrison through, and a slab in the wall still marks the spot. Campbell, Havelock, and Outram met on the slope outside the Mess-house, and the meeting of three such soldiers under such conditions was a memorable event. No red-coated Boswell, unhappily, has told us how the veterans greeted each other. The Kaisarbagh, strongly held by the mutineers, overlooked the little patch of rough soil on which the three famous soldiers stood, and every gun that could be trained upon the group broke into fire. It was to an accompaniment of bellowing cannon, of bursting shells, and of whistling bullets that Campbell, Havelock, and Outram exchanged their first greeting.

Young Roberts, with Captain Norman, accompanied Outram and Havelock back to the Residency, and he has described how he passed from post to post, held with such long-enduring and stubborn courage by the relieved garrison. "When we came," he says, "to the Bailey Guard, and looked at the battered walls and gateway, not an inch without a mark of a round shot or bullet, we marvelled that Aitken and Loughnan could have managed to defend it for nearly five months." It was found difficult to get the relieved garrison to talk of their own experiences; they were too hungry for news from the outside world! Jones-Parry says, "The first man of the garrison I met was my old schoolfellow and chum, Meecham. He was an excellent specimen of the condition of the defenders, for he looked more like a greyhound than a man. He was thin as a lath, and his eyes looked sunken into his head."

Lucknow was relieved; but to reach the Residency had cost Sir Colin Campbell a loss of 45 officers and 496 men. Campbell found his position difficult. He had broken through the besieging force; he had not ended the siege. To hold the Residency meant to be besieged himself. He decided to bring off the Residency garrison, with the women and children, abandoning the shot-wrecked walls and foul trenches to the enemy. To evacuate the Residency, carrying off in safety, through the lines of a hostile force five times as numerous as his own, 600 women and children, and more than 1000 sick or wounded men, was a great feat, but Sir Colin Campbell accomplished it, and did it so adroitly that not a casualty was incurred, and not a serviceable gun abandoned. So completely, in fact, did Sir Colin Campbell deceive the enemy that their guns were pouring their fire angrily on the Residency for at least four hours after the last British soldier had left it!

Havelock died just as he was being carried out of the slender and battered defences he had reached and held so gallantly. He died of an attack of dysentery, brought on, says Major Anson, "by running nearly three-quarters of a mile under fire from the Residency to meet the Commander-in-Chief and greet him as his deliverer."

He lies buried in the Alumbagh, the place Havelock himself won by an assault so daring when advancing to relieve Lucknow. He was buried on the morning of November 25, and round his rude coffin, on which the battle-flag lay, stood his sorrowing comrades, a group of the most gallant soldiers that earthly battlefields have ever known—Campbell, and Outram, and Peel, and Adrian Hope, and Fraser Tytler, and the younger Havelock, with men of the Ross-shire Buffs and of the Madras Fusileers, whom Havelock had so often led to victory. On a tree that grew beside the grave the letter H was roughly carved, to mark where Havelock's body lay. To-day the interior of the Alumbagh is a garden, and a shapely obelisk marks the spot where sleeps the dust of one of the bravest soldiers that ever fought for the honour and flag of England.

CHAPTER IX

THE SEPOY IN THE OPEN

The losses of the beleaguered English during the siege of the Residency were, of course, great. When the siege began the garrison consisted of 927 Europeans—not three out of four being soldiers—and 765 natives. Up to the date of the relief by Havelock—87 days—350 Europeans, more than one out of every three of the whole European force, were killed or died of disease!

It is curious to note how all the swiftly-changing events and passions of the Mutiny are reflected in such of the diaries and journals of the period as have been published; and frequently a view of the actors in the great drama and of their actions is obtained from this source, such as grave historians, much to the loss of their readers, never give us. One of the best diaries of the kind is that of Lady Canning, as published in "The Story of Two Noble Lives," by Augustus J. C. Hare. This journal gives us dainty little vignettes of the principal figures in the Mutiny, with pictures of all the alternating moods of fear and hope, of triumph and despair, as, moment by moment, they were experienced by the little circle of Government House in Calcutta. Here, for example, is a quaint picture of Havelock, which Lady Canning draws when the news reached Calcutta of his death:—

> *Nov.* 27.—We had a grievous piece of news from Alumbagh. Havelock died two days ago. He died of dysentery, worn out in mind and body.... It is curious now to remember how his appointment was abused here, when he was called "an old fossil dug up and only fit to be turned into pipe-clay." I knew him better than almost any one, and used to try and keep him in good-humour when he seemed a little inclined to be affronted. He was very small, and upright, and stiff, very white and grey, and really like an iron ramrod. He always dined in his sword, and made his son do the same. He wore more medals than ever I saw on any one, and it was a joke that he looked as if he carried all his money round his neck. He certainly must have had eleven or twelve of those great round half-crown pieces.

Lady Canning goes on to picture Campbell's march back to Cawnpore, with his great convoy of wounded men and women and children, and her woman's imagination fastens naturally on this long procession of helpless human beings. "Sir Colin," she writes, "has sent off four miles long of women and wounded!" Later on she reports the procession as fourteen miles long! And no doubt the business of transporting such a host of helpless creatures out of a city which contained 60,000 hostile troops, and across nearly fifty miles of an enemy's country, was a feat calculated to impress the human imagination.

Campbell had one tremendous source of anxiety. He had to carry his huge convoy of non-combatants, guns, treasure, and material across the slender, swaying line of boats which bridged the Ganges at Cawnpore before safety was reached. That bridge, indeed, formed his only possible line of retreat. If it were destroyed or fell into the enemy's hands, the tragedy of Cabul—where only one man escaped out of an army—might have been repeated.

Campbell had left Windham to guard the bridge and hold Cawnpore, but Windham had only 500 men—a force scarcely stronger in fighting power than that with which Wheeler held the fatal entrenchments—and within easy striking distance was the Gwalior contingent, numbering, with a fringe of irregulars, some 25,000 men, with forty guns, the most formidable and best-drilled force, on the Sepoy side, in the whole Mutiny. At its head, too, was Tantia Topee, the one real soldier on the enemy's side the Mutiny produced, with quite enough warlike skill to see the opportunity offered him of striking a fatal blow at Campbell's communications. If Windham's scanty force had been crushed, and the bridge destroyed, Campbell's position would have been, in a military sense, desperate, and the tragedy of Cawnpore might have been repeated in darker colours and on a vaster scale. Sound generalship required Campbell to smash the formidable force which threatened Cawnpore before advancing on Lucknow; but Campbell took all risks in order to succour the beleaguered Residency.

Having plucked the beleaguered garrison out of the very heart of the enemy's forces, it may be imagined with what eagerness Campbell now set his face towards Cawnpore again. There was no safety for his helpless convoy till the bridge was crossed. For days, too, all communications with Windham had been intercepted. An ominous veil of unpierced silence hung between the retreating English and their base. Campbell set out from the Alumbagh on the morning of November 27. All day the great column crept along over the desolate plain towards the Ganges. At nightfall they had reached Bunnee Bridge, and that "veil of silence" was for a moment lifted. Or, rather, through it there stole a faint deep sound, full of menace, the voice of cannon answering cannon! Windham was attacked! He was perhaps fighting for his life at the bridge-head!

All through the night those far-off and sullen vibrations told how the fight was being maintained, and with what eagerness the march was resumed next morning may be guessed. Forbes-Mitchell relates how Campbell addressed the 93rd, and told them they must reach Cawnpore that night at all costs. The veteran was fond of taking his Highlanders into his confidence; and he went on to explain:—

> "If the bridge of boats should be captured before we got there we would be cut off in Oude with 50,000 of our enemies in our rear, a well-equipped army of 40,000 men, with a powerful train of artillery, numbering over 40 siege guns, in our front, and with all the women and children, sick and wounded to guard. So, 93rd,"

> said the grand old chief, "I don't ask you to undertake this forced march in your present tired condition without good reason. You must reach Cawnpore to-night at all costs." "All right, Sir Colin," shouted one voice after another from the ranks; "we'll do it!"

The men, it must be remembered, had not had their clothes off or changed their socks for eighteen days, and what a tax on the fortitude of the men that forced march was, can hardly be realised. Alison tells the story very graphically:—

> Not a moment was to be lost. The danger was instant, and the whole army eagerly pressed on towards the scene of danger. At every step the sound of a heavy but distant cannonade became more distinct; but mile after mile was passed over, and no news could be obtained. The anxiety and impatience of all became extreme. Louder and louder grew the roar—faster and faster became the march—long and weary was the way—tired and footsore grew the infantry—death fell on the exhausted wounded with terrible rapidity—the travel-worn bearers could hardly stagger along under their loads—the sick men groaned and died. But still on, on, on, was the cry. Salvoes of artillery were fired by the field battery of the advanced guard in hopes that its sound might convey to the beleaguered garrison a promise of the coming aid. At last some horsemen were seen spurring along the road; then the veil which had for so long shrouded us from Windham was rent asunder, and the disaster stood before us in all its deformity.

The story of Windham's disastrous fight at Cawnpore is a sort of bloody appendix to Campbell's march on Lucknow. It must be told here to make the tale complete.

Windham was a soldier of a fine, if not of the highest type, a man of immense energy and of cool daring which, if it always saw the peril, scorned to turn aside on account of it. His sobriquet was "Redan" Windham, and no one who has read the story of how, on September 8, 1855, he led the British stormers through the embrasures of the Redan can doubt that Windham's courage was of a lion-like quality. He was the first of the stormers of the Second Division to cross the great ditch in front of the Redan, and the first to clamber through an embrasure. When his men—young soldiers belonging to half-a-dozen separate regiments—hung back under the great ramparts of the Redan, Windham thrice ran forward alone with his brandished sword into the centre of the work, calling on the men to follow. He has told the story of how, again and again, he went back to his men, patted them on the back, and begged them to follow him.

Five times he sent to the rear for reinforcements, and it shows the coolness of the man in the hell of that great fight that, determined at last to go himself in search of additional troops, he first turned to an officer standing near and asked his name. Then he said to him, "I have sent five times for support, now bear witness that I am not in a funk"—at which the officer smiled—"but I will now go back myself and see what I can do."

He went back, but before he could bring up new troops, the men still clinging to the Redan gave way, and the attack failed. Windham's judgment was challenged, but he was as brave as his own sword. He no doubt had his limitations as an officer. Russell, a perfectly good critic, says that he "seemed always to have something to do in addition to something that he had done already." There was a certain note of hurry in his character, that is, which does not add to the efficiency of a leader. His failing as an officer, Russell adds, was "reckless gallantry and dash"—grave faults, no doubt, in a general, but faults which are not without their compensations in a mere leader of fighting men. This was the man whom Campbell chose to keep the bridge at Cawnpore while he made his dash for the relief of Lucknow.

Windham's force consisted of 500 men, made up of convalescent artillerymen, some sailors, and four companies of the 64th. Some earthworks had been thrown up to guard the bridge-head, but, in a military sense, the position was scarcely defensible. Windham's orders were to forward with the utmost speed to Campbell all reinforcements as they came up; to keep a vigilant watch on the Gwalior contingent, and hold the bridge to his last man and the last cartridge.

Windham sent on the reinforcements for a time, loyally, but as the Gwalior contingent—which had now been joined by Nana Sahib and all his forces—began to press more menacingly upon him, he strengthened himself by holding the troops as they came up; until, at the moment when the fight commenced, he had a force of some 1700 men. On November 19, the Gwalior contingent and their allies were distributed in a semicircle round Cawnpore—the nearest body being fifteen miles distant, the main body some twenty-five miles off.

Windham, always disposed to attack rather than wait to be attacked, first formed a plan for leaping on these hostile forces in detail. He could move from the interior of the circle; they were scattered round a segment of its circumference. Windham left 300 men to hold the bridge-head, and, with the main body of his force, took a position outside the town, in readiness for his dash. Two divisions of the enemy were about fifteen miles to the north, on either side of a canal running parallel to the Ganges. Windham proposed to place 1200 men in boats on the canal at nightfall, quietly steal up through the darkness, and in the morning leap on the enemy on either bank in turn and destroy them, then fall swiftly back on his base.

It was a pretty plan, but Tantia Topee had his military ideas too. He thrust forward the Gwalior contingent along the road from the west, and on November 25 their leading division crossed the Pando River only three miles from Windham's camp outside Cawnpore. Windham promptly swung round to his left, marched fiercely out—1200 men with eight guns against 20,000 with twenty-five guns—and fell impetuously on the head of the enemy's nearest column. He crumpled it up with the energy of his stroke, and drove it, a confused mass, in retreat, leaving three guns in Windham's hands.

But from a ridge of high ground Windham was able to see the real strength of the enemy. He had crushed its leading division of 3000 men, but behind them was the main body of 17,000 men with twenty guns moving steadily forward.

Windham's killed and wounded already amounted to nearly 100 men, and he had no choice but to fall back. His scanty little battery of six light guns, with undrilled gunners, could not endure the fire of the heavy artillery opposed to them.

Windham, with characteristic tenacity, would not abandon the city and fall back on his entrenchments. He took a position on open ground outside the town, across what was called the Calpee road—the road, that is, running to the north—and waited the development of the enemy's plans. In the town were enormous stores—the supplies for Campbell's force, with Windham's own baggage. He ought, no doubt, to have sent all these back to the entrenchments, and he admitted afterwards that he had blundered in not doing so; and the blunder cost the British force dearly.

The morning of the 27th dawned, and Windham stood to arms. He could get no information as to the enemy's movements. He had no cavalry, and his spies crept back to him horribly mutilated. He could only wait for Tantia Topee's stroke. That general proved throughout the day that he had a good soldierly head, and could frame a clever and daring plan of battle.

Windham expected to be assailed on his left flank. But at ten o'clock the roar of cannon broke out on his right and on his front. A strong rebel force moving on the Calpee road from the north struck heavily on Windham's front, while a yet stronger force coming in from the east threw itself on his right flank. It was in the main an artillery attack, and the rebel fire was of overwhelming fury. At the front, the 88th (the Connaught Rangers) and the Rifles, with a battery of four guns, held their own valiantly. Some companies of the 82nd and the 34th held the right flank, and here, too, the fight was gallantly sustained. Two battles, in brief, were in progress at the same moment, and at each of the assailed points the British numbered scarcely 600 bayonets, with two or three guns, while at each point the artillery fire of the enemy was of terrific severity.

For nearly five hours the tumult and passion of the battle raged. At the front the British ammunition began, at last, to fail, the native drivers deserted, and Windham found it necessary to withdraw two companies from his right flank to strengthen his front. At that moment he discovered that Tantia Topee—who up to this stage had maintained the fight chiefly with his artillery, and had with great skill gathered a heavy mass of infantry on the left flank of the British—was developing a third attack at that point. He thrust his infantry, that is, past Windham's left, and tried to seize the town, so as to cut off the fighting front of the British from the bridge.

Two companies of the 64th were brought up from the scanty garrison at the bridge-head to check this dangerous movement; and then Windham found that the enemy had broken in on his right flank, and were in possession of the lower portions of the town!

Windham was out-generalled, and had no choice but to fall back on his entrenchments, and he had to do this through narrow streets and broken ground while attacked in front and on both flanks by a victorious enemy ten times stronger than himself in bayonets, and more than ten times stronger in artillery. Adye says that the retreat to the entrenchments "was made in perfect order, and not a man was lost in the operation"; but on this subject there is the wildest conflict of evidence. Moore, the chaplain of Windham's force, says "the men got quite out of hand, and fled pell-mell for the fort. An old Sikh officer at the gate tried to stop them and to form them up in some order, and when they pushed him aside and brushed past him he lifted up his hands and said, 'You are not the brothers of the men who beat the Khalsa army and conquered the Punjab!'" Mr. Moore goes on to say that "the old Sikh followed the flying men through the fort gate, and, patting some of them on the back, said, 'Don't run, don't be afraid; there is nothing to hurt you.'" If there was disorder the excuse is that the men were, for the most part, young soldiers without regimental cohesion—they were mere fragments of half-a-dozen regiments—they had been for five hours under an overwhelming artillery fire, and were exhausted with want of food: and a retreat under such conditions, and through a hostile city, might well have taxed the steadiness of the best troops in the world. As a matter of fact, the men of the 64th, the 34th, and the 82nd held together with the steadiness of veterans, and their slow and stubborn retreat, their fierce volleys and occasional dashes with the bayonets, quite cooled the ardour of the mutineers as they followed the retreating British.

At one point, indeed, on the right flank of the British there was a clear case of misconduct, and the culprit was an officer. His name in all the published reports is concealed under the charity of asterisks. Campbell, in his despatch, says:—"Lieut.-Colonel * * * misconducted himself on the 26th and 27th November in a manner which has rarely been seen amongst the officers of Her Majesty's service; his conduct was pusillanimous and imbecile to the last degree, and he actually gave orders for the retreat of his own regiment, and a portion of another, in the very face of the orders of his General, and when the troops were not seriously pressed by the enemy."

Every man who wears a red coat and a pair of epaulettes is not necessarily a hero, and human courage, at best, is a somewhat unstable element. This particular officer had risen to high rank and seen much service, but some failure of nerve, some sudden clouding of brain, in the stress of that desperate fight, made him play—if only for a moment—the part both of an imbecile and a coward, and surrender a position which was essential to the British defence. He was court-martialled after the fight and dismissed the service.

Windham's retreat involved the sacrifice of all the military stores in the town, a great supply of ammunition, the mess plate, and the paymaster's chests and baggage of four Queen's regiments, &c. Some 500 tents, as one item alone, were turned into a huge bonfire that night by the exultant rebels. But, though Windham had fallen back to the entrenchments at the bridge-head, he was as ready for fight as ever. He held a council of his officers that night and proposed to sally out under cover of darkness and fall on the enemy, a proposal which at least proves the unquenchable quality of his courage.

This plan was not adopted, but, it being discovered that a gun had been overturned and abandoned in the streets of the city, Windham sent out 100 men of the 64th, with a few sailors, to bring that gun in. It was a feat of singular daring, carried out with singular success, and this is how the story of it is told by an officer who took part in the adventure:—

> We marched off under the guidance of a native, who said he would take us to the spot where the gun lay. We told him he should be well rewarded if he brought us to the gun, but if he brought us into a trap we had a soldier by him "at full cock" ready to blow his brains out. We passed our outside pickets, and entered the town through very narrow streets without a single Sepoy being seen, or a shot fired on either side. We crept along. Not a soul spoke a word. All was still as death; and after marching this way into the very heart of the town our guide brought us to the very spot where the gun was capsized. The soldiers were posted on each side, and then we went to work. Not a man spoke above his breath, and each stone was laid down quietly. When we thought we had cleared enough I ordered the men to put their shoulders to the wheel and gun, and when all was ready and every man had his pound before him I said "Heave!" and up she righted. We then limbered up, called the soldiers to follow, and we marched into the entrenchment with our gun without a shot being fired.

On the morning of the 28th, Windham, still bent on "aggressive defence," sallied out to fight the enemy in the open—or rather on either flank. On the left front the Rifles and the 82nd, under Walpole, thrashed the enemy in a most satisfactory manner, capturing two 18-pounders. On the right, the 64th and the 34th, under Carthew, fought for hours with desperate courage. General Wilson, in particular, led two companies of the 64th in a very audacious attempt to capture a battery of the enemy. Wilson himself was killed, and two officers of the 64th—Stirling and McCrae—were each cut down in the act of spiking one of the enemy's guns, and the attempt, though gallant as anything recorded in the history of war, failed.

When evening came the British had fallen back to their entrenchments, upon which a heavy fire, both of artillery and small arms, was poured. The enemy was in complete possession of the town, and, planting some guns on the bank of the river, tried to destroy the bridge. "The dust of no succouring columns," says Alison, "could be seen rising from the plains of Oude, and the sullen plunge of round shot into the river by the bridge showed by how frail a link they were bound to the opposite bank, whence only aid could arrive."

Suddenly at this dramatic moment Campbell himself—who had pushed ahead of his column—made his appearance with his staff on the scene. Says Alison:—

> The clatter of a few horsemen was suddenly heard passing over the bridge and ascending at a rapid pace the road which leads to the fort. As they came close under the ramparts, an old man with grey hair was seen to be riding at their head. One of the soldiers recognised the commander-in-chief; the news spread like wildfire: the men, crowding upon the parapet, sent forth cheer after cheer. The enemy, surprised at the commotion, for a few

> moments ceased their fire. The old man rode in through the gate. All felt then that the crisis was over—that the Residency saved, would not now be balanced by Cawnpore lost.

A characteristic incident marked Campbell's arrival. A guard of the 82nd held a hastily constructed *tête de pont* which covered the bridge, and its officer, in answer to Campbell's inquiry as to how matters stood, replied with undiplomatic bluntness that "the garrison was at its last gasp." At this announcement the too irascible Sir Colin simply exploded. "He flew at the wretched man," says Lord Roberts, "as he was sometimes apt to do when greatly put out, rating him soundly, and asking him 'how he dared to say of Her Majesty's troops that they were at the last gasp!'" This, in Campbell's ears, was mere egregious and incredible treason!

With the arrival of Campbell and his convoy, and the splendid little fighting force he commanded, the story of what happened at Cawnpore becomes very pleasant reading. On the morning of the 30th, the further bank of the Ganges was white with the tents and black with the masses of Campbell's force. With what wrath Campbell's soldiers looked across the river and saw all their baggage ascending, in the shape of clouds of black smoke, to the sky may be guessed, but not described. Many wrathful camp expletives, no doubt, followed the upward curling smoke!

Peel's heavy guns were swung round, and opened in fierce duel with the enemy's battery firing on the bridge. One of the first shots fired from one of Peel's 24-pounders struck the gun which Nana Sahib had at last got to bear upon the bridge, and dismounted it. An 8-inch shell next dropped amongst a crowd of his troops, and they quickly fell back. Then the British troops commenced to file across the river, still under the fire of the enemy. The enemy's advance batteries were quickly driven back, and the great convoy began to creep over the bridge.

For thirty-six hours the long procession of sick and wounded, of women and children, of guns and baggage crept across the swaying bridge. On the night of the 29th, the mutineers tried to interrupt the process by sending down fire-rafts upon the bridge. Tried earlier, the scheme might have succeeded, or tried even then with greater skill and daring, it might have had some chance of success; as it was, it failed ignobly, and the endless stream of non-combatants was brought over the river into safety. Campbell, for all his fire of courage—and it may be added of temper—had an ample measure of Scottish coolness, and he kept quietly within his lines for five days till his helpless convoy had been despatched under escort to Allahabad, and was beyond reach of hostile attack. Then, with his force in perfect fighting form, he addressed himself to the task of crushing the enemy opposed to him.

His own force, steadily fed by reinforcements, by this time numbered 5000 infantry, 600 sailors, and 35 guns; that of the enemy amounted to something like 25,000 men with 40 guns. Nana Sahib, with his mass of somewhat irregular troops, occupied the left wing between the city and the river; the Gwalior contingent, still formidable in numbers and military efficiency, occupied the town as a centre, and formed the enemy's right wing, thrust out into the plain towards the canal. It was a very strong position. The enemy's left, perched on high wooded hills, was covered with nullahs and scattered buildings. An attack on their centre could only be made through the narrow and crooked streets of the city, and was therefore almost impossible. But their right lay open to Campbell's stroke, and if turned it would be thrust off the Calpee road, its only line of retreat.

Campbell's strategy was simple, yet skilful. Alison, indeed, says, somewhat absurdly, that it will "bear comparison with any of the masterpieces of Napoleon or Wellington." Kaye, too, says that the plan of this battle "establishes the right of Sir Colin Campbell to be regarded as a great commander." Whether these somewhat high-flown eulogiums are justifiable may perhaps be doubted; but Campbell's plan certainly succeeded. Campbell, in brief, fixed the attention of the enemy on their left wing—the one he did not mean to attack—by opening on it on the morning of the 6th with the roar of artillery. He paralysed the centre with a feigned infantry assault, under Greathed. Then by a swift and unexpected attack he shattered the enemy's right wing, at once smiting it in front and turning its flank.

The drifting clouds of battle-smoke helped him to concentrate, unobserved, on his left, a strong force consisting of Hope, with the Sikhs, the 53rd, the 42nd, the 93rd, and Inglis with the 23rd, the 32nd, and 82nd.

The iron hail of Campbell's guns smote the town cruelly, while the rattle of Greathed's musketry formed a sort of sharp treble to the hoarse diapason of the artillery. Presently, through the white drifting smoke of the guns, came the Rifles, under Walpole, firing on the edge of the town, to Greathed's left. Campbell was still keeping back his real stroke, and this clatter of artillery and musketry, and the clouds of drifting battle-smoke, held the senses of the enemy. Suddenly, from behind a cluster of buildings on the British left, line after line of infantry moved quickly out. It was Hope's and Inglis's brigades, which, in parallel columns of companies, left in front, now—to quote the language of an eye-witness—"shot out and streamed on, wave after wave of glittering bayonets, till they stretched far across into the plain, while the cavalry and horse artillery, trotting rapidly out, pushed on beyond them, raising clouds of dust, and covering their advance."

Campbell's plan was now developed, and the enemy opened all their guns with the utmost fury on the steady lines of the two brigades. At a given signal, the British columns swung round, formed front to the enemy's position, and, in perfect order, as Alison puts it, "swept on with a proud, majestic movement" against a cluster of high brick mounds which covered the bridge across the canal—both bridge and mounds being held in great force by the enemy. "Grouped in masses behind the mounds, the rebels fired sharply, while their guns, worked with great precision and energy, sent a storm of shot and shell upon the plain, over which, like a drifting storm, came the stout skirmishers of the Sikhs and the 53rd, covering their front with the flashes of a bickering musketry, behind whom rolled in a long and serried line the 93rd and 42nd, sombre with their gloomy plumes and dark tartans, followed, some hundred yards in rear, by the thin ranks of Inglis's brigade."

The skirmishers quickly cleared the mounds, and the Sikhs and the Highlanders went forward at a run to the bridge. It was held with fierce courage by the enemy. A sleet of shot swept along its entire length. It seemed to be barred as by a thousand dancing points of flame—the flash of musketry and the red flames of the great guns.

As Sikhs and Highlanders, however, pressed sternly forward, they heard behind them the tramp of many feet and the clatter of wheels. It was Peel with his sailors bringing up a 24-pounder. They came up at a run, the blue-jackets "tailing on" to the ropes, and clutching with eager hands the spokes of the wheels. The gun was swung round on the very bridge itself, and sent its grape hurtling into the ranks of the Sepoys on the further side. Sikhs and Highlanders kindled to flame at the sight of that daring act. With a shout they ran past the gun, and across the bridge; some leaped into the canal, splashed through its waters and clambered up the further bank. The bridge was carried! A battery of field artillery came up at the gallop, thundered across its shaking planks, and, swinging round, opened fire on the tents of the Gwalior contingent, while the two brigades pressed eagerly forward on the broken enemy.

Forbes-Mitchell, who fought that day in the ranks of the 93rd, gives a very picturesque description of the combat. Campbell, who was almost as fond of making speeches as Havelock, and understood perfectly how to stir the blood of his men, gave a brief address to the 93rd before launching the turning movement. He gave the Highlanders one somewhat quaint warning. There was a huge accumulation of rum, Campbell said, in the enemy's camp; it had been drugged, he added, by the enemy, and no man must touch it. "But, 93rd!" he said, "I trust you! Leave that rum alone!"

As a matter of fact, when the men swept with a rush across the canal, they found the rum against which Sir Colin had warned them standing—great casks with their heads knocked out for the convenience of intending drunkards—in front of the enemy's camp, with their infantry drawn up in columns behind them. "There is no doubt," says Forbes-Mitchell, "that the enemy expected the British would break their ranks when they saw the rum, and make a rush for it, and they made careful and tempting provision for that contingency." That expectation forms a somewhat severe commentary on the thirsty character the British private had won for himself in India!

The 93rd, however, virtuously marched past the rum barrels, while the supernumerary rank, as Campbell had ordered, upset the barrels and poured their contents out. It was, fortunately, *not* whisky! Forbes-Mitchell, again, describes how, covered by the heavy fire of Peel's guns, their line advanced, with the pipers playing and the colours in front of the centre company. "By the time," he says, "we reached the canal, Peel's blue-jackets were calling out, '—— these cow-horses'—meaning the gun bullocks. 'Come, you 93rd! Give us a hand with the drag-ropes as you did at Lucknow;'" and a company of the 93rd slung their rifles and dashed to the help of the blue-jackets! The sailors gave a vehement cheer for "the red and blue," and some well-known vocalist in the ranks of the 93rd struck up a familiar camp-song with that title, and, says Forbes-Mitchell, "the whole line, including the skirmishers of the 53rd and the sailors," joined with stentorian voices in singing—

"Come, all you gallant British hearts,
Who love the red and blue!"

The British line swept across the enemy's camp, and so complete was the surprise, so unexpected was the onslaught, that the chupatties were found in the very process of being cooked upon the fires, the bullocks stood tied behind the hackeries, the sick and wounded were lying in the hospitals. The smith left the forge and the surgeon his patient to fly from the avenging bayonets. Every tent was found exactly as its late occupants had sprung from it.

Beyond the camp the Gwalior contingent had rallied, and stood drawn up in steady lines. The eagerly advancing British line—to the wonder of the men—was halted. Suddenly through some fields of tall sugar-cane the 9th Lancers came galloping, and behind them, masked by the close lines of the Lancers, was a field battery. When the enemy saw the gleaming tips of the British lances, they fell instantly into squares of brigades, and opened fire on the cavalry at a distance of about three hundred yards. "Just as they commenced to fire," says Forbes-Mitchell, "we could hear Sir Hope Grant, in a voice as loud as a trumpet, give the command to the cavalry, 'Squadrons outwards!' while Bourchier gave the order to his gunners, 'Action front!' The cavalry wheeled as if they had been at a review on the Calcutta parade-ground, and thus uncovered the guns." The guns, charged with grape, were swung round, unlimbered as quick as lightning within about 250 yards of the squares, and round after round of grape was poured into the enemy with murderous effect, every charge going right through, leaving a lane of dead from four to five yards wide. The Highlanders could see the mounted officers of the enemy, as soon as they caught sight of the guns, dash out of the squares, and fly like lightning across the plain!

The victory, in a word, was complete. The Gwalior contingent was destroyed as a military force: its camp, magazines, and guns fell into the hands of the British, and Campbell urged a furious pursuit of the broken soldiery along the Calpee road. For fourteen miles the cavalry and horse artillery rode at the gallop, capturing ammunition waggons and baggage carts, dispersing and slaying such of the infantry as still tried to keep some formation, till at last the panting rebels flung away their arms, and fled into the jungle, or crouched in the fields of sugar-cane, seeking cover from the red sabres and lances of the horsemen. The enemy's centre had no choice but to abandon the town, and fall hurriedly back and melt into the general stream of fugitives.

Nana Sahib, with the left wing, had the Bithoor road, diverging widely from the Calpee road, for his line of retreat, and Campbell pushed forward a strong force under General Mansfield, his chief of staff, to thrust the flying enemy off that road.

Mansfield was a brave man, singularly expert in the routine work of a military office, but quite unfitted for the rough shock of the battlefield. For one thing, he was very short-sighted, and, as Malleson puts it, "was too proud to trust to the sight of others." He reached the point where he commanded the road, but halted his men, stared with dim and spectacled eyes at the stream of fugitives, with their guns, and allowed it all to flow past him undisturbed and unpursued. Nana Sahib himself, as it happened, rode somewhere amongst the fugitives, unsmitten by British lead! Campbell had to despatch Hope Grant the next day along the Bithoor road, in pursuit of this wing of the fugitives, and that fine soldier overtook the flying enemy after a march of twenty-five miles, captured all their guns, and tumbled them into hopeless ruin.

Campbell's victory was splendid and memorable. With 5000 men he had overthrown 25,000, captured thirty-two guns and the whole of their baggage, and driven his enemy in flying rout along two diverging lines of retreat. And it was a victory won rather by the brains of the general than by the bayonets of the soldiers. Campbell's entire loss in killed was only ninety-nine of all ranks. The army of 25,000 Campbell overthrew so utterly, it must be remembered, included the best-trained and most perfectly-equipped native force in all India—the Gwalior contingent, at least 10,000 strong.

CHAPTER X

DELHI: HOW THE RIDGE WAS HELD

All the passion, the tragedy, and the glory of the Indian Mutiny gathers round three great sieges. We vaguely remember a hundred tales of individual adventure elsewhere on the great stage of the Mutiny; we have perhaps a still fainter and more ghostly mental image of the combats Havelock fought on the road to Lucknow, and the battles by which Campbell crushed this body of rebels or that. But it is all a mist of confused recollections, a kaleidoscope of fast-fading pictures. But who does not remember the three great sieges of the Mutiny—Cawnpore, Lucknow, Delhi? The very names are like beacon lights flaming through leagues of night!

At Cawnpore the British were besieged and destroyed, a tragedy due to Wheeler's fatal blunder in choosing the site where the British were to make their stand for life, and his failure in collecting provisions for the siege. At Lucknow, again, the British were besieged, but triumphed, becoming themselves in turn the besiegers. Success here was due to the genius of Henry Lawrence in organising the defences of the Residency, and his energy in storing supplies before the Mutiny broke out. The brave men who died behind Wheeler's ridges of earth, or in the Slaughter Ghaut at Cawnpore, showed valour as lofty and enduring as that of the men who held the Residency with such invincible courage at Lucknow. But the interval between the tragedy at Cawnpore and the triumph at Lucknow is measured by the difference between the two leaders, Wheeler and Lawrence. Both were brave men, but Lawrence was a great captain.

At Delhi the British, from the outset, were the besiegers, and nothing in British history—not the story of Sir Richard Grenville and the *Revenge*, of the Fusileers at Albuera, or of the Guards at Inkerman—is a more kindling tale of endurance and valour than the story of how for months a handful of British clung to the Ridge outside Delhi, fighting daily with foes ten times more numerous than themselves, and yet besieging—or maintaining the show of besieging—the great city which was the nerve-centre and heart of the whole Mutiny.

At Cawnpore and Lucknow the British fought for existence. At Delhi they fought for empire! While the British flag flew from the Ridge at Delhi it was a symbol that the British *raj* was still undestroyed. It was a red gleaming menace of punishment to all rebels. Had that flag fallen for twenty-four hours, India, for a time at least, would have been lost to England. But it flew proudly and threateningly aloft, undestroyed by a hundred attacks, till at last Nicholson led his stormers through the Cashmere Gate, and the fate of the Mutiny was sealed!

LORD LAWRENCE

Reproduced from the Life of Lord Lawrence by permission R. Bosworth Smith, *Esq.*

The mutineers from Meerut rode into Delhi on May 11. It was the city of the Great Mogul. It appealed by a thousand memories to both the race-pride and the fanaticism of the revolted Sepoys. Here the Mutiny found, not only a natural stronghold, but an official head, and Delhi thus became a far-seen signal of revolt to the whole of Northern India. But on June 7—or less than four weeks after Willoughby in heroic despair blew up the great magazine at Delhi—Sir Henry Barnard's microscopic army made its appearance on the Ridge, and the siege of Delhi began. It was a real stroke of military genius that thus, from the earliest outbreak of the Mutiny, kept a bayonet, so to speak, pointed threateningly at its very heart!

And the hero of the siege of Delhi is not Barnard, or Wilson, or Baird-Smith, or Neville Chamberlain, or Nicholson—but a man who never fired a shot or struck a sword-stroke in the actual siege itself—John Lawrence. Lawrence, and not Havelock, nor Outram, nor Canning, was the true saviour of the British *raj* in India in the wild days of the Mutiny.

John Lawrence was five years younger than his gallant brother Henry, who died in the Residency at Lucknow. He had no visible gleam of the brilliancy which makes Henry Lawrence a character so attractive. Up to middle life, indeed, John Lawrence was a silent, inarticulate, rugged man, with the reputation of being a great worker, but whom nobody suspected to be a genius, and for whom nobody—least of all Lawrence himself—dreamed fame was waiting. He came of that strong-bodied, strong-brained, masterful race of which the North of Ireland is the cradle. But England, Ireland, and Scotland all had a share in the making of John Lawrence. He was actually born in England. His father was a gallant Irish soldier, who led the forlorn hope at the storming of Seringapatam. His mother was a lineal descendant of John Knox, the Scottish reformer. And perhaps the characteristic traits of the three countries never met more happily in a single human character than in John Lawrence. In Ulster he was known amongst his schoolmates as "English John." At Haileybury, in England, he was looked upon as a typical Irishman.

The truth is, he was Englishman, Irishman, Scotchman all in one. He had Celtic glow and fire under a crust of Scottish silence and caution; and he added the Englishman's steady intelligence and passion for justice to Scottish hard-headedness and the generous daring of the Irish character. Or, to put the matter in a different way, in any perilous crisis he could survey the situation with the balanced judgment of an Englishman; could choose his course with the shrewd and calculating sagacity of a Scotchman; then carry it out with Irish fire and daring!

Lawrence shone as a youth neither in studies nor in games, and both as a youth and man he had a magnificent faculty for silence. By blood and genius he was a soldier. But duty was the supreme law of life for him; and at the bidding of what he deemed to be duty, he surrendered a soldier's career and entered the Indian Civil Service. His silent energy, his strong brain, his passion for work, his chivalrous loyalty to righteousness, quickly assured him a great career. He was above the middle height, strongly built, with an eager, forward gait. His massive head gave him a sort of kingly look—the forehead broad, the eyes deep-set and grey, but with a gleam in them as of a sword-blade. The firm lips had a saddened curve; the face was ploughed deep with furrows of thought and work. His voice, when his feelings were aroused, had a singular resonance and timbre, and his whole aspect was that of silent, half-melancholy simplicity and strength.

But Lawrence was exactly the man for a great crisis. He had a kingly faculty for choosing fit instruments. He saw with perfect clearness every detail of the visible landscape; but he had also that subtler vision—which only great poets and great statesmen possess—of the tendencies and forces which underlie external facts and determine their flow. The Celtic element in him, perhaps, gave Lawrence that rare and subtle faculty; but by virtue of his Scottish strain he was essentially a man of action. He could grasp a great purpose with a hand of steel, and hold it unshaken through all the shocks of conflict and adversity.

Lawrence, it may be added, was pre-eminently fortunate in his officers. Partly by the attraction which draws like to like, and partly by his own rare genius for choosing fit instruments, he had gathered round him a group of splendid soldiers and administrators, all in the prime of life. Nicholson, for example, was only thirty-five; Edwardes and Neville Chamberlain only thirty-seven. The general average of age, indeed, on Lawrence's staff was much below that of India in general. All the energy of youth, in brief, was in Lawrence's men; all the sagacity of ripest statesmanship was in Lawrence himself.

Lawrence's contribution to the history of the Mutiny must be compressed into a dozen sentences. In 1857 he was Chief Commissioner of the Punjaub, the "land of the five rivers," with a population of 20,000,000. The Punjaub was newly-conquered territory; its population was the most warlike in India; its frontiers marched for 800 miles with those of Afghanistan, and the hill passes were held by wild Moslem clans always ready to storm down with clattering shield and gleaming spear on the fat, defenceless plains at their feet. In eight years, under the *régime* of the Lawrences, the Punjaub was rendered orderly, loyal, and prosperous; while the Punjaub Frontier Force, a body of 12,000 men, which kept the mountain tribes in order, was perhaps the first body of native troops which ever followed British officers into battle.

Then came the cataclysm of the Mutiny. As with the shock of an earthquake, British rule in Northern India seemed to crumble to the ground, and British officers who yesterday were rulers of kingdoms and cities, were to-day fugitives, or fighting in tiny and broken clusters for their lives. The Mutiny, too, cut Oude and the Punjaub off from the centre of authority at Calcutta. For weeks no whisper from the outside world reached Lawrence. He was left to keep his own head and shape his own policy.

His policy may be told almost in a sentence. He anticipated mutiny, and outpaced it. He disarmed with iron resolution and swift decision all the Sepoy regiments whose loyalty was doubtful, and put all the forts, arsenals, treasuries, and strategic points in the Punjaub under the guard of British bayonets. Then he organised a movable column of European troops—scanty in dimensions, but of the finest fighting quality—under the command, first, of Neville Chamberlain, and next of Nicholson; and this force stood ready to strike at any point where mutiny threatened to lift its head. In the Punjaub, that is, mutiny was anticipated, robbed of weapons and left helpless, and under the ceaseless menace of the light-footed, almost ubiquitous, movable column.

Next, having dismissed into air, as with a gesture of his hand, the army whose loyalty was tainted, Lawrence had to create another native army, with loyalty above reproach. And from the wild mountain clans and the Sikhs—themselves a conquered people—Lawrence actually created a new army, nearly 50,000 strong, with which he was able to crush the very Sepoys who, under British leadership, had been the conquerors of the Punjaub!

MAJOR-GENERAL SIR HERBERT B. EDWARDES, K.C.B., K.C.S.I.

From a lithograph

Lawrence's genius and masterful will, too, determined the whole strategy to be employed for the suppression of the Mutiny. He settled the question that Delhi must be instantly besieged. He formed a military base for the siege at Umballa, a distance of a hundred miles, and he kept sleepless guard over that long line of communications. He fed the besieging force with supplies and munitions of every kind; reinforced it with, first, his own frontier troops, the famous Guides and the Ghoorkas, and, later, with his own movable column. He cast into the scale against Delhi, in effect, his last coin, his last cartridge, and his last man. And in that terrible game, on which hung the fate of the British rule in India, Lawrence won! "Through him," wrote Lord Canning, "Delhi fell." And the fall of Delhi rang the knell of the Mutiny.

Once, it is true, even John Lawrence's iron courage seemed to give way, or, rather, the strain of the peril threw his cool judgment off its balance. The fate of India visibly hung on Delhi. The force on the Ridge was absurdly inadequate for its task, and Lawrence conceived the idea that, to succeed at Delhi, it would be necessary to abandon Peshawur, give up the Punjaub to Dost Mohammed, and retire across the Indus. There were three European regiments, with powerful artillery, and the best native troops locked up beyond the Indus. On the Ridge at Delhi they would decide the issue of the siege. "If Delhi does not fall," Lawrence argued, "Peshawur must go. Let us abandon the Punjaub for the sake of Delhi."

It is still thrilling to read the sentences in which Herbert Edwardes protested against this evil policy. To abandon Peshawur, he urged, would be to fail not only at Delhi, but all over India. "Cabul would come again!" Lawrence quoted Napoleon against Edwardes. Did not Napoleon ruin himself in 1814 by holding fast to the line of the Elbe instead of falling back to the Rhine? But Edwardes knew the Eastern mind. India is not Europe. To waver, to seem to withdraw, to consent to disaster, was to be ruined. To abandon the Punjaub, Edwardes warned Lawrence, was to abandon the cause of England in the East. "Every hand in India would be against us. Don't yield an inch of frontier!... If General Reed, with all the men you have sent him, cannot get into Delhi, let Delhi go. The Empire's reconquest hangs on the Punjaub." Then he quotes Nelson against Lawrence. "Make a stand! 'Anchor, Hardy, anchor!'" The quotation was, perhaps, not very relevant; but it is curious to note how one brave spirit seems to speak to another across half a century, and give a new edge to its courage.

There can be no doubt that Edwardes showed, at this moment, not only the more heroic temper, but the sounder judgment of the two. Canning settled the dispute. "Hold on to Peshawur to the last," he wrote; and the question was decided. But Lawrence's momentary lapse into indecision only sets in more dazzling light his courage afterwards. It was after he had seriously meditated abandoning the Punjaub that he despatched the immortal movable column, under Nicholson, 4200 strong, with a powerful battering-train, to Delhi, thus feeding the gallant force on the Ridge with his own best troops, and yet not giving up "an inch of the frontier," or abating one whit of his own haughty rule in the Punjaub!

General Anson, as we have seen, was commander-in-chief in India when the Mutiny broke out. He was a brave man, had fought as an ensign at Waterloo, and had seen forty-three years' bloodless service after that great battle. But his gifts were rather social than soldierly. He was a better authority on whist and horses than on questions of tactics and strategy, and he was scarcely the man to face an army in revolt. Lawrence acted as a military brain and conscience for Anson, and determined that Delhi must be attacked; though, as a matter of fact, Anson had only three regiments of British troops, almost no artillery, and absolutely no transport at his command.

On May 16 Anson held a council of war with his five senior officers at Umballa, and the council agreed unanimously that, with the means at Anson's command, nothing could be done. It is a curious fact, showing the speed with which, from this point, events moved, that, within less than two months from the date of that council, all its members were dead—either killed in battle, or killed by mere exposure and strain! But Lawrence's views prevailed. "Pray, only reflect on the whole history of India," he wrote to Anson. "Where have we failed when we have acted vigorously? Where have we succeeded when guided by timid counsels?"

Anson and his advisers gave that highest proof of courage which brave men can offer: they moved forward without a murmur on an adventure which they believed to be hopeless. From an orthodox military point of view it was hopeless. Only, the British empire in India has been built up by the doing of "hopeless" things.

On May 24 Anson reached Kurnal, where his troops were to arrive four days afterwards. On the 26th Anson himself was dead, killed by cholera after only four hours' illness!

Sir Henry Barnard, who succeeded him, had been Chief of the Staff in the Crimea. He was an utter stranger to India, having landed in it only a few weeks before. He was a brave soldier, and a high-minded English gentleman; but he was, perhaps, even less of a general than Anson. His force consisted of 2400 infantry, 600 cavalry, and 22 field-guns. Barnard had to fight one fierce and bloody combat before he reached the Delhi Ridge. This took place on June 7. It was the first time the British and the mutineers had met in the shock of battle; and the Sepoys who had revolted at Meerut, and the British troops who had been so strangely held back from crushing the revolt at the moment of its outbreak, now looked grimly at each other across a narrow interval of sun-baked turf. Lord Roberts says that when, as night fell on June 6, it was known that the troops were to move forward and attack the rebel force which stood in their path to Delhi, the sick in hospital declared they would remain there no longer, and "many quite unfit to walk insisted upon accompanying the attacking column, imploring their comrades not to mention they were ill, for fear they should not be allowed to take part in the fight!"

The rebels fought with an obstinacy unsurpassed in the whole record of the Mutiny; but British troops in such a mood as we have described, were not to be stayed. The 75th carried the rebel guns at the point of the bayonet; Hope Grant with his scanty squadrons of horse swept round their left flank. The British lost less than 200 killed and wounded, the rebels lost over 1000 men and 13 guns; and, as night fell, Barnard took possession of the famous Ridge. Then from the streets of the revolted city, the crowds looked up and saw the British flag, a gleaming and fluttering menace, a stern prophecy of defeat and retribution, flying from the Flagstaff Tower.

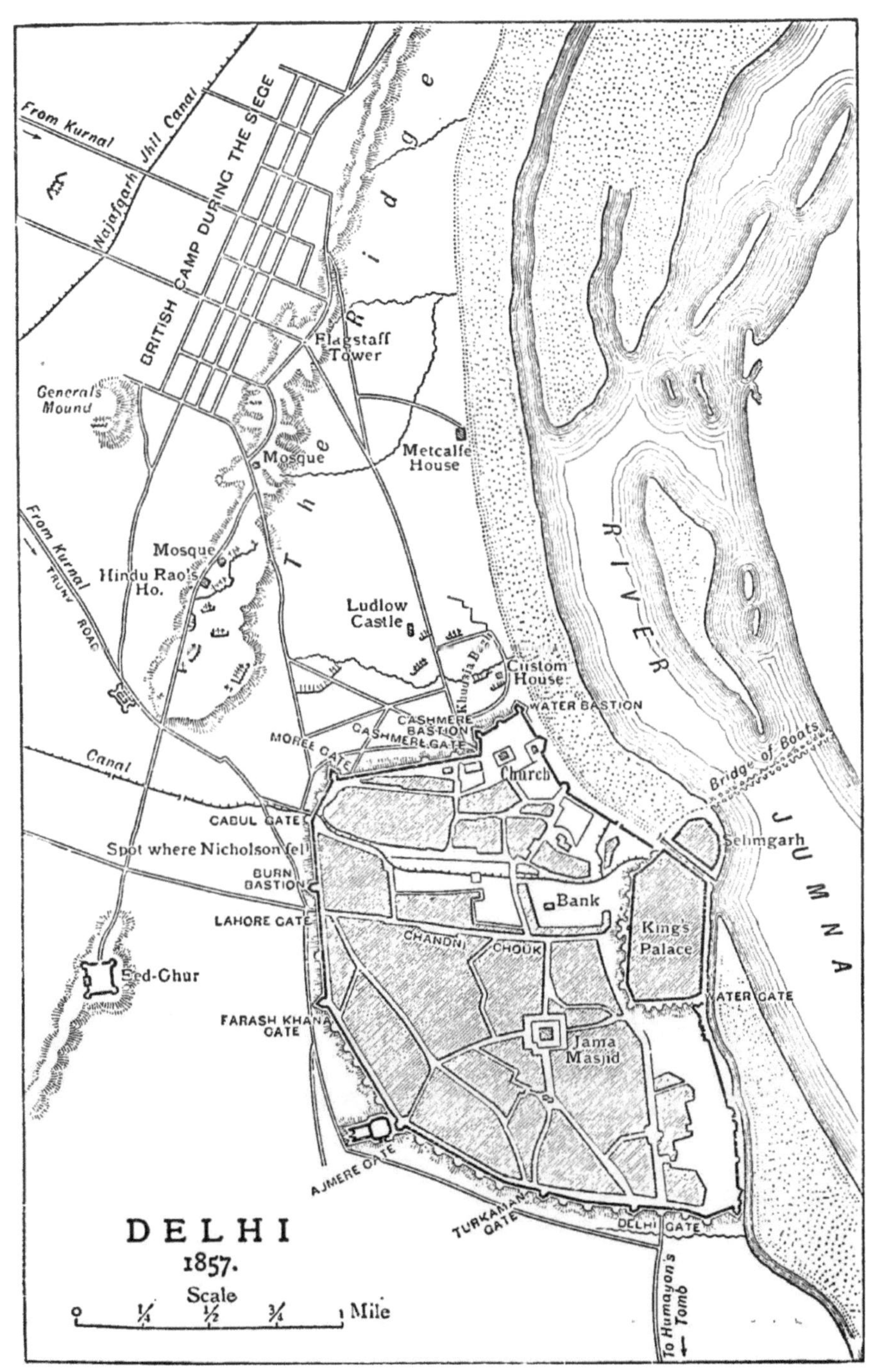

DELHI, 1857.

Walker & Cockerell sc.

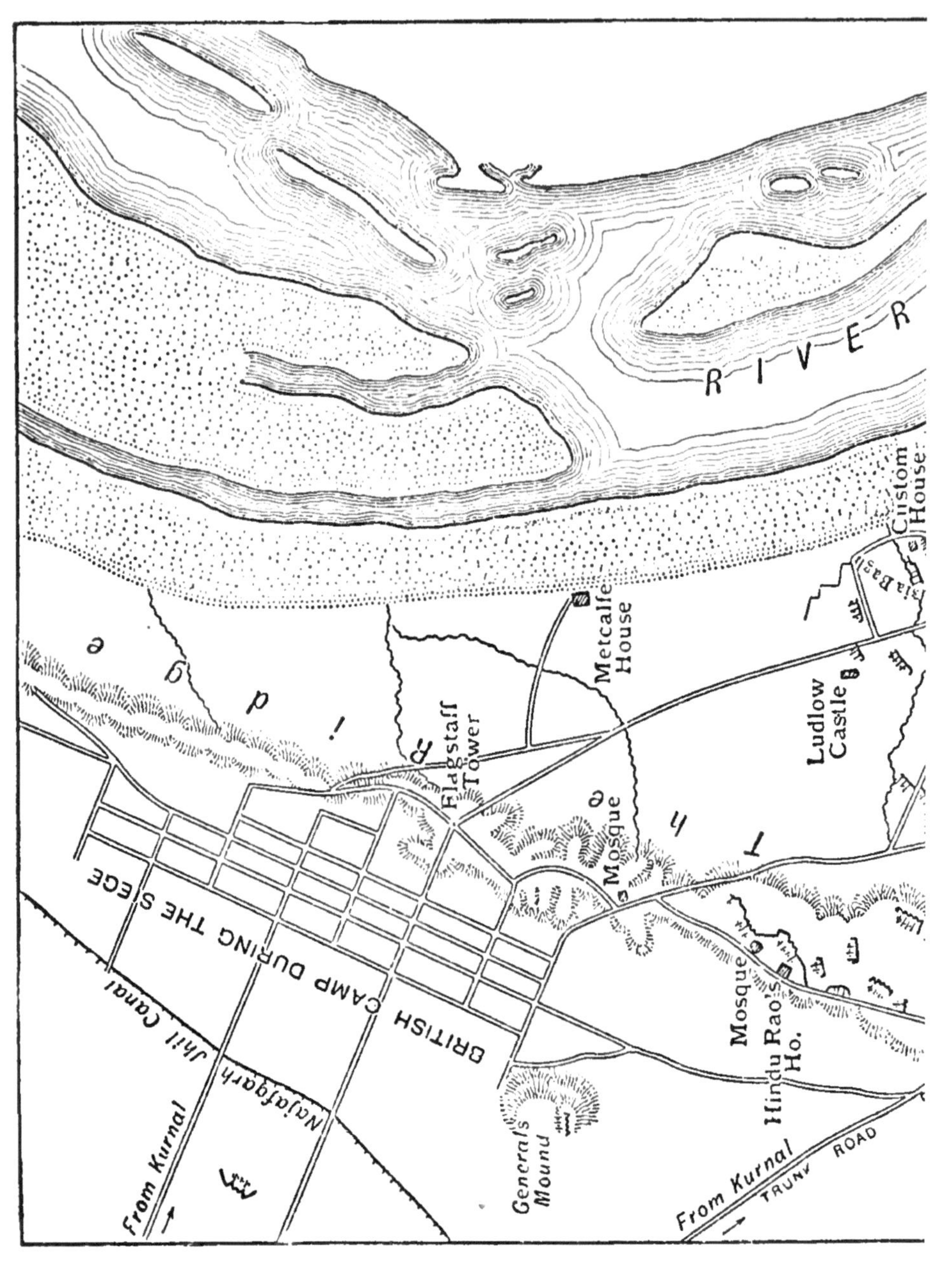

Delhi, 1857 (*Enlarged - Top*)

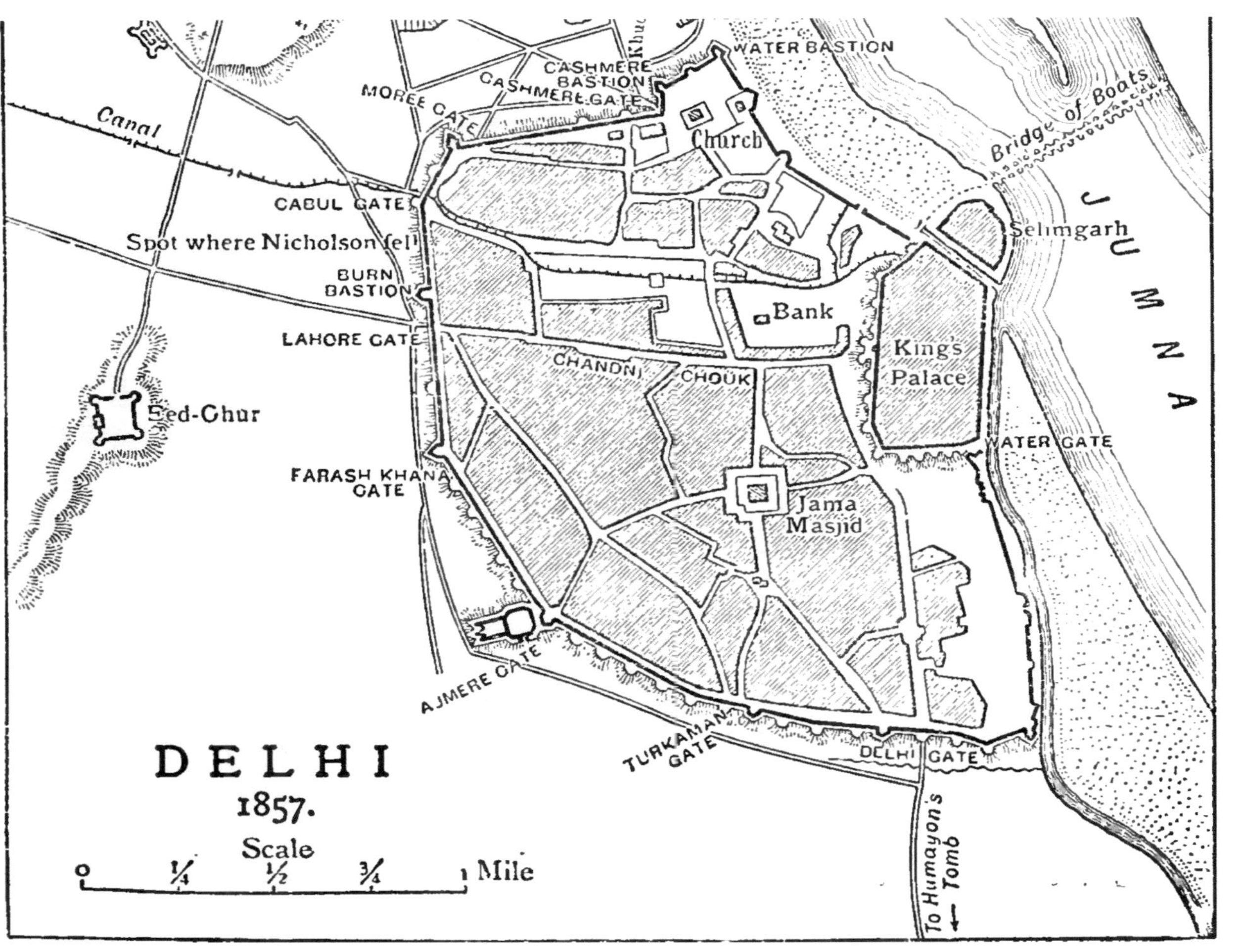

Delhi, 1857 (*Enlarged - Bottom*)

Delhi lies on the right bank of the Jumna; and nearly six miles of massive stone wall twenty-four feet high, with a ditch twenty-five feet broad and nearly as many feet deep in front, sweep round the city, forming a bow, of which the river is the string. Napier, afterwards Lord Napier of Magdala, had employed his rare skill as an engineer in strengthening the defences of the city. The walls were knotted with bastions, mounting 114 heavy guns. Behind them was a huge fanatical population and over 40,000 revolted Sepoys, with some 60 field-guns and exhaustless magazines of warlike supplies. Every week, from one revolted station after another, new waves of mutineers flowed into the city. Some 3000 British soldiers, with a few battalions of native troops, and 22 light guns, stood perched on the Ridge to undertake the desperate feat of besieging this huge stronghold!

The historic Ridge, it may be explained, is a low hill, not quite sixty feet high, and some two miles long, running obliquely towards the city walls. Its left touches the Jumna itself, at a distance of more than two miles from the city; its right was within 1200 yards of the hostile walls. At the middle of the Ridge stood the Flagstaff Tower. On its right extremity the Ridge overlooked the trunk road, and was surrounded by a fringe of houses and gardens, making it the weak point of the British position. The various buildings along the crest of the Ridge, Hindu Rao's house, the observatory, an old Pathan mosque, the Flagstaff Tower, &c., were held by strong pickets, each with one or more field-guns. The external slope of the Ridge was covered with old buildings and enclosures, giving the enemy dangerous shelter in their attacks. The main body of the British was encamped on the reverse slope of the Ridge.

Delhi, it will be seen, was in no sense "invested." Supplies and reinforcements flowed in with perfect safety on its river front throughout the whole siege. All that Barnard and his men could do was to keep the British flag flying on the Ridge, and hold their ground with obstinate, unquenchable courage, against almost daily assaults, until reinforcements reached them, and they could leap on the city.

The first reinforcement to arrive took the surprising shape of a baby! One officer alone, Tytler, of the 38th Native Infantry, had brought his wife into the camp; she was too ill to be sent to the rear, and, in a rough waggon for bed-chamber, gave birth to a son, who was solemnly named "Stanley Delhi Force." The soldiers welcomed the infant with an odd mixture of humour and superstition. A British private was overheard to say, "Now we shall get our reinforcements. This camp was formed to avenge the blood of innocents, and the first reinforcement sent us is a new-born infant!"

The next day the famous Guides sent by Lawrence from his Frontier Force marched into camp, three troops of cavalry and six companies of infantry, under Daly, an officer of great daring and energy. This little force had marched 580 miles in twenty days, a feat of endurance unsurpassed in Indian history. The cavalry consisted mainly of Afghans, tall, swarthy, fierce-looking. The Ghoorkas were sturdy, undersized little Highlanders, born fighters all of them, and ready to follow their commanding officer, Major Reid, on any dare-devil feat to which he might lead them. The battalion numbered 490 men, and of these no less than 320—or three out of four—were killed or wounded during the siege. On the day of the assault

(September 14) no fewer than 180 of them, who were lying sick or wounded in the hospital, volunteered for the assault, and came limping and bandaged into the ranks of their comrades, to join in the mad rush through the Cashmere Gate!

The revolted Sepoys, on their side, were full of a fierce energy quite unusual to them, and on the very first day they flung themselves in great numbers, and with great daring, on the detachment holding Hindu Rao's house. Two companies of the 60th held this post, with two guns from Scott's battery; and for half the afternoon the quick flashes, the white smoke of cannon, and the incessant rattle of musketry round the assailed post told with what fury the attack was being urged, and how stubbornly the defence was being maintained.

At last the cavalry of the newly-arrived Guides was sent at the enemy. They rode in upon the Sepoys with magnificent courage, broke them into flying fragments, and pursued them, wounding and slaying, to the walls of the city. Their victory was brilliant, but it was dearly bought, their commander, Quentin Battye, being mortally wounded. He was little more than a lad, but was almost worshipped by his dark-faced horsemen. He had been an English public-school boy, and, Lord Roberts says, was curiously fond of quotations. Almost his last words, spoken to a friend, were, "Good-bye! 'Dulce et decorum est pro patria mori.' That's how it is with me, old fellow!" The victories of England are still won, as in Wellington's days, on the playing grounds of its great schools.

The Guides found in the camp a soldier of mingled yet splendid fame who had been their leader in many a gallant charge—Hodson, of Hodson's Horse. Hodson had been, rightly or wrongly, under a cloud; but the crisis of the Mutiny naturally gave, to the most daring horseman and the most brilliant light cavalry leader in India, a great opportunity. He was now at the head of a body of irregular horse, and one of Barnard's most trusted officers. He was tall, fair-haired, with bloodless complexion, heavy curved moustache, and keen, alert, and what some one called "unforgiving" eyes.

When the Guides, as they rode into the camp, met Hodson, a curious scene took place. They crowded round him with wild gesticulations and deep-voiced, guttural shouts. "They seized my bridle," says Hodson himself, "my dress, hands, and feet, and literally threw themselves down before the horse with tears streaming down their faces!" Hodson was the ideal leader for fierce irregulars like the Guides, a brilliant swordsman, of iron nerve, and courage as steadfast as the blade of his own sword. And with leaders like Daly, and Hodson, and Reid, and Battye, Sikhs and Ghoorkas made soldiers that might have charged through Russian Life Guards, or broken a square of Pomeranian Grenadiers!

On June 10 the Sepoys delivered another attack, in great strength, on Hindu Rao's house, which they looked upon as the key of the British position, and which was held on this day by the Ghoorkas under Reid. The Sepoys hoped that the Ghoorkas would join them, and, as they came on, instead of firing, they waved their hands, and shouted, "Don't fire. We are not firing. We want to speak to you. Come and join us." "Oh yes! we are coming," answered the sturdy little Ghoorkas, with fierce, jesting humour, and, running forward to within thirty yards of the

Sepoys, they poured a quick and deadly fire upon them, driving them back with great slaughter. From that stage of the siege, Hindu Rao's house, perhaps the most fiercely attacked point in the British front, was held by Reid and his Ghoorkas, and a better officer or better men were not to be found on the Ridge.

The more eager spirits among the British were burning to leap on the city, and, on June 12, a plan of attack was actually prepared by the engineer officers and Hodson, and approved by Barnard. The whole force was to be divided into three columns; one was to break its way through the Cashmere Gate, a second through the Lahore Gate, a third was to fling itself on the walls, and attempt an escalade—practically, the same plan by which the city was finally carried. It was a project, considering the force available for its execution, almost insane in its daring; and Barnard, though he consented to it, took no decided and methodical steps to carry it out.

It would almost seem, indeed, as if physical strain, want of sleep, and the terrible responsibility he was carrying, had affected Barnard's head. The situation might well have taxed—and over-taxed—the brain of a greater general than Barnard. The light guns of the British, firing at a distance of a thousand yards, could make no impression on the walls. Their strength was dwindling daily; that of the enemy was growing fast. And it was natural that the British temper, under such conditions, should become explosive, and that the more daring spirits were eager, in the face of any risks, to come to the sword's point with their enemies. The General's nerve was curiously shaken. Hope Grant tells how Sir Henry Barnard sent for him on the evening of the 12th: "He hushed me into a whisper, and asked me if I thought any person could possibly overhear us, adding, 'There is treason around us.' Then he explained, 'I mean to attack the town to-night.'" Barnard's manner produced on Hope Grant's mind the impression that his brain was slightly off its balance.

At one o'clock that night the troops were suddenly paraded, ammunition served out, and leaders assigned to the three columns. But the 75th Foot had, somehow, been left at the extreme front without orders, and before they could be brought up the grey dawn was breaking, and the proposed attack had to be abandoned. Lord Roberts says that this "blunder" was "a merciful dispensation, which saved the British from an irreparable disaster." That was not Hodson's judgment. In his journal he says: "The attack was frustrated by the fears and absolute disobedience to orders of ——, the man who first lost Delhi, and has now, by his folly, prevented its being recaptured." But Hodson was more impatient and blunt-spoken than is permissible to even a gallant soldier, and his diary reflects, perhaps, rather the condition of his liver than the deliberate judgment of his head. Thus he writes: "That old woman ——, has come here for nothing apparently, but as an obstacle; —— is also a crying evil to us!"

On the 12th, indeed, the Sepoys themselves were attacking Flagstaff Tower with great fury, but were repelled with steady valour. On June 14, General Reed arrived in camp; he was in chief divisional command, and should at once have taken over the charge of the siege from Barnard; but a ride of 500 miles had left him little better than a physical wreck, and Barnard still remained in command.

On the 13th, 14th, and 15th there were new attacks pluckily urged by the Sepoys, and repelled with cool and stern courage by the British. "They came on," is Hodson's summary, "very boldly, and got most heartily thrashed." On the 17th the British were attacked along their whole front, and from almost every direction, and an attempt was made to construct a battery which would enfilade the Ridge. Two small columns, under Tombs and Reid, were sent out with a dash, broke up the proposed battery in brilliant style, and drove the troops that covered it in wild and bloody flight to the city walls.

Week after week the fighting went on most gallantly, and the story gleams with records of shining pluck; it rings with the clash of steel on steel; it thrills to the rattle of musketry volleys and the deeper voice of the cannon. Thus Hope Grant tells how, on the night of the 19th, from sunset till half-past eleven, he kept back, by repeated charges of squadrons of the 9th Lancers and the Guides, with the help of some field-guns, an attack on the rear of the British position.

The fighting was close and furious. As Daly came up through the darkness into the fight, Tombs said, "Daly, if you don't charge, my guns are taken;" and Daly, shaking his reins, and followed by a handful of his Guides, dashed on the enemy, and saved the guns. Colonel Yule, of the 9th Lancers, was killed; Daly himself was severely wounded; and the enemy, in the dark, worked round the flanks of the British guns, and two of the pieces were on the point of being taken.

Hope Grant collected a few men, and rode fiercely into the enemy's ranks. His horse was shot, and, galloping wildly into the mass of Sepoys, fell dead. Hope Grant was thus left unhorsed in the darkness, and in the midst of the enemy! His orderly, a fine, tall Sowar, who had remained loyal when his regiment mutinied, was in a moment by his side, and cried, "Take my horse; it is your only chance of safety." Hope Grant refused the generous offer, and, taking a firm grasp of the horse's tail, bade the Sowar drag him out of the *mêlée*. The next day Hope Grant sent for the Sowar, warmly praised his gallant conduct, and offered him a reward in money. The brave fellow drew himself up with dignity, salaamed, and said, "No, Sahib, I will take no money."

Seaton describes how, during that wild night combat, they watched, from the Ridge above, the flashes of the guns, rending the gloom with darting points of flame, and listened to the shouts, the clash of weapons, the crackle of the musketry that marked the progress of the fight. Presently there came a sudden glare, then a roar that for a moment drowned all other sounds. One of the British limbers had blown up. The fight was going badly. Then, out of the darkness, came the cry of a human voice, "Where is the General?" It was an officer asking reinforcements, and three companies of the 1st Fusileers, who were standing hard by, silent and invisible in the dusk, were sent down to the fight. They moved forward at the curt word of command: presently the rolling crash of their volleys was heard; a line of red, dancing points of fire through the darkness marked their progress, and the guns were saved!

June 23 was the centenary of Plassey, and a prediction, widely spread amongst the Sepoys, announced that on that day the *raj* of the British was to end. As it happened, that particular day was also a great religious festival for the Hindus, whilst it was the day of the new moon, and so was held by Mohammedans as a fortunate day. Accordingly an attack of great fury, and maintained for eight long hours, was made on the British right. Some reinforcements, amounting to 850 men, were on the 22nd within twenty miles of Delhi, and a staff officer was despatched to hurry them on; and they actually reached the Ridge in time to take part in the final effort which drove back the enemy. Roberts says that "no men could have fought better than did the Sepoys. They charged the Rifles, the Guides, and the Ghoorkas again and again." But nothing could shake the cool and obstinate—the almost scornful—valour of the British.

Every available man in the camp was at the front, and when the 2nd Fusileers and the 4th Sikhs, who formed the approaching reinforcement, came pressing on with eager speed to the crest of the Ridge, over which the battle-smoke was drifting in dense white clouds, they were at once sent into the fight, and the enemy was finally driven back with a loss of over 1600 men. It is not easy to picture the exhaustion of the British at the close of a fight so stern and prolonged. "When I arrived at Hindu Rao's," wrote an eye-witness, "I found every one exhausted. There were the 1st Fusileers and some Rifles all done up. I went on to the new advanced battery; it was crowded with worn-out men. The artillerymen, likewise done up, had ceased firing; another party of Rifles in a similar state in another position. 120 men of the 2nd Fusileers, who had marched twenty-three miles that morning and had had no breakfast, were lying down exhausted. Three weak companies of Ghoorkas were out as skirmishers; but they, too, were exhausted, and the remainder were resting under a rock. The heat was terrific, and the thermometer must have been at least 140 degrees, with a hot wind blowing, and a frightful glare." Of ten officers in the 2nd Fusileers five were struck down by *coup de soleil.*

The next day Neville Chamberlain, Lawrence's favourite officer, rode into the camp, and assumed the post of adjutant-general.

On July 3 Baird Smith reached the Ridge, and took charge of the engineering operations of the siege. On July 5 Sir Henry Barnard died, killed by the burden of a task too great for him, and Reed assumed command. He held it for less than ten days, and then passed it over to Archdale Wilson, who had shared in the discredit of Meerut, and who, though a brave man, had scanty gifts of leadership.

Twice over during those days of fierce and prolonged battle a time had been fixed for assaulting the city, and twice the plan had been spoiled by an earlier counter-attack of the enemy. Baird Smith, on his arrival, approved of the scheme for an assault, and urged it on Reed, who hesitated over it during the brief period of his command, and then handed it over as a perplexing legacy to his successor Wilson. The proposal to leap on Delhi was finally abandoned; but Baird Smith, the coolest brain employed in the siege, recorded long afterwards his deliberate judgment that "if we had assaulted any time between the 4th and 14th of July we should have carried the place."

On July 9, an attack of great strength, and marked by great daring, was made by the enemy, and was almost lifted into success by the disloyalty of a detachment of the 9th Irregular Cavalry. They were on outpost duty, watching the trunk road. They allowed the enemy to approach the British position without giving warning, and when Hills, who commanded two guns in front of the General's mound, ran out of his tent and leaped on his horse, he found a troop of Carabineers in broken flight, sweeping past him, and the enemy almost on his guns. He shouted "Action front!" then, to give his gunners a chance of firing, rode single-handed into the enemy's squadrons, a solitary swordsman charging a regiment!

Hills actually cut down the leading man, and wounded the second; then two troopers charging him at once, he was rolled over, man and horse, and the troops swept over him. Hills struggled, bruised and half-dazed, to his feet, picked up his sword, and was at once attacked by two of the rebel cavalry and a foot soldier. Hills coolly shot the first horseman riding down upon him, then catching the lance of the second in his left hand, thrust him through the body with his sword. He was instantly attacked by the third enemy, and his sword wrenched from him. Hills, on this, fell back upon first principles, and struck his opponent in the face repeatedly with his fist. But he was by this time himself exhausted, and fell. Then, exactly as his antagonist lifted his sword to slay him, Tombs, who had cut his way through the enemy, and was coming up at a gallop to help his comrade, with a clever pistol-shot from a distance of thirty paces killed the Sepoy. It was a Homeric combat, and both Tombs and Hills received the Victoria Cross.

The enemy meanwhile had galloped past the guns, eager to reach the native artillery, which they hoped would ride off with them. The 9th Lancers, however, had turned out in their shirt-sleeves, and they, riding fiercely home, drove off the enemy.

It is always interesting to listen to the story of a gallant deed, as told by the doer himself. The reckless valour which Lieutenant Hills showed in charging, single-handed, a column of rebel cavalry, in order to secure for his gunners a chance of opening fire, can hardly be described by a remote historian. But Hills has told the story of his own deed, and an extract from his tale, at least, is worth giving:—

> I thought that by charging them I might make a commotion, and give the gun time to load, so in I went at the front rank, cut down the first fellow, slashed the next across the face as hard as I could, when two Sowars charged me. Both their horses crashed into mine at the same moment, and, of course, both horse and myself were sent flying. We went down at such a pace that I escaped the cuts made at me, one of them giving my jacket an awful slice just below the left arm—it only, however, cut the jacket. Well, I lay quite snug until all had passed over me, and then got up and looked about for my sword. I found it full ten yards off. I had hardly got hold of it when three fellows returned, two on horseback. The first I wounded, and dropped him from his horse. The second charged me with a lance. I put it aside, and caught him an awful gash on the head and face. I thought I had killed him. Apparently he must have clung to his horse, for he disappeared. The wounded man then came up, but got his skull split. Then came

> on the third man—a young, active fellow. I found myself getting very weak from want of breath, the fall from my horse having pumped me considerably, and my cloak, somehow or other, had got tightly fixed round my throat, and was actually choking me. I went, however, at the fellow and cut him on the shoulder, but some "kupra" (cloth) on it apparently turned the blow. He managed to seize the hilt of my sword, and twisted it out of my hand, and then we had a hand-to-hand fight, I punching his head with my fists, and he trying to cut me, but I was too close to him. Somehow or other I fell, and then was the time, fortunately for me, that Tombs came up and shot the fellow. I was so choked by my cloak that move I could not until I got it loosened. By-the-bye, I forgot to say that I fired at this chap twice, but the pistol snapped, and I was so enraged I drove it at the fellow's head, missing him, however.

The Sepoys had planted a battery of guns at a point in their front called Ludlow Castle, and maintained from it a constant fire on Metcalfe House. Their skirmishers, too, crept up with great audacity, and maintained a ceaseless fire on the British pickets. It was necessary to silence this battery, and early in the morning of August 12, without call of bugle or roll of drum, a force of British, Sikhs, and Ghoorkas, with a handful of cavalry, stole down the slope of the Ridge in order to carry the offending guns. The order was given for profoundest silence, and almost like a procession of shadows the little column crept over the Ridge through the gloom, and disappeared in the midst of the low-lying ground on its way to the rebel guns.

Undetected in the sheltering blackness, the column reached the sleeping battery. A startled Sepoy, who caught through the haze and shadow a sudden glimpse of stern faces and the gleam of bayonets, gave a hasty challenge. It was answered by a volley which ran like a streak of jagged flame through the darkness, and with a rush the British—their officers gallantly leading, and Sikh and Ghoorka trying to outrace their English comrades—swept on to the battery. The Sepoys succeeded in discharging two guns on their assailants; but Lord Roberts records that the discharge of the third gun was prevented by a gallant Irish soldier named Reegan. He leaped with levelled bayonet over the earthwork, and charged the artilleryman, who was in the very act of thrusting his port-fire on to the powder in the touch-hole of the gun. Reegan was struck at on every side, but nothing stopped him, and the fierce lunge of his bayonet slew the artilleryman and prevented the discharge of the gun. Captain Greville, followed by two or three men, flung himself on another gun, and slew or drove off its gunners.

Hodson characteristically says, "It was a very comfortable little affair!" As a matter of fact, it was, for a dozen fierce minutes, a deadly hand-to-hand combat. "The rebel artillerymen," says Roberts, "stood to their guns splendidly, and fought till they were all killed." The rebels, too, were in great force, and as the passionate *mêlée* swayed to and fro, and the muskets crackled fiercely, and angry thrust of bayonet was answered by desperate stroke of tulwar, the slaughter was great. Some 250 Sepoys were slain, while the British only lost one officer and nineteen men, though nearly a hundred more were wounded. But the battery was destroyed, and four guns brought back in triumph to the camp.

The return of the force was a scene of mad excitement. A wounded officer sat astride one gun, waving his hand in triumph. A soldier, with musket and bayonet fixed, bestrode each horse, and dozens of shouting infantrymen—many with wounds and torn uniform, and all with smoke-blackened faces—clung, madly cheering, to the captured pieces.

On August 7 there rode into the British camp perhaps the most famous and daring soldier in all India, the man with whose memory the siege of Delhi, and the great assault which ended the siege, are for ever associated—John Nicholson.

Nicholson was of Irish birth, the son of a Dublin physician, who had seen twenty years' service in India—service brilliant and varied beyond even what is common in that field of great deeds. There is no space here to tell the story of Nicholson's career, but as he rode into the British camp that August morning, he was beyond all question the most picturesque and striking figure in India. He was a man of splendid physique, and is said to have borne an almost bewildering resemblance to the Czar Nicholas. He was six feet two in height, strongly built, with a flowing dark-coloured beard, colourless face, grey eyes, with dark pupils, in whose depths, when he was aroused, a point of steady light, as of steel or of flame, would kindle. Few men, indeed, could sustain the piercing look of those lustrous, menacing eyes. His voice had a curious depth in it; his whole bearing a singular air of command and strength—an impression which his habit of rare and curt speech intensified. "He was a man," says one who knew him well, "cast in a giant mould, with massive chest and powerful limbs, and an expression, ardent and commanding, with a dash of roughness; features of stern beauty, a long black beard, and sonorous voice. His imperial air never left him." "Nicholson," says Lord Roberts, "impressed me more profoundly than any man I had ever met before, or have ever met since."

Nicholson, like the Lawrences, like Havelock, and Herbert Edwardes, and many of the Indian heroes of that generation, was a man of rough but sincere piety, and this did not weaken his soldiership—it rather gave a new loftiness to its ideals and a steadier pulse to its courage. "If there is a desperate deed to be done in India," Herbert Edwardes told Lord Canning, "John Nicholson is the man to do it"; and exactly that impression and conviction Nicholson kindled in everybody about him.

"He had," says Mrs. Steel, "the great gift. He could put his own heart into a whole camp, and make it believe it was its own." Such a masterful will and personality as that of Nicholson took absolutely captive the imagination of the wild, irregular soldiery of which he was the leader.

What was Nicholson's fighting quality, indeed, may be judged, say, from the fashion in which he smashed up the mutinous Sepoys at Mardan (as told in Trotter's "Life" of him), and chased them mile after mile towards the hills of Swat, Nicholson leading the pursuit on his huge grey charger, "his great sword felling a Sepoy at every stroke!" His faculty for strategy, and for swift, sustained movement is, again, told by the manner in which he intercepted and destroyed the Sealkote mutineers at the fords of the Ravi on their way to Delhi, The mutineers were two days' march ahead of him, and Nicholson made a forced march of forty-four miles in a single day, and under a July sun in India, to get within stroke of them. Nicholson's little force started at 9 P.M. on July 10, and marched twenty-six miles without a break; after a halt of two hours they started on their second stage of eighteen miles at 10 A.M. During the hottest hour of the afternoon the force camped in a grove of trees, and the men fell, exhausted, into instant slumber.

Presently an officer, awakening, looked round for his general. "He saw Nicholson," says Trotter, "in the middle of the hot, dusty road, sitting bolt upright on his horse in the full glare of that July sun, waiting like a sentinel turned to stone for the moment when his men should resume their march!" They might take shelter from the heat, but he scorned it. A march so swift and fierce was followed by an attack equally vehement, Nicholson leading the rush on the enemy's guns in person, and with his own sword cutting literally in two a rebel gunner in the very act of putting his linstock to the touch-hole of his cannon.

The worship of force is natural to the Eastern mind; and, in 1848, when Nicholson was scouring the country between the Attock and the Jhelum, making incredible marches, and shattering with almost incredible valour whole armies with a mere handful of troops, the mingled admiration and dread of the native mind rose to the pieties of a religion. "To this day," a border chief told Younghusband, twelve years after Nicholson was dead, "our women at night wake trembling, and saying they hear the tramp of Nikalsain's war-horse!" A brotherhood of Fakirs renounced all other creeds, and devoted themselves to the worship of "Nikkul-Seyn." They would lie in wait for Nicholson, and fall at his feet with votive offerings.

Nicholson tried to cure their inconvenient piety by a vigorous application of the whip, and flogged them soundly on every opportunity. But this, to the Fakir mind, supplied only another proof of the great Irishman's divinity; and, to quote Herbert Edwardes, "the sect of Nikkul-Seynees remained as devoted as ever. *Sanguis martyrum est semen Ecclesiæ!* On one occasion, after a satisfactory whipping, Nicholson released his devotees on the condition that they would transfer their adoration to John Becher; but as soon as they attained their freedom they resumed their worship of the relentless Nikkul-Seyn." The last of the sect, says Raikes, dug his own grave, and was found dead in it shortly after the news came that Nicholson had fallen at Delhi.

Nicholson's ardour had made him outride the movable column he was bringing up to reinforce the besiegers; but on August 14, with drums beating and flags flying, and welcomed with cheers by the whole camp, that gallant little force marched in. It consisted of the 52nd, 680 strong, a wing of the 61st, the second Punjaub Infantry, with some Beloochees and military police, and a field battery.

Work for such a force, and under such a leader, was quickly found. The siege train intended to breach the walls of Delhi was slowly creeping along the road from the Punjaub, and with unusual daring a great force of mutineers marched from Delhi to intercept this convoy. The movement was detected, and on August 25 Nicholson, with 1600 infantry, 400 cavalry, and a battery of field guns, set out to cut off the Sepoy force.

BRIGADIER-GENERAL JOHN NICHOLSON

From a portrait in the East India United Service Club

The rain fell in ceaseless, wind-blown sheets, as only Indian rain can fall. The country to be crossed was mottled with swamps. The roads were mere threads of liquid mud, and the march was of incredible difficulty. The enemy was overtaken at Nujutgurh, after a sort of wading march which lasted twelve hours. "No other man in India," wrote a good soldier afterwards, "would have taken that column to Nujutgurh. An artillery officer told me that at one time the water was over his horses' backs, and he thought they could not possibly get out of their difficulties. But he looked ahead, and saw Nicholson's great form riding steadily on as if nothing was the matter."

The rebels, 6000 strong, held an almost unassailable position, edged round with swamps and crossed in front by a deep and swift stream with an unknown ford. In the dusk, however, Nicholson led his troops across the stream. As they came splashing up from its waters he halted them, and, with his deep, far-reaching voice, told them to withhold their fire till within thirty yards of the enemy. He then led them steadily on, at a foot-pace, over a low hill, and through yet another swamp, while the fire of the enemy grew ever fiercer.

When within twenty yards of the enemy's guns, Nicholson gave the word to charge. A swift volley, and an almost swifter rush, followed. The British in a moment were over the enemy's guns, Nicholson still leading, his gleaming sword, as it rose and fell in desperate strokes, by this time turned bloody red. Gabbett, of the 61st, ran straight at one of the guns, and his men, though eagerly following, could not keep pace with their light-footed officer. He had just reached the gun, fully twenty paces in advance of his men, when his foot slipped, he fell, and was instantly bayoneted by a gigantic Sepoy. With a furious shout—a blast of wrathful passion—his panting men came up, carried the gun, and bayoneted the gunners.

Nicholson had the true genius of a commander. The moment he had carried the guns he swung to the left; and led his men in a rush for a bridge across the canal in the enemy's rear, which formed their only line of retreat to Delhi. An Indian force is always peculiarly sensitive to a stroke at its line of retreat, and the moment Nicholson's strategy was understood the Sepoy army resolved itself into a flying mob, eager only to outrun the British in the race for the bridge. Nicholson captured thirteen guns, killed or wounded 800 of the enemy, and drove the rest, a mob of terrified fugitives, to Delhi, his own casualties amounting to sixty.

His men had outmarched their supplies, and they had at once to retrace their steps to Delhi. They had marched thirty-five miles, under furious rains and across muddy roads, and had beaten a force three times stronger than their own, holding an almost impregnable position, and had done it all in less than forty hours, during twenty-four of which they had been without food. It was a great feat, and as the footsore, mud-splashed soldiers came limping into the camp all the regimental bands on the Ridge turned out to play them in.

The few hours preceding Nicholson's arrival at the Ridge were the darkest hours of the siege, and some at least of the British leaders were hesitating whether the attempt to carry the city ought not to be abandoned. The circumstances, indeed, were such as might well strain human fortitude to the breaking point. The British force of all arms, native and European, was under 6000. Its scanty and light artillery commanded only two out of the seven gates of Delhi. The siege, in fact, was, as one writer puts it, "a struggle between a mere handful of men on an open ridge and a host behind massive and well-fortified walls." Cholera was raging among the British. The 52nd on August 14 marched into camp 680 strong with only six sick. On September 14—only four weeks later, that is—the effectives of the regiment were only 240 of all ranks. Nearly two men out of every three had gone down!

There was treachery, too, in Wilson's scanty force. Their plans were betrayed to the enemy. The slaughter amongst the British officers in the native regiments was such as could only be explained by the fact that they were shot down by their own men from behind, rather than by their open foes in the front. The one good service General Reed did during his brief interval of command was to dismiss from the camp some suspected regiments.

Archdale Wilson's nerve, like that of Barnard and of Reed, his predecessors, was shaken by the terrific strain of the siege, and he contemplated abandoning it. "Wilson's head is going," wrote Nicholson to Lawrence on September 7; "he says so himself, and it is quite evident he speaks the truth." It was due chiefly to John Lawrence's clear judgment and iron strength of will that a step so evil and perilous was not taken. Lawrence had flung his last coin, his last cartridge, his last man into the siege, and he warned Wilson that the whole fate of the British in India depended on an immediate assault. "Every day," he wrote, "disaffection and mutiny spread. Every day adds to the danger of the native princes taking part against us." The loyalty of the Sikhs themselves was strained to the breaking point. Had the British flag fallen back from the Ridge, not merely would Delhi have poured out its armed host, 50,000 strong, but every village in the north-west would have risen, and the tragedy of the Khyber Pass might have been repeated, on a vaster scale, upon the plains of Hindustan. The banks of the Jumna might have seen such a spectacle as Cabul once witnessed.

But there were brave men on the Ridge itself, trained in Lawrence's school, and in whom the spirit of John Lawrence burned with clear and steady flame. Baird Smith and Neville Chamberlain, Norman and Nicholson, and many another, knew that the fortunes and honour of England hung on the capture of Delhi. Lord Roberts tells a curious and wild story that shows what was Nicholson's temper at this crisis:—

> I was sitting in Nicholson's tent before he set out to attend the council. He had been talking to me in confidential terms of personal matters, and ended by telling me of his intention to take a very unusual step should the council fail to arrive at any fixed determination regarding the assault. "Delhi must be taken," he said, "and it is absolutely essential that this should be done at once; and, if Wilson hesitates longer, I intend to propose at to-day's meeting that he should be superseded." I was greatly startled, and ventured to remark that, as Chamberlain was *hors de combat* from his wound, Wilson's removal would leave him (Nicholson) senior officer with the force. He smiled as he answered, "I have not overlooked that fact. I shall make it perfectly clear that, under the circumstances, I could not possibly accept the command my-

> self, and I shall propose that it be given to Campbell of the 52nd. I am prepared to serve under him for the time being, so no one can ever accuse me of being influenced by personal motives."

Roberts puts on record his "confident belief" that Nicholson would have carried out this daring scheme, and he adds that, in his deliberate judgment, Nicholson was right. Discipline in a crisis so stern counts for less than the public honour and the national safety.

It is to be noted that on a still earlier date, September 11—Nicholson had written to Lawrence telling him Wilson was talking of withdrawing the guns and giving up the siege. "Had Wilson carried out his threat of withdrawing the guns," adds Nicholson, "I was quite prepared to appeal to the army to set him aside, and elect a successor. I have seen lots of useless generals in my day; but such an ignorant, croaking obstructive as he is, I have never hitherto met with!"

Fortunately, Wilson found a tonic in the spirit of the men who sat round his council-table. "The force," he wrote to the Chief Commissioner, "will die at their post." Reinforcements came creeping in, till the forces on the Ridge rose to 8748 men, of whom, however, less than half were British. The battering-train from Umballa, too, safely reached the camp. It consisted of six 24-pounders, eight 18-pounders, and four 8-inch howitzers, with 1000 rounds of ammunition per piece. The huge convoy, with its tumbrils and ammunition-carts, sprawled over thirteen miles of road, and formed an amazing evidence of the energy and resources of John Lawrence.

Now at last the siege really began. Ground was broken for the new batteries on September 7, at a distance of 700 yards from the walls, and each battery, as it was armed, broke into wrathful thunder on the city. Each succeeding battery, too, was pushed up closer to the enemy's defences. Thus Major Scott's battery was pushed up to within 180 yards of the wall, and the heavy guns to arm it had to be dragged up under angry blasts of musketry fire. No fewer than thirty-nine men in this single battery were struck down during the first night of its construction! A section of No. 1 Battery took fire under the constant flash of its own guns, and, as the dancing flames rose up from it, the enemy turned on the burning spot every gun that could be brought to bear. The only way to quench the fire was to take sand-bags to the top of the battery, cut them open, and smother the fire with streams of sand.

A Ghoorka officer named Lockhart called for volunteers, and leaped upon the top of the battery, exposed, without shelter, to a storm of cannon balls and musket bullets. Half-a-dozen Ghoorkas instantly followed him. Four out of the seven men—including Lockhart himself—were shot down, but the fire was quenched.

The fire of the batteries was maintained with amazing energy and daring until September 13. Colonel Brind, for example, records that he never took off his clothes or left his guns from the moment they opened on the 8th to the 14th inst.

CHAPTER XI

DELHI: THE LEAP ON THE CITY

On September 13 four engineer officers—Medley and Lang, Greathed and Home—undertook the perilous task of examining the breaches in the enemy's defences. Medley and Lang were detailed to examine the Cashmere Bastion, and Lang asked to be allowed to go while it was yet daylight. Leave was granted; and, with an escort of four men of the 60th, he crept to the edge of the cover on the British front, then coolly ran up the glacis and sat down upon the top of the counterscarp, under a heavy fire, studying the ditch and the two breaches beyond, and returned unhurt, to pronounce the breach practicable! It was necessary, however, to ascertain the depth of the ditch, and Lang and Medley were sent again, after nightfall, on this business.

Medley himself may tell the story of the daring adventure:—

> It was a bright, starlight night, with no moon, and the roar of the batteries, and clear, abrupt reports of the shells from the mortars, alone broke the stillness of the scene; while the flashes of the rockets, carcasses, and fireballs lighting up the air ever and anon made a really beautiful spectacle. The ghurees struck ten, and, as preconcerted, the fire of the batteries suddenly ceased. Our party was in readiness. We drew swords, felt that our revolvers were ready to hand, and, leaving the shelter of the picquet, such as it was, advanced stealthily into the enemy's country.... With the six men who were to accompany us, Lang and I emerged into the open, and pushed straight for the breach. In five minutes we found ourselves on the edge of the ditch, the dark mass of the Cashmere Bastion immediately on the other side, and the breach distinctly discernible. Not a soul was in sight. The counterscarp was sixteen feet deep, and steep. Lang slid down first, I passed down the ladder, and, taking two men out of the six, descended after him, leaving the other four on the cope to cover our retreat.
>
> Two minutes more and we should have been at the top of the breach. But, quiet as we had been, the enemy were on the watch, and we heard several men running from the left towards the breach. We therefore reascended, though with some difficulty, and, throwing ourselves down on the grass, waited in silence for what was to happen. A number of figures immediately appeared

> on the top of the breach, their forms clearly discernible against the bright sky, and not twenty yards distant. We, however, were in the deep shade, and they could not, apparently, see us. They conversed in a low tone, and presently we heard the ring of their steel ramrods as they loaded. We waited quietly, hoping that they would go away, when another attempt might be made. Meanwhile, we could see that the breach was a good one, the slope being easy of ascent, and that there were no guns on the flank. We knew by experience, too, that the ditch was easy of descent. After waiting, therefore, some minutes longer, I gave the signal. The whole of us jumped up at once and ran back towards our own ground. Directly we were discovered a volley was sent after us. The balls came whizzing about our ears, but no one was touched.

The other engineers performed their task with equal coolness and daring, and at midnight all the breaches were reported practicable, and it was resolved that the assault should be made in the morning.

Nicholson, at the head of a column of 1000 men—of whom 300 belonged to the 75th—was to carry the breach near the Cashmere Bastion. The second column, under Brigadier Jones, composed of the 8th, the 2nd Bengal Fusileers, and the 4th Sikhs—850 in all—was to assail the gap near the Water Bastion. The third column, 950 strong, under Campbell, of the 52nd, was to blow in the Cashmere Gate and fight its way into the city. The fourth column, under Major Reid, made up of the Guides' Infantry, Ghoorkas, and men from the picquets, was to break in an entrance by the Lahore Gate. A reserve column, 1000 strong, under Brigadier Longfield, of the 8th, was to feed the attack at any point where help was required. Five thousand men were thus to fling themselves on a great city held by 50,000!

It was three o'clock in the morning, the stars still burning in the measureless depths of the Indian sky, when the columns stood in grim silence ready for the assault. The chaplain of the forces records that in not a few of the tents the service for the day was read before the men went out into the darkness to join the columns. The lesson for the day, as it happened, was Nahum iii., and the opening verse runs, "Woe to the bloody city! It is full of lies and robbery.... Behold, I am against thee, saith the Lord of Hosts."

How do men feel who gather at such an hour and for such a deed? Lord Roberts quotes from a brother officer's diary a curious little picture of British soldiers preparing themselves for one of the most daring exploits in the history of war:—

> We each of us looked carefully to the reloading of our pistols, filling of flasks and getting as good protection as possible for our heads, which would be exposed so much going up the ladders. I wound two puggaries or turbans round my old forage cap, with the last letter from the hills in the top, and committed myself to the care of Providence. There was not much sleep that night in our camp. I dropped off now and then, but never for long, and whenever I woke I could see that there was a light in more than one of

> the officers' tents, and talking was going on in a low tone amongst the men, the snapping of a lock or the springing of a ramrod sounding far in the still air, telling of preparation for the coming strife. A little after midnight we fell in as quickly as possible, and by the light of a lantern the orders for the assault were then read to the men. Any officer or man who might be wounded was to be left where he fell; no one was to step from the ranks to help him, as there were no men to spare. If the assault were successful he would be taken away in the doolies, or litters, and carried to the rear, or wherever he could best receive medical assistance. If we failed, wounded and sound should be prepared to bear the worst. No prisoners were to be made, as we had no one to guard them, and care was to be taken that no women or children were injured. To this the men answered at once by "No fear, sir." The officers now pledged their honour, on their swords, to abide by these orders, and the men then promised to follow their example.
>
> At this moment, just as the regiment was about to march off, Father Bertrand came up in his vestments, and, addressing the Colonel, begged for permission to bless the regiment, saying, "We may differ, some of us, in matters of religion, but the blessing of an old man and a clergyman can do nothing but good." The colonel at once assented, and Father Bertrand, lifting his hands to heaven, blessed the regiment in a most impressive manner, offering up at the same time a prayer for our success, and for mercy on the souls of those soon to die.

The dash on the city was to have taken place at three o'clock in the morning, but it was difficult to collect all the men from the picquets who were to take part in the assault, and day was breaking before the columns were complete. The engineers, closely examining the breaches, found that during the night the Sepoys had blocked up the gaps with sand-bags and had improvised *chevaux de frise*. The attack was accordingly held back for a few minutes while the British batteries reopened for the purpose of smashing the new defences.

The sun was clear of the horizon when, at a signal, the batteries ceased. A sudden silence fell on the slope of the Ridge and on the enemy's wall. A thrill ran through the waiting columns, as each man, like a hound on the leash, braced himself up for the desperate rush. Nicholson had been standing, silent and alone, in front of his column; and now with a gesture of his hand he gave the signal. A shout, sudden, and stern, and fierce, broke through the air. It came from the 60th Rifles, who with a vehement cheer ran out to the front in skirmishing order, and in a moment the four columns were in swift and orderly movement. Then the enemy's guns from every point broke into flame!

It is impossible to compress into a few paragraphs of cold type the story of that great assault; the fire and passion of the charge, the stubborn fury of the defence, the long, mad struggle through the streets. And the fact that four desperate combats at as many separate points broke out at once makes it still more difficult to give any single connected picture of the scene.

Nicholson led column No. 1 steadily forward till it reached the edge of the jungle. Then the engineers and storming party went forward at a run. They reached the crest of the glacis, and stood there under a perfect blaze of musketry. The stormers had outrun the ladder parties! The ditch gaped sixteen feet wide below them. The breach in front was crowded with dark figures, shouting, firing, hurling stones, all in a tempest of Eastern fury. The ladders were quickly up, and were dropped into the ditch. The men leaped down, and almost with the same impulse swept up the further side—Nicholson's tall figure leading—and men and officers, contending madly with each other who should be first, raced up the broken slope of the breach, dashed the Sepoys back in confused flight, and gained the city!

The second column was as gallantly led as the first, and met with an almost fiercer resistance. At the signal its storming party ran out from the shelter of the Customs house. The two engineer officers, Greathed and Ovenden, and twenty-nine men out of the thirty-nine who formed the ladder parties were instantly shot down; but the attack never paused for an instant. The men of the 8th, the Sikhs, and the Fusileers came on with a silent speed and fury that nothing could stop. The ditch was crossed, as with a single effort. One officer—little more than a lad—Ensign Phillips, with soldierly quickness, and with the help of a few riflemen, swung round the guns on the Water Bastion, and opened fire with them on the Sepoys themselves.

The assault of the third column, directed at the Cashmere Gate, is, perhaps, the most picturesque and well-known incident in the wild story of that morning. This column did not find a breach; one had to be made! Campbell brought up his column within sight of the Cashmere Gate, but under cover; then, at the signal, a little cluster of soldiers ran out towards the gate. Its first section consisted of Home, of the Engineers, with two sergeants and ten sappers, each man carrying a bag containing twenty-five pounds of gunpowder. Behind them ran a firing party of the 52nd, under Salkeld. The sight of that little, daring handful of men, charging straight for the gate, so amazed the Sepoys that for a few moments they stared at them without firing. Then, from the wall on either side of the gate, from above the gate itself, and from an open wicket in its broad expanse, broke a sustained and angry blaze of musketry!

To run steadily on in the teeth of such a fire was a feat of amazing courage. But, Home leading, the little cluster of heroes never faltered. The bridge in front of the gate had been almost completely destroyed, a single beam being stretched across the ditch; and, in single file, each man carrying his bag of powder, Home's party—by this time reduced to nearly one-half of its number—crossed, flung down the bags of powder at the foot of the gate, and then leaped into the ditch for cover, leaving the firing party behind to make the explosion.

Salkeld came up at a run, carrying the port-fire in his hand, his men, with bent heads, racing beside him. Salkeld fell, shot through the leg and arm; but, like the runner in Greek games, he handed the port-fire as he fell to Corporal Burgess, who in turn, as he bent over the powder, was shot dead. Lord Roberts says that in falling he yet ignited the powder. Malleson, on the other hand, says that Sergeant Carmichael snatched the port-fire from the dying hand of Burgess, lit the fuse, and then, in his turn, fell mortally wounded. On this another brave fellow named Smith, thinking Carmichael had failed, ran forward to seize the port-fire, but saw the fuse burning, and leaped into the ditch, just in time to escape the explosion.

In a moment there was a blast as of thunder, and—not the gate unfortunately, but merely the little wicket in it, had vanished! The bugler from the ditch sounded the advance; but such was the tumult of battle now raging that the storming parties of the 52nd, waiting eagerly to make their rush, heard neither the explosion nor the bugle-call. Campbell, their colonel, however, had seen the flame of the explosion, and gave the word. The storming party and the supports, all intermixed, ran forward at the double, they crossed, man after man, the single beam remaining of the bridge, and crept through the wicket. They found within the gate an overturned cannon, and some blackened Sepoy corpses. The main body followed, and from the two breaches and the Cashmere Gate the three columns met, breathless, confused, but triumphant, in the open space between the Cashmere Gate and the church.

The fourth column alone of the assaulting parties practically failed. A battle is always rich in blunders; and the guns, which were to have accompanied the column, somehow failed to arrive, and Reid, its commander, pushed on without them. He had to face an unbroken wall 18 feet high, lined with guns and marksmen. Reid himself fell, wounded and insensible, and there was some confusion as to who should take his place as leader. It was expected that the Lahore Gate would have been opened from within by the advance of the first column, but, before the Lahore Gate was reached from within the city by the British, the fourth column found itself unable to sustain the murderous fire from the walls, and fell back into cover.

The Sepoys, in their exultation, actually ventured upon a sally, and Hope Grant had to bring up the scanty cavalry of the camp to check the advance of the enemy.

The cavalry could not charge, for this would bring them under the fire of the walls; they would not withdraw, for this would uncover the camp. They could only sit grimly in their saddles, and hold back the enemy by the menace of their presence, while men and horses went down unceasingly under the sleet of fire which broke over them. "For more than two hours," says Hodson, "we had to sit on our horses, under the heaviest fire, without the chance of doing anything. My young regiment behaved admirably, as did all hands. The slaughter was great. Lamb's troop lost twenty-seven men out of forty-eight, and nineteen horses, and the whole cavalry suffered in the same proportion."

Hope Grant tells how he praised the 9th Lancers for their cool steadiness, and the men answered from the ranks that they were ready to stand as long as he chose. "Hodson," says one officer who was present, "sat like a man carved in stone, apparently as unconcerned as the sentries at the Horse Guards, and only by his eyes and his ready hand, whenever occasion offered, could you have told that he was in deadly peril, and the balls flying among us as thick as hail!"

Delhi in shape roughly resembles an egg, and, in the assault we have described, the British had cracked, so to speak, the small end. Inside the Cashmere Gate was a comparatively clear space, a church, a Hindoo temple, and a mosque being scattered along its southern boundary. These owed their existence to the somewhat mixed piety of James Skinner, a gallant soldier, who played a brilliant part in Clive's wars. His mother was a Hindoo lady, his wife was a Mohammedan; and, being severely wounded in some engagement, Skinner vowed, if he recovered, he would build three places of worship—a church, a temple, and a mosque! And the three buildings which stand opposite the Cashmere Gate are the fruits of that very composite act of piety. The three assaulting columns, in broken order and sadly reduced in numbers, but in resolute fighting mood, were re-formed in the open space in front of these buildings.

The third column, under Colonel Campbell, cleared the buildings on its left front, and then pushed forward on its perilous way straight through the centre of the city towards the Jumma Musjid, a huge mosque that lifted its great roof high above the streets and gardens of the city more than two miles distant. The first and second columns, now practically forming one, swung to the right, and, following the curve of the "egg" to which we compared Delhi, proceeded to clear what was called the Rampart Road, a narrow lane running immediately within the wall round the whole city. It was intended to push along this lane till the Lahore Gate was reached and seized. The Lahore Gate is the principal entrance into the city, the main street—the Chandin Chouk, the Silver Bazaar—runs from it to the King's Palace, bisecting the "egg" which forms the city. If this gate were carried, Delhi was practically in the British possession.

The column, led by Jones, pushed eagerly on. The Moree Gate and the Cabul Gate were seized, the guns on the ramparts were captured, and the leading files of the advance came in sight of the Lahore Gate. A lane, a little more than two hundred and fifty yards long, led to it; but that narrow, crooked path was "a valley of death" more cruel and bloody than that down which Cardigan's Light Cavalry rode in the famous charge at Balaclava. The city wall itself formed the boundary of the lane on the right; the left was formed by a mass of houses, with flat roofs and parapets, crowded with riflemen. The lane was scarcely ten yards wide at its broadest part; in places it was narrowed to three feet by the projecting buttresses of the wall.

About a hundred and fifty yards up the lane was planted a brass gun, sheltered by a bullet-proof screen. At the further extremity of the lane, where the ground rose, was a second gun, placed so as to cover the first, and itself covered by a bullet-proof screen. Then, like a massive wall, crossing the head of the lane, rose the great Burn Bastion, heavily armed, and capable of holding a thousand men. A force of some 8000 men, too, had just poured into the city through the Lahore and Ajmeer Gates, returning from the sally they had made on Reid's column; and these swarmed round the side and head of the lane to hold it against the British.

Never, perhaps, did soldiers undertake a more desperate feat than that of fighting a way through this "gate of hell," held by Sepoys, it will be noted, full of triumph, owing to their repulse of the attack of the fourth column under Reid already described. But never was a desperate deed more gallantly attempted.

The attacking party was formed of the 1st Bengal Fusileers; and, their officers leading, the men ran with a dash at the lane. They were scourged with fire from the roofs to the left; the guns in their front swept the lane with grape. But the men never faltered. They took the first gun with a rush, and raced on for the second. But the lane narrowed, and the "jam" checked the speed of the men. The fire of the enemy, concentrated on a front so narrow, was murderous. Stones and round shot thrown by hand from the roofs and parapets of the houses were added to musketry bullets and grape, and the stormers fell back, panting and bleeding, but still full of the wrath of battle, and leaving the body of many a slain comrade scattered along the lane.

Two or three men refused to turn back, and actually reached the screen through which the further gun was fired. One of these was Lieutenant Butler, of the 1st Bengal Fusileers. As he came at the run through the white smoke he struck the screen heavily with his body; at that moment two Sepoys on the inner side thrust through the screen with their bayonets. The shining deadly points of steel passed on either side of Butler's body, and he was pinned between them as between the suddenly appearing prongs of a fork! Butler, twisting his head, saw through a loophole the faces of the two Sepoys who held the bayonets, and who were still vehemently pushing, under the belief that they held their enemy impaled. With his revolver he coolly shot them both, and then fell back, pelted with bullets, but, somehow, unhurt, to his comrades, who were reforming for a second charge at the head of the lane.

On came the Fusileers again, a cluster of officers leading, well in advance of their men. Major Jacob, who commanded the regiment, raced in that heroic group. Speke was there, the brother of the African explorer; Greville, Wemyss, and the gallant Butler once again. The first gun in the lane was captured once more, and Greville, a cool and skilful soldier, promptly spiked it. But the interval betwixt the first gun and the second, had to be crossed. It was only a hundred yards, but on every foot of it a ceaseless and fiery hail of shot was beating. The officers, as they led, went down one by one. Jacob, one of the most gallant soldiers of the whole siege, fell, mortally wounded. Jacob's special quality as a soldier was a strangely gentle but heroic coolness. The flame of battle left him at the temperature of an icicle; its thunder did not quicken his pulse by a single beat, and his soldiers had an absolute and exultant confidence in the quick sight, the swift action, the unfaltering composure of their gallant commander. Some of his men halted to pick him up when he fell, but he called to them to leave him, and press forward. Six other officers, one after another, were struck down; the rush slackened, it paused, the men ebbed sullenly back; the second attack had failed!

Nicholson, as the officer in general command of the assaulting columns, might well have remained at the Cashmere Gate, controlling the movements of the columns; but his eager, vehement spirit carried him always to the fighting front. He first accompanied Campbell's column on its perilous march, but then rejoined his own proper column just as it came in sight of the Lahore Gate. The officers immediately about him—men themselves of the highest daring—advised that, as the attack of the fourth column had failed, it would be wise strategy to hold strongly the portion of the city they had carried and reorganise another general assault. They had done enough for the day. Their men had lost heavily, and were exhausted. They were in ignorance of the fortunes of the other columns.

But Nicholson's fiery spirit was impatient of half measures or of delays. He was eager, moreover, to check the dangerous elation caused amongst the Sepoys by their repulse of the fourth column. So he resolutely launched a new assault on the Lahore Gate. How gallantly the officers led in an attack which yet their judgment condemned has been told.

Nicholson watched the twice-repeated rush of the Fusileers, and the fall, one by one, of the officers who led them. When the men for a second time fell back, Nicholson himself sprang into the lane, and, waving his sword, called on his men, with the deep, vibrating voice all knew, to follow their general. But even while he spoke, his sword pointing up the lane, his face, full of the passion of battle, turned towards the broken, staggering front of his men, a Sepoy leaned from the window of a house close by, pointed his musket across a distance of little more than three yards at Nicholson's tall and stately figure, and shot him through the body. Nicholson fell. The wound was mortal; but, raising himself up on his elbow, he still called on the men to "go on." He rejected impatiently the eager help that was offered to him, and declared he would lie there till the lane was carried. But, as Kaye puts it, he was asking dying what he had asked living—that which was all but impossible.

Colonel Graydon tells how he stooped over the fallen Nicholson, and begged to be allowed to convey him to a place of safety; but Nicholson declared "he would allow no man to remove him, but would die there." It was, in fact, a characteristic flash of chivalry that made Nicholson at last consent to be removed. He would allow no one to touch him, says Trotter, "except Captain Hay, of the 60th Native Infantry, with whom he was not upon friendly terms. 'I will make up my difference with you, Hay,' he gasped out. 'I will let you take me back.'"

The lane was strewn with the British dead. To carry it without artillery was hopeless. There were no better soldiers on the Ridge than the 1st Bengal Fusileers—"the dear old dirty-shirts" of Lord Lake. When they, on the morning of that day, broke through the embrasures of the Cashmere battery, one of their officers has left on record the statement that "the Sepoys fled as they saw the white faces of the Fusileers looking sternly at them." They fled, that is, not from thrust of steel and flash of musket, but before the mere menace of those threatening, war-hardened countenances! The 1st, as a matter of fact, had their muskets slung behind, to enable them to use their hands in climbing the breach, and so, when they came up the crest of the breach and through the embrasures, the men had no muskets in their hands. The threat written on their faces literally put the Sepoys to flight. Where such men as these had failed, what troops could succeed?

The column fell slowly and sullenly back to the Cabul Gate, the wounded being sent to the rear. Lord Roberts tells us that, being sent by Wilson to ascertain how affairs were going on in the city, he observed as he rode through the Cashmere Gate a doolie by the side of the road without bearers, and with evidently a wounded man inside. He says:—

> I dismounted to see if I could be of any use to the occupant, when I found, to my grief and consternation, that it was John Nicholson, with death written on his face. He told me that the bearers had put the doolie down and had gone off to plunder; that he was in great pain, and wished to be taken to the hospital. He was lying on his back, no wound was visible, and but for the pallor of his face, always colourless, there was no sign of the agony he must have been enduring. On my expressing a hope that he was not seriously wounded, he said, "I am dying; there is no chance for me." The sight of that great man lying helpless and on the point of death was almost more than I could bear. Other men had daily died around me, friends and comrades had been killed beside me, but I never felt as I felt then—to lose Nicholson seemed to me at that moment to lose everything.

Nicholson's fall, it is striking to note, impressed every one in that tiny and heroic army at Delhi exactly as it impressed Roberts. He lingered through all the days of slow, stubborn, resolute fighting, which won Delhi; but day by day the news about Nicholson's fluctuating life was almost more important than the tidings that this position or that had been carried. Nicholson was a man with Clive's genius for battle and mastery over men, while in the qualities of chivalry and honour he deserved to be classed with Outram or Havelock. He was only thirty-seven when he died; what fame he might have won, had he lived, no man can tell. He was certainly one of the greatest soldiers the English-speaking race has produced.

Many monuments have been erected to Nicholson; one over his actual grave, another—with an unfortunately elaborate inscription—in the parish church at Lisburn. But the fittest and most impressive monument is a plain obelisk erected on the crest of the Margalla Pass, the scene, in 1848, of one of his most daring exploits. There in the wild border pass stands the great stone pillar, and round it still gathers many a native tradition of the daring and might of the great sahib. Sir Donald Macnab says that when the worshippers of "Nikkul-Seyn" in Hazara heard of his death, "they came together to lament, and one of them stood forth and said there was no gain from living in a world that no longer held Nikalsain. So he cut his throat deliberately and died." The others, however, reflected that this was not the way to serve their great guru; they must learn to worship "Nikalsain's God"; and the entire sect actually accepted Christianity on the evidence of Nicholson's personality!

Campbell's column, meanwhile, had fought its way across two-thirds of the city, and come in sight of the massive arched gateway of the Jumma Musjid. But the engineers that accompanied the column had fallen; Campbell had no artillery to batter down the great gate of the mosque, and no bags of powder with which to blow it up. He was, however, a stubborn Scottish veteran, and he clung to his position in front of the mosque till he learnt of the failure to carry the Lahore Gate. Then, judging with soldierly coolness that it would be impossible to hold unsupported the enormously advanced position he had won, he fell back in leisurely fashion till he came into touch with the reserve column at the Cashmere Gate.

The British columns had been fighting for over six hours, and had lost 66 officers and 1104 men, or very nearly every fourth man in the assaulting force. Amongst the fallen, too, were many of the most daring spirits in the whole force, the men who were the natural leaders in every desperate enterprise. Less than 4000 of the brave men who followed Nicholson and Jones and Campbell across the breaches or through the Cashmere Gate that morning remained unwounded, and there were 40,000 Sepoys yet in Delhi! Of the great "egg," too, which formed the city, the British held only the tiny northern extremity.

Under these conditions Wilson's nerve once more failed him. He doubted whether he ought to persist in the assault. Was it not safer to fall back on the Ridge? Repeatedly, in fact, through the days of stubborn fighting which followed, Wilson meditated the fatal policy of retreat. He was worn-out in mind and body. His nerve had failed at Meerut when the Mutiny first broke out; it threatened to fail again here at Delhi, in the very crisis of the assault. To walk a few steps exhausted him. And it was fortunate for the honour of England and the fate of India that Wilson had round him at that crisis men of sterner fibre than his own. Some one told Nicholson, as he lay on his death-bed, of Wilson's hesitations. "Thank God," whispered Nicholson. "I have strength yet to shoot him if necessary!"

Wilberforce, in his "Unrecorded Chapter of the Indian Mutiny," gives a somewhat absurd, and not too credible, account of the incident which, according to him, kept Wilson's nerve steady at that crisis. The 52nd, after so many hours of fighting, had fallen back on the reserve at the Cashmere Gate, and Wilberforce, who belonged to that regiment, was occupied with a brother officer in compounding a "long" glass of brandy and soda to quench his thirst. His companion poured in so generous an allowance of brandy that he was afraid to drink it. He says:—

> Not liking to waste it, we looked round us, and saw a group of officers on the steps of the church, apparently engaged in an animated conversation. Among them was an old man, who looked as if a good "peg" (the common term for a brandy and soda) would do him good. Drawing, therefore, nearer the group, in order to offer the "peg" to the old officer, we heard our colonel say, "All I can say is that I won't retire, but will hold the walls with my regiment." I then offered our "peg" to the old officer, whom we afterwards knew to be General Wilson. He accepted it, drank it off, and a few minutes after we heard him say, "You are quite right—to retire would be to court disaster; we will stay where we are!"

"On such little matters," Wilberforce gravely reflects, "great events often depend!" The course of British history in India, in a word, was decisively affected by that accidental glass of brandy and soda he offered to General Wilson! It tightened his shaken nerves to the key of resolution! Wilberforce's book belongs rather to the realm of fiction than of grave history, and his history-making glass of brandy and soda may be dismissed as a flight of fancy. It was the cool judgment and the unfaltering daring of men like Baird Smith and Neville Chamberlain, and other gallant spirits immediately around Wilson, which saved him from the tragedy of a retreat. When Wilson asked Baird Smith whether it was possible to hold the ground they had won, the curt, decisive answer of that fine soldier was, "We *must* hold it!" And that white flame of heroic purpose burnt just as intensely in the whole circle of Wilson's advisers.

The British troops held their position undisturbed on the night of the 14th. The 15th was spent in restoring order and preparing for a new assault. There is a curious conflict of testimony as to whether or not the troops had got out of hand owing to mere drunkenness. It is certain that enormous stores of beer, spirits, and wine were found in that portion of the city held by the British. Lord Roberts says, "I did not see a single drunken man throughout the day of assault, and I visited every position held by our troops within the walls of the city." This bit of evidence seems final. Yet it would be easy to quote a dozen witnesses to prove that there was drunkenness to a perilous extent amongst the troops, and it is certain that Wilson found it expedient to give orders for the destruction of the whole of the vast stores of beer and spirits which had fallen into his hands.

A new plan of attack was devised by the engineers. Batteries were armed with guns captured from the enemy, and a destructive fire maintained on the chief positions yet held in the city. The attacks, too, were now directed, not along the narrow streets and winding lanes of the city, but through the houses themselves. Thus wall after wall was broken through, house after house captured, the Sepoys holding them were bayoneted, and so a stern and bloody path was driven to the Lahore Gate.

On the 16th the famous magazine which Willoughby had blown up, when Delhi fell into the hands of the rebels early in May, was captured, and it was found that Willoughby's heroic act had been only partially successful. The magazine, that is, was less than half destroyed, and the British found in it no fewer than 171 guns, mostly of large calibre, with enormous stores of ammunition. The Sepoys read their doom in the constant flight of shells from the British batteries in the city. They read it, in almost plainer characters, in the stubborn daring with which a path was being blasted through the mass of crowded houses towards the Lahore Gate. And from the southern extremity of the city there commenced a great human leakage, a perpetual dribble of deserting Sepoys and flying budmashes.

Lord Roberts served personally with the force driving its resolute way across houses, courtyards, and lanes, towards the Lahore Gate, and he tells, graphically, the story of its exploits. On September 19, the men had broken their way through to the rear of the Burn Bastion. Only the width of the lane separated them from the bastion itself. The little party, 100 strong—only one-half of them British—gathered round the door that opened on the lane, the engineer officer burst it open, and Gordon, of the 75th Foot, leading, the handful of gallant men dashed across the lane, leaped upon the ramp, raced up it, and jumped into the bastion. They bayoneted or shot its guards, and captured the bastion without losing a man!

The next day, with great daring, Roberts and Lang of the Engineers, following a native guide, crept through the tangle of courtyards and lanes, till they reached the upper room of a house within fifty yards of the Lahore Gate. "From the window of this room," says Roberts, "we could see beneath us the Sepoys lounging about, engaged in cleaning their muskets and other occupations; while some, in a lazy sort of fashion, were acting as sentries over the gateway and two guns, one of which pointed in the direction of the Sabzi Mandi, the other down the lane behind the ramparts, leading to the Burn Bastion and Cabul Gate. I could see from the number on their caps that these Sepoys belonged to the 5th Native Infantry." The troops were brought up silently by the same route, and leaped suddenly on the gate, capturing it, and slaying or putting to terrified flight the Sepoys whom Lang and Roberts had watched in such a mood of careless and opium-fed unconcern only a few minutes before.

The party that captured the Lahore Gate then moved up the great street running from it through the Silver Bazaar—its shops all closed—till they reached the Delhi Bank, which they carried. Another column forced its way into the Jumma Musjid, blowing in its gates without loss.

CHAPTER XII

DELHI: RETRIBUTION

There remained the great palace, the last stronghold of the Mutiny, a building famous in history and in romance. The 60th Rifles were launched against it, the gates were blown open, and the troops broke their way in. They found it practically deserted. The garrison had fled, the king and his household were fugitives, and the clash of British bayonets, the tramp of British feet, rang through the abandoned halls and ruined corridors of the palace of the Mogul.

The flight of the garrison from the imperial palace had been hastened by a very gallant feat of arms. Between the palace and the bridge crossing the Jumna is a strong fort, a sort of outwork to the palace, called the Selingarh. An officer, Lieutenant Aikman, with a party of Wilde's Sikhs, had been despatched to reconnoitre along the river front. Aikman, who knew the ground thoroughly, and who was of a daring temper, determined to make a dash at the Selingarh, and so prevent the escape of the king and his court across the river. With his handful of Sikhs, Aikman carried the Selingarh with one fierce rush, and seized the passage connecting the rear gate of the palace with the fort, thus plugging up that opportunity for flight. The king, with his court, as it happened, had fled already, but as Aikman held the rear gate of the palace, while the 60th Rifles blew in its front gates, all who remained in it were made prisoners.

That the imperial palace should have been carried almost without loss of life seems wonderful. It proves how completely the spirit of the Sepoys had been broken by the fiery valour of the British assaults. Yet even the capture of the palace was marked by some curious, though isolated, examples of courage on the part of the rebels.

Hope Grant, for example, records that a sentry was found at one of the palace gates dressed and equipped according to regulation, and marching up and down on his beat with his musket on his shoulder. "In a museum at Naples," he adds, "is to be seen the skull and helmet of a man who was found buried at his post in a sentry-box in the midst of the lava. The inscription states the occupant to have been a 'brave soldier'; but nothing could have been braver or cooler than the conduct of this Sepoy, who must have known that his fate was sealed." Roberts, who shared in the rush for the palace gates, adds another curious example of Sepoy courage. They found the recesses in the long passage which led to the palace buildings packed with wounded men, but about thirty yards up the passage stood a Sepoy in the uniform of a grenadier of the 37th Native Infantry. The man stood quietly as the British came along the passage, with his musket on his hip. Then he coolly raised his musket and fired at the advancing party, sending his bullet through the helmet of the leading Englishman. Next, dropping his musket to the level, he charged single-handed down on the entire detachment of the 60th, and was killed!

Colonel Jones, who commanded the Rifles, sent a pencilled note to Wilson announcing, with soldier-like brevity, "Blown open the gate and got possession of the palace."

At sunrise on the morning of September 21 a royal salute rang over Delhi, its pulses of deep sound proclaiming to all India that the sacred city, the home and stronghold of the revolt, was once more in British hands. That same day Wilson moved in from his rough camp on the Ridge, and established his headquarters in the Dewan-i-khas, the king's private hall of audience.

But if Delhi was captured, the King of Delhi, with all the leading figures in the Mutiny, yet remained free, and might easily become the centre of new troubles. The rebel commander-in-chief felt that the game was up when the Burn Bastion was carried, and he fled from the city that night, carrying with him most of his troops. He urged the king to flee with him, and to renew the war in the open country, where his name would have all the magical charm of a spell on the imagination of the common people. But the unhappy king was old and tired. His nerve had been dissolved in the sloth and sensualities of an Indian court. His favourite wife strongly opposed flight, in the interests of her child, whom she hoped to see succeeding the king.

The unhappy monarch, in a word, could neither flee nor stay, and he took refuge in a stately cluster of famous buildings named Humayon's Tomb, some seven miles out of Delhi. Hodson, the daring and famous captain of Light Horse, ascertained this, and with some trouble extracted from Wilson permission to attempt the capture of the king, with strict instructions to promise him his life. Taking fifty picked men from his regiment, Hodson rode out on one of the most audacious expeditions ever undertaken.

The road to Humayon's Tomb at one point runs underneath a strong tower, where the king had at first taken refuge, and which was still filled with his adherents. Fierce dark faces looked down from its parapets and from every arrow-slit in its walls as Hodson, with his little cluster of horsemen, rode past. But in the Englishman's stern face and cool, unflurried bearing there was something which awed those who looked on him, and not a shot was fired as the party rode by on their stern errand.

Hodson and his men reached the spot where the tomb lifts its dome of stainless marble high in the air. In one of the chambers of that great pillar sat, trembling, the last heir of the house of Timour; in the cloisters at its foot were some thousands of the servants and hangers-on of the palace, armed and excited.

For two hours Hodson sat in his saddle before the gate, his men posted—a slender chain of cavalry—round the tomb, while messengers passed to and fro between him and the king. "Picture to yourself," said Hodson's brother, when telling the story, "the scene before that magnificent gateway, with the milk-white domes of the tomb towering up from within. One white man, amongst a host of natives, determined to secure his prisoner or perish in the attempt!"

The king at last consented to come out and deliver himself to Hodson, but only on condition that he repeated with his own lips Wilson's promise of safety for his life. Presently the king came out, carried in a bullock-carriage, and Hodson spurred his horse forward and demanded the king's arms. The king asked him whether he were Hodson Bahadur, and if he promised him his life. Hodson gave the required promise, but added grimly that if any attempt were made at a rescue he would shoot the king down like a dog! Then the procession, at a foot walk, moved on to the city, thousands of natives following and gazing in wonder at the lordly figure of that solitary Englishman carrying off their king alone. But Hodson's calm and dauntless bearing acted as a spell on the crowd.

Bit by bit the multitude slunk away, and, with his fifty horsemen and his group of prisoners, Hodson rode up to the Lahore Gate. "What have you got in that palkee?" asked the officer on duty. "Only the King of Delhi!" said Hodson. The clustering guard at the gate were with difficulty kept from cheering. The little group moved up the stately Silver Bazaar to the palace gate, where Hodson delivered over his royal prisoners to the civil officer in charge. "By Jove, Hodson," said that astonished official, "they ought to make you Commander-in-Chief for this!" When Hodson reported his success to Wilson, that general's ungracious and characteristic comment was, "Well, I'm glad you've got him. But I never expected to see either you or him again!"

Hope Grant tells how he went to see the fallen monarch in his prison:—

> He was an old man, said by one of the servants to be ninety years of age, short in stature, slight, very fair for a native, and with a high-bred, delicate-looking cast of features. Truly the dignity had departed from the Great Mogul, whose ancestors had once been lords of princely possessions in India. It might have been supposed that death would have been preferable to such humiliation, but it is wonderful how we all cling to the shreds of life. When I saw the poor old man he was seated on a wretched charpoy, or native bed, with his legs crossed before him, and swinging his body backwards and forwards with an unconscious dreamy look. I asked him one or two questions, and was surprised to hear an unpleasantly vulgar voice answering from behind a small screen. I was told that this proceeded from his begum, or queen, who prevented him from replying, fearful lest he might say something which should compromise their safety.

Sir Richard Temple, who prepared the evidence for the trial of the ex-king of Delhi, paid many visits to the ill-fated monarch during his confinement. "It was a strange sight," he says, "to see the aged man, seated in a darkened chamber of his palace; the finely chiselled features, arched eyebrows, aquiline profile, the sickly pallor of the olive complexion, nervous twitching of the face, delicate fingers counting beads, muttering speech, incoherent language, irritable self-conscious-ness—altogether made up a curious picture. Here sat the last of the Great Moguls, the descendant of emperors two centuries ago ruling the second largest population in the world; who had himself, though a phantom sovereign, been treated with regal honours. He was now about to be tried for his life by judges whose forefathers had sued for favour and protection from his imperial ancestors."

But there still remained uncaptured the two sons and the grandson of the king. The princes had a very evil fame. They had tortured and slain English prisoners. They had been the leading figures in the Mutiny. Their hands were red with innocent blood, the blood of little children and of helpless women. The princes—Mirza Mogul, at one time the commander-in-chief of the rebel forces, Mirza Khejoo Sultan, and Mirza Aboo Bukir, the son of the late heir-apparent—with some 6000 or 7000 followers, had occupied Humayon's Tomb after the king's capture, partly in a mood of fatalistic despair, and partly with the expectation that they might find the same mercy the king had found.

Macdowell, who was second in command of Hodson's Horse, tells how, on September 21, he got a note from Hodson, "Come sharp; bring 100 men." He rode off at once, and, on meeting, Hodson explained that he had ascertained that the three princes were in Humayon's Tomb, and he meant to bring them in.

Hodson rode to the tomb, halted his troop outside it, and sent in a messenger demanding the surrender of the princes. They asked for a promise of their lives, but Hodson sternly refused any such pledge. As Hodson and Macdowell sat, side by side, on their horses, they could hear the stormy shouts of the followers of the princes begging to be led out against the infidels. But Hodson's audacity and iron resolve prevailed, as they prevailed the day before in the case of the king. The princes sent word that they were coming; and presently a small bullock-cart made its appearance. The princes were in it, and behind came some 3000 armed retainers.

Hodson allowed the cart to come up to his line, ordered the driver to move on, and then formed up his troop, by a single, quick movement, between the cart and the crowd. The troopers advanced at a walk upon the crowd, that fell sullenly and reluctantly back. Hodson sent on the cart containing the princes in charge of ten of his men, while he sternly, and step by step, pressed the crowd back into the enclosure surrounding the tomb; then, leaving his men outside, Hodson, with Macdowell and four troopers, rode up the steps into the arch, and called on the crowd to lay down their arms. "There was a murmur," says Macdowell, who tells the story. "He reiterated the command, and (God knows why, I never can understand it!) they commenced doing so." He adds:—

> Now, you see, we didn't want their arms, and under ordinary circumstances would not have risked our lives in so rash a way. But what we wanted was to gain time to get the princes away, for we could have done nothing, had they attacked us, but cut our way back, and very little chance of doing even this successfully. Well, there we stayed for two hours, collecting their arms, and I assure you I thought every moment they would rush upon us. I

> said nothing, but smoked all the time, to show I was unconcerned; but at last, when it was all done, and all the arms collected, put in a cart, and started, Hodson turned to me and said, "We'll go now." Very slowly we mounted, formed up the troop, and cautiously departed, followed by the crowd. We rode along quietly. You will say, why did we not charge them? I merely say, we were one hundred men, and they were fully 6000. I am not exaggerating; the official reports will show you it is all true. As we got about a mile off, Hodson turned to me and said, "Well, Mac, we've got them at last"; and we both gave a sigh of relief. Never in my life, under the heaviest fire, have I been in such imminent danger. Everybody says it is the most dashing and daring thing that has been done for years (not on my part, for I merely obeyed orders, but on Hodson's, who planned and carried it out).

Hodson and Macdowell quickly overtook the cart carrying the princes, but a crowd had gathered round the vehicle, and pressed on the very horses of the troopers. "What shall we do with them?" said Hodson to his lieutenant. Then, answering his own question, he added, "I think we had better shoot them here. We shall never get them in!" And Hodson proceeded to do that daring, cruel, much-abused, much-praised deed.

He halted his troop, put five troopers across the road, in front and behind the cart, ordered the princes to strip; then, taking a carbine from one of his troopers, he shot them with his own hand, first, in a loud voice, explaining to his troopers and the crowd who they were, and what crimes they had done. The shuddering crowd gazed at this tall, stern, inflexible sahib, with his flowing beard, white face, and deep over-mastering voice, shooting one by one their princes; but no hand was lifted in protest.

Hodson showed no hurry. He made the doomed princes strip, that the act might seem an execution, not a murder. He shot them with his own hand, for, had he ordered a trooper to have done it, and the man had hesitated, a moment's pause might have kindled the huge swaying breathless crowd to flame.

Critics in an overwhelming majority condemn Hodson's act. Roberts, whose judgment is mildest, says his feeling is "one of sorrow that such a brilliant soldier should have laid himself open to so much adverse criticism." Hodson himself wrote on the evening of the same day, "I made up my mind at the time to be abused. I was convinced I was right, and when I prepared to run the great physical risk of the attempt I was equally game for the moral risk of praise or blame. These have not been, and are not, times when a man who would serve his country dare hesitate as to the personal consequences to himself of what he thinks his duty."

Perhaps, however, Hodson was scarcely a cool judge as to what "duty" might be in such a case. The outrages which accompanied the Mutiny had kindled his fierce nature into a flame. "If ever I get into Delhi," he had said, weeks before, "the house of Timour won't be worth five minutes' purchase!" Hodson's "five minutes" proved inadequate; but, writing afterwards, on the very day he shot the princes, he recorded, "In twenty-four hours I disposed of the principal members of the house of Timour the Tartar. I am not cruel, but I confess I did rejoice in the opportunity of ridding the earth of these ruffians."

Macdowell writes the epitaph of the princes: "So ended the career of the chiefs of the revolt and of the greatest villains that ever shamed humanity."

The bodies were driven into Delhi and cast on a raised terrace in front of the Kotwallee. Cave-Browne, who was chaplain to the forces at the time, comments on the curious fact that this was the very spot where the worst crimes of the princes had been committed. "It was," he says, "a dire retribution! On the very spot where, four months ago, English women and children had suffered every form of indignity and death, there now lay exposed to the scoff and scorn of the avenging army, three scions of the royal house, who had been chief among the fiends of Delhi."

The story of the siege of Delhi is one of the most wonderful chapters in the history of war. The besieging army never amounted to 10,000 men; it sometimes sank below 5000. For weeks the British had thus to face an enemy exceeding themselves in number sometimes by a ratio of ten to one, and with an overwhelming superiority of artillery. They fought no fewer than thirty-two battles with the enemy, and did not lose one! For three months every man, not sick, in the whole force had to be under arms every day, and sometimes both by night and day. The men were scorched by the heat of the sun, wasted with dysentery and cholera, worn out with toil.

A new and strange perplexity was added to the situation by the fact that many of the native troops on the Ridge were notoriously disloyal. The British officers sometimes ran as much danger of being shot by their own troops behind them as by the Sepoys in front. Early in July the 4th Sikhs were purged of Hindustanis, as these could not be trusted. General Barnard had to abandon one plan of assault on Delhi, because at the last moment he discovered a conspiracy amongst the native soldiers in the camp to join the enemy. The strength of the force was sapped by sickness as well as by disloyalty.

On August 31, for example, out of under 11,000 men 2977 were in hospital. Of their total effective force, nearly 4000—or two out of every five—were killed, or died of wounds received in battle. Yet they never lost heart, never faltered or murmured or failed. And after twelve weeks of such a struggle, they at last stormed in open day a strong city, with walls practically unbreached, and defended by 30,000 revolted Sepoys. This is a record never surpassed, and seldom paralleled, in history!

Months afterwards, Lawrence, looking from the Ridge over the scene of the long and bloody struggle, said to his companion with a sigh, "Think of all the genius and bravery buried here!" The environs of Delhi, the reverse slope of that rocky crest from which the British guns thundered on the rebel city, are indeed sown thick with the graves of brave men who died to maintain the British Empire in India.

CHAPTER XIII

THE STORMING OF LUCKNOW

With the fall of Delhi the tale of the Great Mutiny practically ends. Lucknow, it is true, remained to be captured. The broken forces of the mutineers had to be crushed in detail. A new system of civil administration had to be built up. The famous Company itself vanished—the native prophecy that the *raj* of the Company would last only a hundred years from Plassey thus being curiously fulfilled; and on September 1, 1858—less than a year after Delhi fell—the Queen was proclaimed throughout India as its Sovereign. But Hodson, who in addition to being a great soldier had a wizard-like insight into the real meaning of events, was right when, on the evening of the day on which the British flag was hoisted once more over the royal palace at Delhi, he wrote in his journal: "This day will be a memorable one in the annals of the empire. The restoration of British rule in the East dates from September 20, 1857."

Yet there would be a certain failure in the dramatic completeness of the story were it to end leaving Lucknow in the hands of the rebels. The tale of the storming of the capital of Oude must be added as a pendant to that other great siege which planted the British flag on the walls of Delhi.

There was, in a sense, no "siege" of Lucknow by the British. There was no investment, no formal approaches, no zigzag of trenches. It was a storm, rather than a siege—though the fighting stretched from March 2 to March 21, 1858. But it was the last of the great military operations of the campaign which crushed the Mutiny. The fall of the city left the historic revolt without a centre. The war, henceforth, always excepting the brilliant campaign of Sir Hugh Rose in the Central Provinces, became a guerilla campaign; a campaign of petty sieges, of the hunting down of one Sepoy leader after another, of the rout of this petty body of mutineers, or of that. It is curious to note how great civilians and great soldiers differed in judgment as to the policy of undertaking the recapture of Lucknow at that particular moment. Colin Campbell's strategy was to conduct a cool campaign in the hills of Rohilcund, and leave Lucknow alone for the present. That city would serve as a sort of draining ground, a centre into which all the mutineers would flow; and when cool weather came, Campbell, imprisoning Lucknow in a girdle of converging columns, would destroy or capture the mutineers in one vast "bag." This was leisurely and wary strategy; but it overlooked the political elements in the problem. It was the scheme of a soldier rather than of a statesman. Lucknow, left for months undisturbed, would be a signal of hope for every revolted chief and mutinous Sepoy. It might well take the place of Delhi as the brain and heart of the Mutiny. It would be a sign to all India that the British did not feel themselves strong enough, as yet, to strike at the centre of the rebel power.

The civilian was wiser than the soldier, and Lord Canning's views prevailed. But it is worth noting that Colin Campbell's plan of "bagging" all the mutineers with one vast, far-stretching sweep in Lucknow would have been carried into effect on Lord Canning's lines, but for a double blunder, which marked Campbell's own conduct of the siege.

It was a great task to which the British Commander-in-chief now addressed himself. Lucknow was a huge honeycomb of native houses; a city more than twenty miles in circumference, with a turbulent population calculated variously at from 300,000 to 1,000,000 people. It had a garrison of 130,000 fighting men, with an overwhelming force of artillery. The Sepoy leaders, too, who knew the value of the spade in war, had spent months in making the city, as they believed, impregnable. Both Havelock and Colin Campbell, in fighting their way to the Residency, had broken into the city from the eastern front; and the Sepoys, with a touching simplicity, took it for granted that the third attack on the city would follow the lines of the earlier assaults. The British, that is, would cross the canal, and force a path to the Residency through the great gardens and stately buildings which occupied the space betwixt the mass of the city and the Goomtee; and they accordingly barred this approach by a triple line of formidable defences. The first was a vast flanked rampart, on the inner side of the canal, and to which the canal served as a wet ditch. The second was a great circular earthwork, like the curve of a railway embankment, which enclosed the Mess-house. Behind it rose what was, in fact, the citadel of Lucknow, the Kaisarbagh, or King's Palace. Both these lines stretched from the river on one flank, to the mass of houses which constituted the town, on the other flank. They might be pierced, they could not be turned; and they bristled from flank to flank with heavy guns. The third line was a stupendous earthwork, covering the whole north front of the King's Palace. Its guns swept the narrow space betwixt the palace and the river with their fire.

Each great building along this line of advance was itself a fortress, and everything which ingenuity could suggest, and toil execute, had been done to make the defence formidable. The task of fighting a way across these triple lines, and through this tangle of fortified houses, each girdled with rifle-pits, and loopholed from foundation to roof, might well have been deemed impossible.

In the previous November Colin Campbell had rescued the garrison of the Residency; but he was compelled to surrender Lucknow itself to the rebels. With great wisdom and audacity, however, he clung to the Alumbagh, planting Outram there, with a force of about 4000 men. The Alumbagh, thus held, was a sort of pistol levelled at the head of Lucknow, or a spear threatening its heart. It was a perpetual menace; a sign that the British still kept their hold of the revolted city, and, on some bloody errand of revenge, would speedily return to it. The task of holding a position so perilous exactly suited Outram's cool brain and serene courage. He had nothing of Nicholson's tempestuous valour, or of Hodson's audacious daring. He lacked initiative. The temper which made Nelson, at Copenhagen, put the telescope to his blind eye, when his admiral was trying to call him off from the fight, was one which Outram could hardly have understood; and it was a temper which certainly never stirred in his own blood. But, given a definite task, Outram might be trusted to do it with perfect intelligence, and, if necessary, to die cheerfully in the doing of it.

For three months he held that perilous post in front of Lucknow, a tiny handful of troops bearding a great revolted city, with a garrison of 100,000 fighting men. He was attacked on front and rear and flank, and, more than once, with a force of over 60,000 men. No less than six great attacks, indeed, can be counted. But Outram held his post with exquisite skill and unshaken valour. His troops were veterans; his officers were fighters of unsurpassed quality. Brasyer commanded his Sikhs; Barrow and Wale led his scanty squadrons of horse; Vincent Eyre, Olpherts, and Maude, commanded his guns. With such troops, and such leaders, Outram, for more than three months, held his daring post in front of Lucknow, and beat back, with vast loss of life, the attacks hurled upon him. And the Alumbagh, thus victoriously held, served as a screen, behind which Campbell's forces gathered for the leap on Lucknow.

Colin Campbell was happily delivered from the evil condition which had hitherto fettered all the operations of the British. He was not required to attempt, with a handful of men, the task of a great army. He had under his hands the finest fighting force any British general in India had yet commanded, an army of 31,000 men, with 164 guns. Of these, 9000 were Ghoorkas—the Nepaulese contingent under Jung Bahadur. It was late in reaching the field, and Campbell doubted whether he ought to wait for the Ghoorkas. But here, again, the civilian proved wiser than the soldier. "I am sure," wrote Lord Canning, "we ought to wait for the Jung Bahadur, who would be driven wild to find himself deprived of a share in the work." It was a political gain of the first order to show the greatest fighting prince in India arrayed under the British flag against the Mutiny.

Hope Grant, with the present Lord Roberts as his A.A.G., commanded the cavalry; Archdale Wilson the guns; Napier—afterwards of Magdala fame—the engineers. Outram, Lugard, and Walpole commanded the three infantry divisions. It was a fine army, admirably officered and led, and made a perfect fighting machine. And of all Campbell's generals, no one, perhaps, served him better than did Robert Napier. He supplied the plan of attack, which made the Sepoy defences worthless, and enabled Lucknow to be carried, practically, in fourteen days, and at a loss of only 125 officers and men killed, and less than 600 wounded.

The east front, which was to be attacked, resembled, roughly, a boot laid on its side. A great canal, running north and south, is the sole of the "boot"; the river Goomtee curves round the toe, and, running back sharply to the south, defines the top of the foot, and stretches up to what may be described as the ankle. The road across the Dilkusha bridge pierces the centre of what we have called the "sole," and the triple line of Sepoy defences barred this line of approach. Napier's plan was to bridge the Goomtee, pass a strong force, with heavy guns, in a wide sweep round the "toe" of the boot, on the northern bank of the river. The heavy guns, when placed in position on the north bank, would take in reverse all the Sepoy defences, and smite with a direct and overwhelming fire the chief positions—the

Mess-house, the Secundrabagh, and the Residency, &c., which the Sepoys held. The Sepoy generals had constructed no defences on the north bank of the river, though it was strongly held by the rebel cavalry. Outram was to command the force operating from the north bank of the river. When his guns had swept the Sepoy defences from flank to flank, then the British left would advance, cross the Dilkusha bridge, and fight its way up to the Kaisarbagh and the Residency, Outram, with his flanking gun-fire, always pushing ahead.

LIEUTENANT-GENERAL SIR JAMES OUTRAM, BART., G.C.B.

From a painting by Thomas Brigstock

The British right and left were thus like the two blades of a pair of scissors, thrust through the web of the Sepoy defences; and when the "scissors" closed, those defences would be cut clean through from east to west.

Campbell began his operations on the morning of March 3. Forbes-Mitchell, who stood in the ranks of the 93rd, looked out with a soldier's eye over the domed mosques and sky-piercing minarets of the doomed city, sharp-cut against the morning sky. "I don't think," he writes, "I ever saw a prettier scene." Forbes-Mitchell was not an artist, only a hard-fighting private in the 93rd; but Russell of the *Times*, who was familiar with all the great cities of the world, was just as deeply impressed as Forbes-Mitchell with the aspect that Lucknow wore that fateful morning, when the red tide of war was about to fill and flood its streets. This is how Russell describes the scene: "A vision of palaces, minarets, domes, azure and golden, cupolas, colonnades, long façades of fair perspective, in pillar and column, terraced roofs—all rising up amid a calm, still ocean of the brightest verdure. Look for miles and miles away, and still the ocean spreads, and the towers of the fairy city gleam in its midst. Spires of gold glitter in the sun. Turrets and gilded spheres shine like constellations. There is nothing mean or squalid to be seen. Here is a city more vast than Paris, as it seems, and more brilliant, lying before us."

But there was the grim face of war hidden beneath the mask of smiling beauty which Lucknow presented that March morning. The soldiers, as they stood in their ranks, could see, line beyond line, the frowning Sepoy defences; while, in the foreground, Peel, with his blue-jackets, was getting his heavy 16-pounders into position for the fierce duel about to begin. Colin Campbell's movement on his left, however, was but a feint, designed to mislead the enemy's generals. On the night of the 4th the construction of two bridges across the Goomtee was begun. On the morning of the 5th one of them was completed, and the British infantry crossed, and threw up earthworks to defend the bridge-head. By midnight on the 5th both bridges were complete, with their approaches, and by four o'clock the troops were crossing. Hope Grant, in command of the cavalry, covered their front, and drove back the enemy's horse.

The Queen's Bays, a young regiment that had never yet been engaged, were in the advance. They got out of hand in their ardour, and rode recklessly on a body of Sepoy horse, smashed them with their charge, followed them over-eagerly into broken ground, and under heavy gun-fire. They came back broken from that wild charge, their major, Percy Smith, was killed, and the Bays themselves suffered badly.

Outram, meanwhile, had got round what we have called the "toe" of the boot, and, swinging to the left, followed the curve of the river bank till a point was reached which took the first line of the Sepoy defences beyond the river in reverse. Twenty-two heavy guns had been brought, by this time, across the river, and sites were chosen for two powerful batteries. Nicholson, of the Engineers, tells how he rode with Outram to the river bank, to choose the position of the first battery. "Got close," he writes, "to the end of the enemy's lines, and found we could see into the rear of these works. Poor creatures! They have not a grain of sense. They have thrown up the most tremendous works, and they are absolutely useless." A stroke of clever generalship, in a word, had turned the Sepoy lines into mere paper screens.

A building, called the Chaker Kothi, or Yellow House, had to be carried, as it commanded the site of one of the batteries. Most of the Sepoys holding the building fled when the British attacking party came on, but nine of them stubbornly clung to their post, and they fired so fast, and with so deadly an aim, that they shot down more than their own number before the position was carried. It was only, indeed, by firing salvos from a troop of horse artillery that this stubborn little garrison was driven out of the building at last. Then, from the summit of the Yellow House, a three-storey building, a flag—one of the colours of the Bengal Fusileers—was set up, a signal to the British left wing that Outram's batteries were in position.

On the morning of the 9th, Outram's guns opened on the first line of the Sepoy defences, that to which the canal served as a wet ditch, with a fire that swept it from flank to flank. Campbell was pouring the fire of Peel's guns upon the Martinere, which served as a sort of outwork to the long canal-rampart, and at two o'clock the Highland regiments—the 42nd leading, the 93rd in support—were launched on the enemy's position. The men of the 93rd were too impatient to be content with "supporting" the 42nd, and the two regiments raced down the slope side by side. Earthworks, trenches, rifle-pits were leaped or clambered over, and almost in a moment the Sepoys were in wild flight across the canal. The Highlanders, with the 4th Punjaub Rifles, followed them eagerly, and broke through the enemy's first line.

Outram's first battery, as we have said, was sweeping this line with a cruel flank fire. The Sepoys had been driven from their guns in the batteries that abutted on the river, and they seemed to be deserted. Adrian Hope's men were attacking, at that moment, the farther, or southern, end of the line; and Butler, of the 1st Bengal Fusileers, with four privates, ran down to the bank of the river and tried to attract the attention of the British left, some third of a mile distant; but in vain. The river was sixty yards wide, the current ran swiftly, the farther bank was held by Sepoy batteries; and though no Sepoys could be seen, yet it might well be that scores were crouching under its shelter. Butler, however, with the ready daring of youth, threw off his coat and boots, scrambled down the river bank, plunged into the stream and swam across it. He climbed up the farther bank, mounted the parapet of the abandoned work, and, standing there, waved his arms to the distant Highlanders. It was not a very heroic figure! His wet uniform clung to his limbs, the water was running down hair and face. The Sepoys nigh at hand, opened a sharp fire upon him. But still that damp figure stood erect and cool, showing, clear against the sky-line.

Butler was seen from the British left, and the meaning of his gestures understood; but a staff officer, with more punctiliousness than common sense, objected to the troops moving along the line till orders had been received to that effect. So a brief delay occurred. Still that damp figure stood aloft, shot at from many points, but vehemently signalling. Now the Highlanders and Sikhs came eagerly on, and Butler, having handed over to them the battery which, wet and unarmed, he had captured, scrambled down into the river, and swam back to rejoin his regiment. It was a gallant feat, and the Victoria Cross, which rewarded it, was well earned.

That night the British were content with holding the enemy's first line. On the 10th Campbell, who, for all his hot Scottish temper, was the wariest and most deliberate of generals, was content with pushing Outram's batteries still farther up the north bank, so as to command the Mess-house and the Begum's Palace. On the left, the building known as Banks' House was battered with artillery, and carried. The two blades of the scissors, in a word, had been thrust far up into the city, and now they were to be closed! Betwixt the positions held to the right and to the left, stood the great mass of buildings known as the Begum Kothi, the Begum's Palace. This was strongly held, and the fight which carried it was the most stubborn and bloody of the whole operations of the siege.

The guns played fiercely upon it for hours; by the middle of the afternoon a slight breach had been effected, and it was resolved to assault. Forbes-Mitchell says that the men of the 93rd were finishing their dinner when they noticed a stir amongst the staff officers. The brigadiers were putting their heads together. Suddenly the order was given for the 93rd to "fall in." "This was quietly done, the officers taking their places, the men tightening their belts, and pressing their bonnets firmly on their heads, loosening the ammunition in their pouches, and seeing that the springs of their bayonets held tight." A few seconds were spent in these grim preparations, then came the sharp word of command that stiffened the whole regiment into an attitude of silent eagerness. The Begum's Palace was to be rushed.

It was a block of buildings of vast size and strength. The breach was little more than a scratch in the wall of the gateway, which it needed the activity of a goat to climb, and which only British soldiers, daringly led, would have undertaken to assault in the teeth of a numerous enemy. And there were nearly 5000 Sepoys within that tangle of courts! The storming party consisted of the 93rd and the 4th Punjaub Rifles, led by Adrian Hope. The 93rd led, the Punjaubees were in support, and the rush was fierce and daring. It is said that the adjutant of the 93rd, McBean, cut down with his own sword no less than eleven of the enemy, in forcing his way through the breach; and he won the Victoria Cross by his performance. He was an Inverness ploughman when he enlisted in the 93rd, and he rose through all its ranks until he commanded the regiment.

Captain M'Donald was shot dead while leading his men. His senior lieutenant took the company on, until the charging crowd was stopped by a ditch eighteen feet wide, and from twelve to fourteen feet deep. The stormers leaped, with hardly a pause, into the ditch, but it seemed impossible to climb up the farther bank. Wood, of the Grenadier company, however, clambered on the shoulders of a tall private, and, claymore in hand, mounted the farther side. The spectacle of a Highland bonnet and menacing claymore, making its appearance above the ditch, proved too much for the Sepoys. They fled, and Wood pulled up man after man by the muzzle of his rifle—the rifles, it may be mentioned as an interesting detail, were all loaded, and on full cock! Highlanders and Punjaubees, racing side by side, had now broken into the great palace. Every doorway was barred and loopholed, and the Sepoys fought desperately; but the Highlanders, with the Punjaubees in generous rivalry, broke through barrier after barrier, till they reached the inner square, filled with a mass of Sepoys. "The word," Forbes-Mitchell says, was "keep well together, men, and use the bayonet," and that order was diligently obeyed. The combat raged for over two hours, the pipe-major of the 93rd blowing his pipes shrilly during the whole time. "I knew," he said afterwards, "our boys would fight all the better while they heard the bagpipes." When the main fight was over, in the inner court of the Begum's Palace, alone, over 860 of the enemy lay dead. Colin Campbell himself described it as "the sternest struggle which occurred during the siege."

That most gallant, but ill-fated soldier, Adrian Hope, personally led one of the storming parties. It is said that he got in through a window, up to which he was lifted, and through which he was pushed by his men. He was sent headlong and sprawling upon a group of Sepoys in the dark room inside. That apparition of the huge, red-headed Celt tumbling upon them, sword and pistol in hand, was too much for the Sepoys, and they fled without striking a blow!

Perhaps the most gallant soldier that perished within the blood-splashed courts of Begum Kothi was Hodson, of "Hodson's Horse." Robert Napier tells the story of how, when he was in the act of reconnoitring the breach, he found Hodson suddenly standing beside him, and saying, laughingly, "I am come to take care of you." The two watched the rush of the stormers up the breach, and listened to the sound of the fierce tumult within the walls. Presently, arm-in-arm, they quietly climbed the breach, and found the last embers of the conflict still spluttering within. Napier was called away by some duty and Hodson went forward alone.

At the back of the mosque ran a narrow lane, bordered by rooms in which many of the flying Sepoys had found shelter. Forbes-Mitchell says they had broken open the door of one of these rooms, and saw it was crowded with Sepoys. He placed some of his party on each side of the door, and sent back two men to the breach to get a few bags of gunpowder, with slow matches fixed, intending to light one of these and fling it into the room, by way of summarily clearing out the Sepoys. At that moment Hodson came quickly up, sword in hand. "Where are the rebels?" he demanded grimly. Forbes-Mitchell's narrative runs: "I pointed to the door of the room, and Hodson, shouting, 'Come on,' was about to rush in. I implored him not to do so, saying 'It's certain death; wait for the powder; I've sent men for powder-bags.' Hodson made a step forward, and I put out my hand to seize him by the shoulder to pull him out of the line of the doorway, when he fell back, shot through the chest. He gasped out a few words, either, 'Oh, my wife,' or 'Oh, my mother'—I cannot now rightly remember—but was immediately choked by blood."

Colonel Gordon-Alexander, who took part in the assault, and saw Hodson come on the scene, gives a similar account of the manner in which Hodson received his wound; but it illustrates the unreliability of human testimony to notice how he and Forbes-Mitchell, who were both actors in the tragedy, flatly contradict each other from this point. Gordon-Alexander says that a man of his company, whom he had sent over to warn Hodson, "never stopped, but ran in at the door and pinned the man who had shot Hodson, with his bayonet, before he had time to reload. There was only one other Sepoy in the doorway, and he was bayoneted, too." Forbes-Mitchell says that after Hodson had been carried off, the bags of powder, with slow matches in them, were brought up. "These we lit, and then pitched the bags in through the door. Two or three bags very soon brought the enemy out, and they were bayoneted. One of the 93rd, a man named Rule, rushed in among the rebels, using both bayonet and butt of his rifle, shouting, 'Revenge for Hodson!' and he killed more than half the men single-handed." But, according to Gordon-Alexander, there were only two Sepoys in the room, and no powder-bags were necessary to drive them out!

Hodson was a soldier of real genius, but was pursued through life, and to his very grave, by a swarm of baseless calumnies. When he was buried, Colin Campbell himself stood by the grave, and, as the coffin of the dead soldier sank from sight, the British commander-in-chief burst into tears. Those tears, rolling down the cheeks of so great and fine a soldier, are Hodson's best vindication and memorial.

Meanwhile, some other formidable buildings—the Secundrabagh, the Shah Nujeef, &c.—had fallen, almost without resistance, into the hands of the British. Outram was steadily pushing on along the northern bank, and scourging with his flank fire each position the Sepoys held. The 12th and the 13th were employed by the engineers in pushing on a line of advance through the houses, to the left of the main road, thus avoiding the fire of the Sepoys. On the morning of the 14th the Imambarah, a mass of minarets, flat roofs, and long, ornamental frontage, was stormed by Brasyer's Sikhs. Outram, by this time, had seized the iron bridge to the west of the Residency. He was in a position to cork the neck of the bottle, that is, and to make flight impossible for the great mass of the Sepoys. But this splendid position was thrown away by the first of the two great blunders which mar Colin Campbell's conduct of the siege.

Outram asked permission to force the bridge, and take the Sepoys, still holding the Kaisarbagh and the Residency, in the rear. Campbell consented, but forbade him crossing, if, in the process, he would lose a single man. Now, the bridge was held in force by the Sepoys, and guarded by a battery, and to force it would necessarily risk many lives. But war is a business of risks, and the gain beyond was enormous. A soldier like Nicholson, or Neill, or Hodson, would have interpreted Campbell's order generously; or they would have stormed the bridge without orders, and would have trusted to the justification which success always gives. But Outram was of a less audacious type. An order, to him, was *sacro-sanct*. He made no attempt to cross the bridge, but looked on, while the defeated Sepoys streamed past in thousands, escaping to the open country, there to kindle the fires of a costly guerilla warfare.

The preparations to pass the bridge, it may be added, were marked by fine valour on the part of one of Outram's engineers. Outram himself had, at the beginning of the operations, thrown a barricade across the bridge, to prevent the Sepoys crossing. When, in turn, he himself had to force his way across, it was necessary to remove this barricade, and to do it in broad daylight, and under a fierce and sustained fire from the Sepoys. Wynne, of the Engineers, and a sergeant named Paul, undertook the perilous task. They crept forward, crouching under the parapet of the bridge; then, kneeling down, they removed one sand-bag after another from the barricade, passing each bag back along the line of men, from hand to hand. But, as the level of the barricade sank, the two gallant engineers were exposed more fully to the Sepoy muskets. The fire was furious. Yet Wynne and his companion coolly pulled down the barricade, bag by bag, till the lowest tier was reached, and then ran back unharmed.

Meanwhile, events elsewhere had moved too fast for the British commander-in-chief. Brasyer's Sikhs, with some companies of the 10th Foot, had stormed the Imambarah. The flying Sepoys took refuge in the next and strongest of all the Sepoy works, the citadel of the whole defence, the Kaisarbagh, a blaze of gilded spires, cupolas and domes, all turned into a vast fortification. The Sikhs and the 10th followed vehemently and closely, while some of the men of the 90th, led by young Havelock, carried a palace close to the Kaisarbagh, from which they commanded three of its bastions. They opened on them a fire so deadly that the Sepoys fled from their guns. The engineers wished to stay any further attack; the programme for the day was exhausted, and, in Colin Campbell's leisurely tactics, nothing further was meant to be done that day.

But the stormers were eager; Sikhs and Highlanders alike had the fire of victory in their blood. They clambered through an embrasure, and forced their way into the Kaisarbagh, Havelock running back and bringing up some companies of the 10th Foot. Brasyer pushed out beyond the Kaisarbagh, indeed, to the Mess-house. Franks and Napier brought up new troops, and the Kaisarbagh itself was swept from end to end.

All the wealth of India seemed to have been gathered within that great mass of gilded walls, and all this was now given up to mad and wasteful plunder. The men, to use Russell's phrase, were "drunk with plunder." They literally waded through court after court, piled high with embroidered cloths, gold and silver brocade, arms rough with jewels, shawls heavy with gold, banners, cloaks, pictures, vases. The men had the wealth of kings under their feet!

It was a day of great deeds. Two successive lines of defensive works, vast as railway embankments, garrisoned by an army, and backed by a great citadel, had been carried in succession. And yet the chief military gain of this great feat was lost, owing to Colin Campbell's absurd order, which held Outram back from carrying the iron bridge, and enabled the flying Sepoys to escape in thousands, to relight the flame of war throughout the whole of Oude.

It is amusing to know that Colin Campbell was at first disgusted, rather than delighted, with the daring rush which, with such indecent and unscientific haste, carried the Kaisarbagh. He is said, indeed, to have sent orders to Franks to evacuate the great post. Franks, however, was both a fine soldier and a hot-blooded Irishman, and he declined, in the bluntest form of speech, to give up the great stronghold his men had carried with a dash so brilliant.

Campbell's imagination, it seems, was haunted by the sense that each Sepoy position, when it was carried, was an abandoned powder-magazine, packed thick with the possibilities of dreadful explosions. And facts justified that uncomfortable belief. The story of one such fatal explosion may be briefly told. In the Jumma Musjid no less than nine cart-loads of gunpowder were discovered. The powder was packed in tin cases, and it was resolved to destroy it by flinging the cases down a well. A line of men was formed, and the cases passed quickly from hand to hand. The first case flung down struck against the side of the well, and exploded. The flame ran from case to case along the whole line till it reached the carts. The cases in the very hands of the men exploded, the nine cart-loads went off in one terrific blast of flame and sound, and, with one exception, the whole party—numbering twenty-two men, with two engineer officers in command—was killed. The only man who escaped was the one that threw that fatal first case down the well!

When the Kaisarbagh and the Mess-house fell, and the third line of Sepoy defences was thus carried, Lucknow was practically in the British power. But on the next day, March 15, Colin Campbell, wary and war-wise soldier though he was, committed a second blunder, which helped to rob the success of some of its best fruits. He realised the blunder he committed when he held back Outram, and to remedy it he perpetrated a further mistake. He despatched his two cavalry brigades in pursuit of the flying Sepoys, and despatched them on the wrong roads. The absence of the cavalry created a huge gap in the British lines on the north of the Goomtee, and a great body of Sepoys, said to be more than 20,000 strong, escaped through it unharmed. "In this way," says Lord Roberts, "the campaign, which should then have come to an end, was protracted for nearly a year by the fugitives spreading themselves over Oude, and occupying forts and other strong positions, from which they were able to offer resistance to our troops till the end of May 1859; thus causing needless loss of thousands of British soldiers." That is a severe condemnation to be written by one great soldier on another.

Brigadier Campbell, with a strong body of horse and guns, hovered outside the Musabagh, ready to cut up the Sepoys when Outram had driven them out of that building. For some mysterious reason, and to the open disgust of the whole British army, he failed to cut up the flying Sepoys. It was, for his command, a day of inertness and failure; yet it was lit up by one splendid dash of personal daring. A small mud fort covered, at one point, the road along which the Sepoys were flying, and Campbell sent forward a party of cavalry—a troop of the 7th Hussars and a squadron of Hodson's Horse, with two guns—to clear the Sepoys out of it. The guns flung a couple of shells over the walls of the fort, and it had the effect of a match flung into a beehive! The bees flew out, eager to sting! Some fifty rebels, headed by the village chief, a giant in size, suddenly rushed from the gate of the fort on the guns. They were upon the Hussars before they could be put in motion to charge, and the three troop officers were in an instant struck down. A cluster of the Sepoys bent over one of the three, Banks, slashing and thrusting at him, when Hegart, in command of the Hussars, rode single-handed to his rescue.

He broke through the group, shooting right and left with his revolver, wheeled and dashed through them again. He had shot three, and knocked over a fourth with the hilt of his sword, when two Sikhs galloped up to his aid, and Banks was saved, only to die of his wounds a few days later. When Hegart emerged from the fight everything he had about him, says Hope Grant, bore traces of his gallant struggle. His saddle and his horse were marked with sword-slashes, his sword-hilt was dinted, his martingale was cut, the silk pocket handkerchief with which his sword was tied to his wrist was severed as cleanly as with a razor.

The capture of Lucknow, in a space of time so brief, and at a cost so slight, was due in part, of course, to the splendid leadership of the officers and the daring of the men. But it was due, in even greater measure, to the skill of the engineers. It was an engineer's plan that sent Outram, with his heavy guns, across the Goomtee, round the "toe" of the boot, and so took the lines of the Sepoys in reverse. It was clever engineering, again, which broke a way for the advance of the British left wing through the houses to the left of the great road. The Sepoys had taken it for granted that the advance of the British would be up that road, and they had turned it into a Valley of Death. Every parapeted housetop that looked down on the road was crowded with muskets. The road itself was merely a double line of crenellated walls, inaccessible to scaling ladders, swept by grape and case-shot from every cross street, pelted by musketry from every mosque roof and palace gable, and raked from end to end with the fire of great guns. But all these elaborate and terrible defences were made useless by the fact that the British engineers tore a road for their advance through the houses to the left of the great road, until the Kaisarbagh itself was reached and seized. The whole siege, indeed, is a lesson in the value of science in war. Brains count for more, in such a struggle, than even bullets.

The Residency itself fell with almost ludicrous tameness. Outram, on the 16th, forced his way across the Iron Bridge, and the Residency, though crowded with Sepoys, was yielded with scarcely a musket shot being fired in defence. The position which the Sepoys tried, in vain, for more than eighty days to carry, was taken by the British in less than as many minutes!

Lucknow did not fall, however, without one eccentric and highly illogical flash of valour being shown by the Sepoys. The Moulvie of Fyzabad was the most obstinate and daring of the leaders thrown up by the great Mutiny. He was a soldier, indeed, who, on the Sepoys' side, rivals Tantia Topee himself for generalship; while, for personal daring, he leaves the Nana's general hopelessly behind. The Moulvie had made his escape from Lucknow, but in a mood of sudden wrath, turned his face towards the city again. He returned, and occupied a strong building, from which he was only expelled with much hard fighting by the 93rd and the 4th Punjaub Infantry. The fight was hopeless from the outset; the city had fallen, further resistance was a mere idle waste of life. Yet the Sepoys showed a more desperate courage in this combat than at any other point throughout the siege. For so much does the influence of one brave man count!

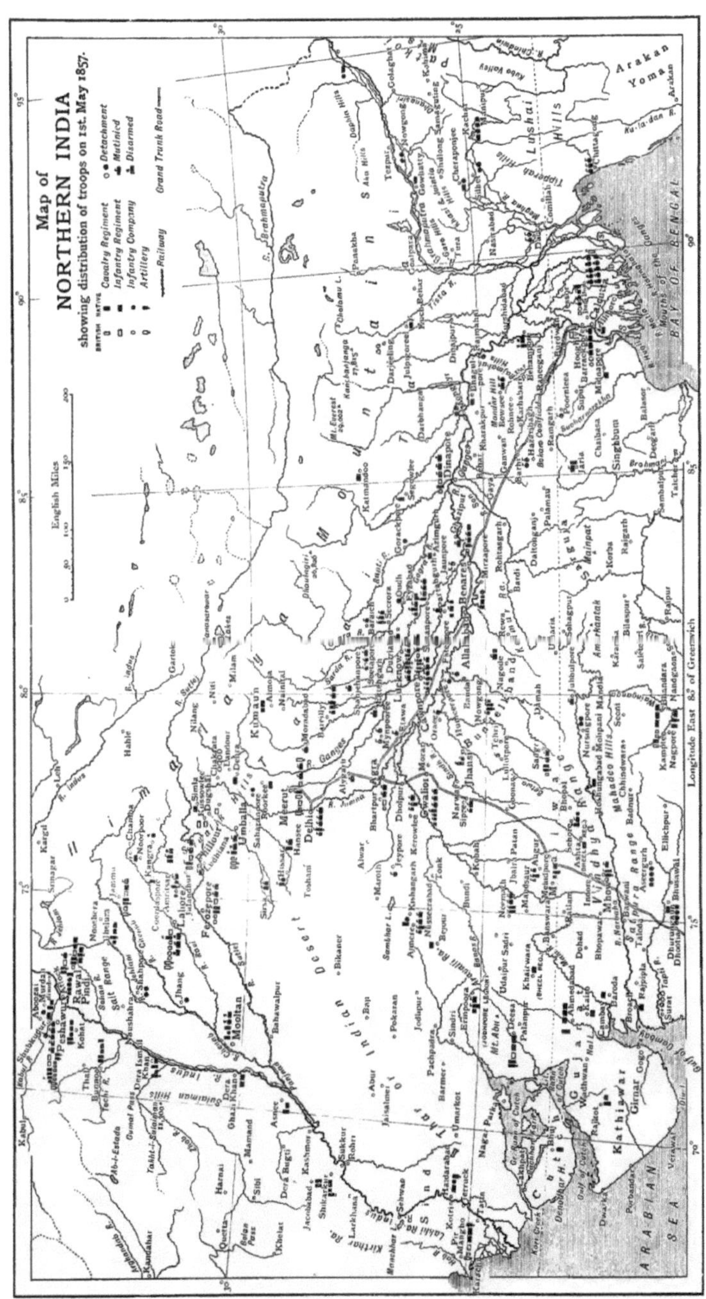

MAP OF NORTHERN INDIA SHOWING DISTRIBUTION OF TROOPS ON 1ST. MAY 1857.

By permission, from Captain Trotter's Life of John Nicholson, John Murray 1898.

Walker & Cockerell sc.

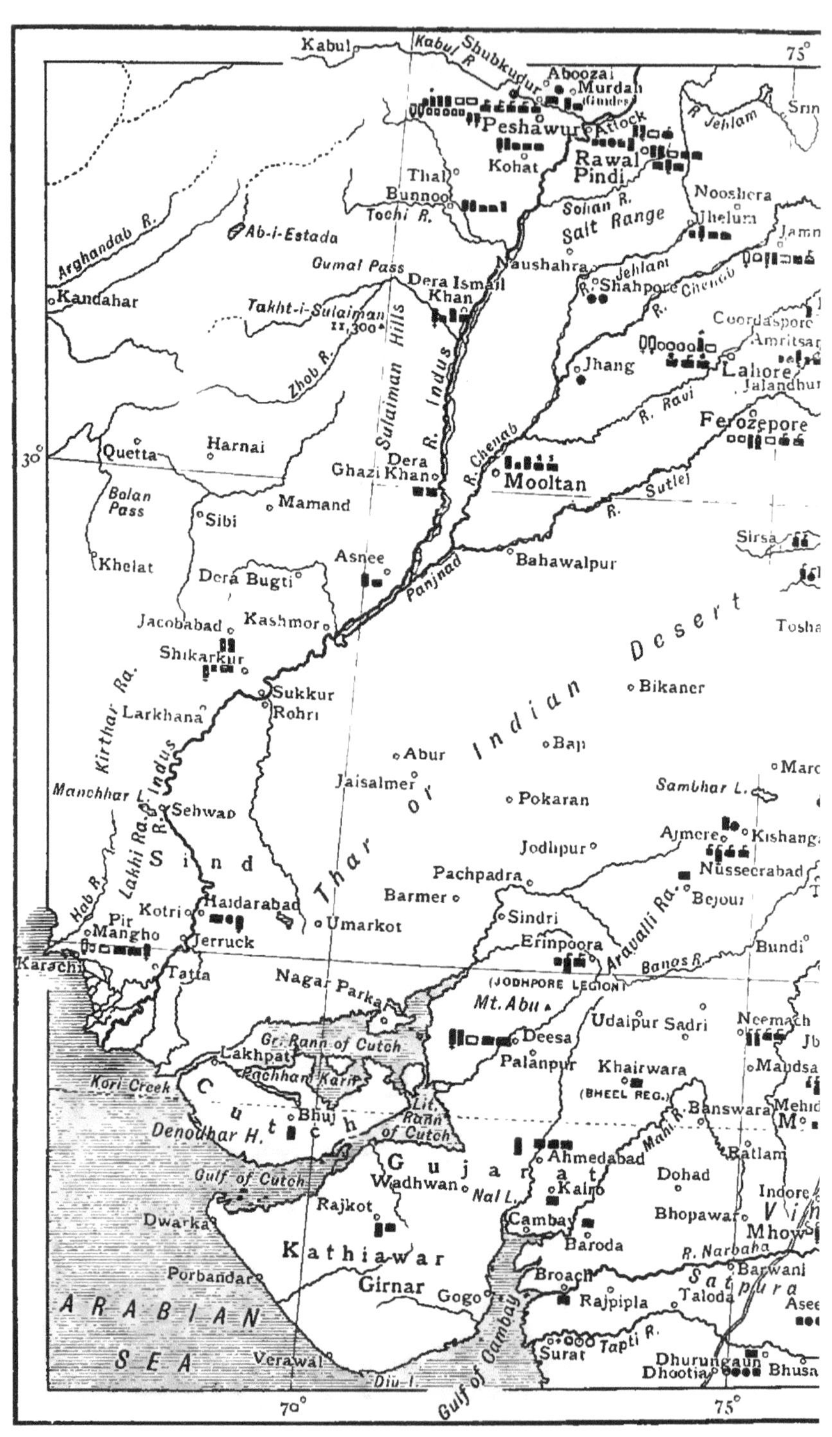

Map of Northern India (*Enlarged - Left*)

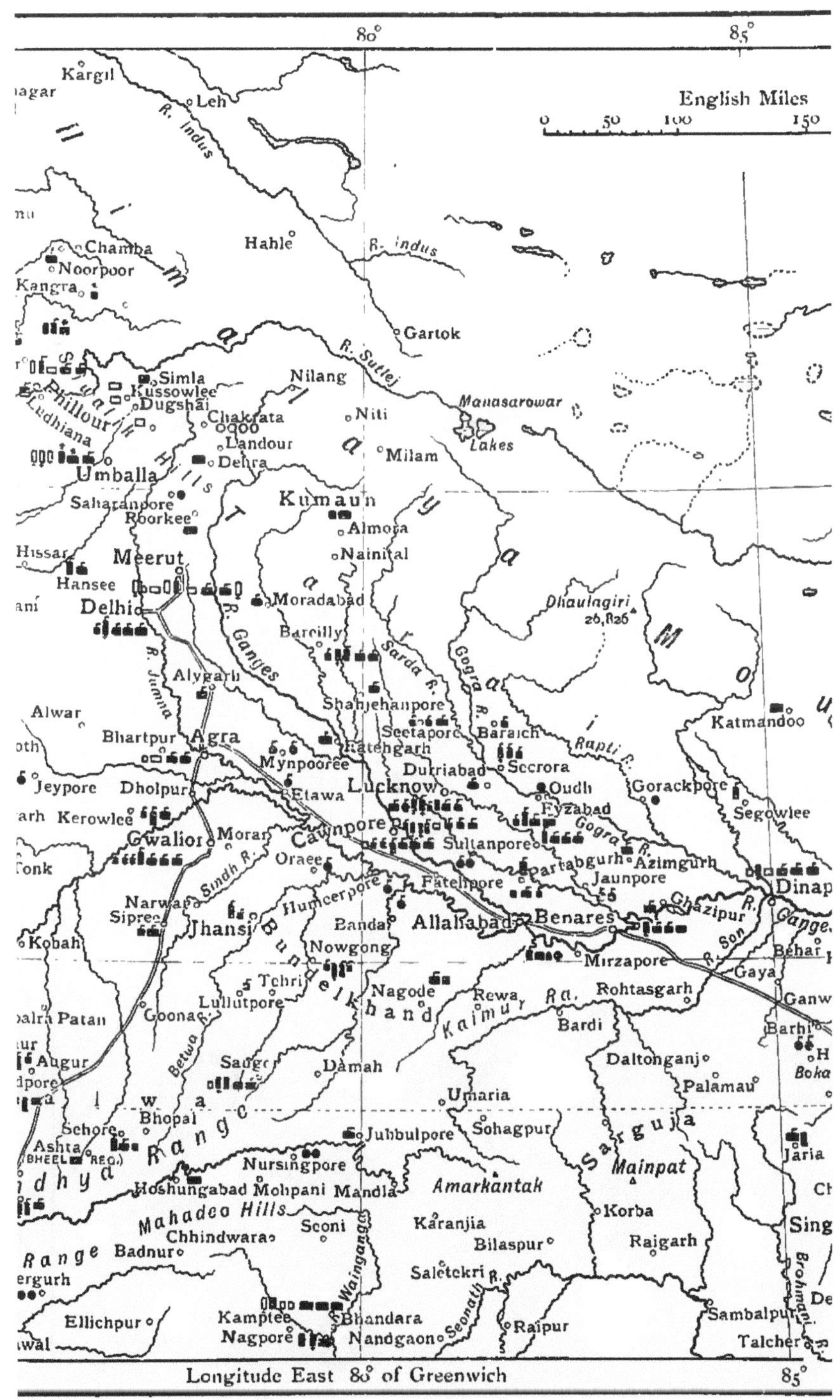

Map of Northern India (*Enlarged - Middle*)

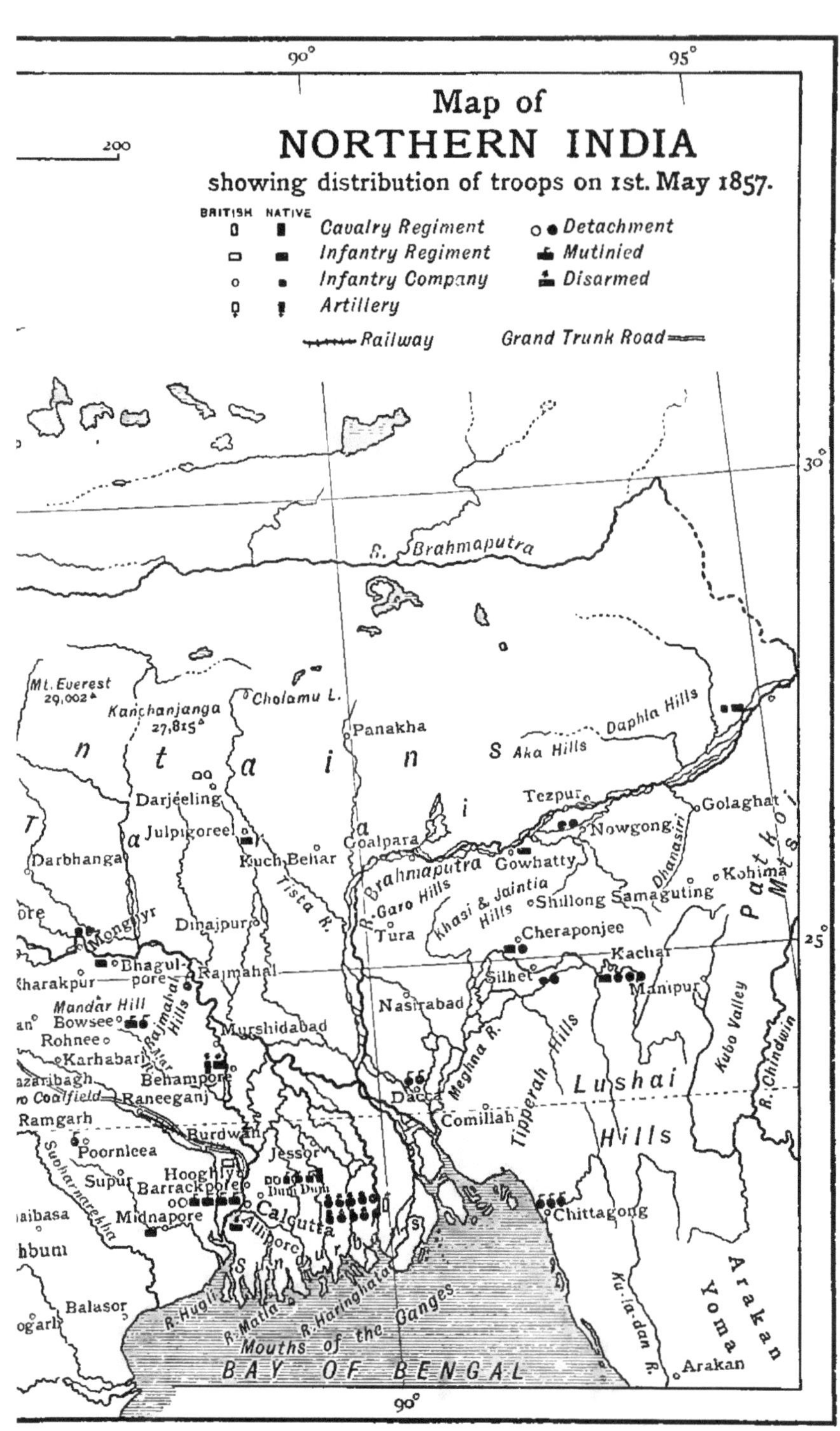

Map of Northern India (*Enlarged - Right*)

INDEX

Symbols

A

B

C

D

E

F

G

H

I

J

K

L

M

N

O

P

Q

R

Y

9 789358 007770

Printed by Libri Plureos GmbH in Hamburg,
Germany